The Wild Garden

Collected Writings From 1990–1993

The Wild Garden

Collected Writings From 1990–1993

Satsvarūpa dāsa Goswami

Persons interested in the subject matter of this book are invited to correspond with our secretary:

GN Press, Inc.
R.D. 1, Box 837-K
Port Royal, PA 17082

Printed in the United States of America
ISBN 0-911233-54-7

Library of Congress Cataloging-in-Publication Data

Gosvāmi, Satsvarūpa Dāsa
The Wild Garden: collected writings from 19901993 by Satsvarūpa Dāsa Goswami.
p. cm.
ISBN 0911233547 $13.00
1. International Society for Krishna Consciousness.
I. Title.
BL1285.84.G665 1994
294.5'512--dc20 947134
CIP

Contents

Foreword	vii
Preface	ix
Vṛndāvana	1
Other Places	65
Poetry	153
Sādhana	185
Prabhupāda	253
Prayer	283
Writing	301
A Mixed Bouquet	343

Foreword

The Wild Garden is collected from unpublished manuscripts written over a three-year period. Much of the writing was done between travels and was written not as a book, but as individual writing sessions.

A writing session has its own integrity. It starts at the beginning and reaches its own conclusion without being dependent on any other previously written session and without having to fit into a predetermined theme. Writing sessions can be written in small blocks of time—workable for a life filled with travel and preaching. By removing the external pressures of time and theme, Satsvarūpa Mahārāja was able to address whatever was on his mind at the moment he sat down to write. *The Wild Garden* has been selected from these sessions.

The Wild Garden is divided into sections. The first two sections, "Vṛndāvana" and "Other Places," contain sessions written on the road that are sensitive to the places where they were written. Other writing sessions have been categorized according to topic: "Poetry," "*Sādhana*," "Prabhupāda," "Prayer," and "Writing." At the end of the book, you will find "A Mixed Bouquet," twelve small pieces that speak for themselves.

Each piece in the book has been numbered. They have not been arranged necessarily in the order that they were written. Please read them as individual pieces. Please also feel free to skip around in the book as you read. This is not a book intended to be read from front cover to back, but to be discovered, like a wild garden.

The Editors

Preface

I am coming to this page to write, not to make a show. It doesn't have to be a perfect lesson written by a perfect teacher. How can I say I am perfect? Then should I not write until I am perfect? Should I not show anyone my writing until I have beaten it into a well-formed essay?

But today I am sitting in a field. It's here as nature has designed it—all weeds and wildflowers and herbs and the uncontrolled sky with the sun boring through the woolly clouds. It is a wild garden.

This collection is my wild garden. It is writing that has grown from itself. It is my stooping down to examine my garden up close and noticing the rain on the back of my hand.

These plants are not my enemies. I have learned something from each of them. They have helped me on my way in Kṛṣṇa consciousness. Their dull purple heads rippling in the wind have reminded me that I am a recipient of Kṛṣṇa's mercy. The simple white flowers have reminded me that I want to be simple. The blaze of dandelions moving from green to yellow to puffball has reminded me of my own cycles and how quickly the seasons pass.

I want to cry like a lover of Kṛṣṇa. I am one who has not yet become free. I want to close my eyes and feel Kṛṣṇa in my heart and in that way burn up all remaining *anarthas*. When will I even approach that stage of Kṛṣṇa consciousness?

In the meantime, I look up and see something new. What appeared like one variety of dandelion is actually two. If I look again without curiosity and submission, all I see is a field of weeds. Nature supplies many healing herbs which the uninterested person thinks are only weeds, but Kṛṣṇa says, "I am the healing herb."

What is my point? This is just an extended metaphor to describe my wild garden. You'll see. Just stay with me and you will understand.

Satsvarūpa dāsa Goswami

Vṛndāvana

1

May that Gopīnātha, whose flute attracts the *gopīs*, dwell in your heart. May His flute music dispel all your ignorance. May the blessing of *yoga-māyā* descend upon you. May we pray for that downpour of mercy. Let us wait for it as the *cakora* bird waits for the moonshine. Like the *cātaka* bird, let us wait and not drink any water except that which falls from the monsoon cloud.

O Vṛndāvana-dhāma, you are the holiest of all holy places. I bow down on the Vraja earth before the *tulasī* in our yard. Tonight I sense a tiny bit of your inner meaning. Please forgive me for dwelling so much on your external features and even complaining sometimes while I live here. You know I talk of your fields and water and animals because it's all I can see. I do it because I know this too is a feature of Vraja. I am too poor to know the wealth of the inner realm. I am faithless and fallen. Please see some good in my attempts.

Why do I think my body is a testing-stone for reality? Is Vṛndāvana as I perceive it? My body is just one of billions, all perceiving through their limited, material senses. I can't change Vṛndāvana just by writing about it; I can't capture it. I can't become a *gopa* or a *gopī* or any kind of devotee just by talking about it. I have to worship and I have to love.

Please don't keep me as an outsider who writes without the slightest trace of your mercy. If I roll in your dust, if I walk your lanes and say what I see—even though I am blind—I have faith that it is a useful act. It makes my language chaste. I have come here with faith. Foolishly, I may have thought I entered Vṛndāvana by plane and taxi. Foolishly, I remain outside. But even outer Vṛndāvana is holy. I pray that you won't kick me away. Please let me enter. Please let me pick up dust and crumbs and see the divine light. All glories to Rādhā and Kṛṣṇa. All glories to all the Vrajavāsīs. All glories to the forest and *sādhus* and living creatures. All glories to Vṛndāvana. Please let us continue reading of your glories and of the glories of your eternal residents, and please let us die here thinking of them.

2

When you go on *parikrama*, you just have to follow the crowd. Everyone walks in the same direction. In my mind, I bow down at the roots of a certain tree in Rāman Retī. Most of the roots extend above ground. Someone put a small pile of bricks in the area where the roots are exposed and people sometimes sit around the tree and draw diagrams in the sand. Less religious people squat and pass stool nearby. But I am mentally offering obeisances to that tree, full *daṇḍavats:* "Please grant me *bhakti.*"

3

Listen—you can hear many voices. It sounds like they are chanting prayers. I have heard them out there since 3:30 this morning—masses of people walking together. Maybe it's one of those near-the-end-of-Kārttika *parikramas* where thousands of pilgrims arrive as if from nowhere. But Madhu said it might be people gathering for a nationwide strike called for by Hindu politicians protesting the mosque in Ayodhya. I hear ladies singing. It's probably a *parikrama.*

Kṛṣṇa, I often feel emptiness, inertia, a brick wall when I try to approach You. It reminds me of the wall circling this house. It is flimsy and low. The top four layers of bricks aren't even cemented in place, just piled up. People take them away. The wall is so low that a dog can hop over it. It's not the Great Wall of China. Is my brick wall like that? Easily dismantled?

There is a little person inside me who encourages me to keep writing it down. Śrīla Prabhupāda said that Kṛṣṇa wrote his books. Kṛṣṇa is in everyone's heart. Because we have become conditioned not to listen to Him, we have to approach a spiritual master to teach us how to hear and respond. "Since one cannot visually experience the presence of the Supersoul, He appears before us as a liberated devotee. Such a spiritual master is no one other than Kṛṣṇa Himself" (Cc., *Ādi* 1.58). A fortunate person takes his dictation from the guru. A fool listens to his own speculations. "He is a seminal thinker," they say.

The voices are a little louder now. I can't hear the sounds of bare feet on the earth—this house is close to the *parikrama* trail—but I sense movement, excitement, everything flowing past in the dark. Śrīla Prabhupāda liked to quote a police report about an early San Francisco Ratha-yātrā: "This is not a window-breaking crowd." The parikramers are like that.

4

Tejaḥ-prakāśa Prabhu and his wife are inviting us to stay at their house. We'll move there in three weeks. I had thought I would stay in the guesthouse "forever," so I put pictures on the walls, straw mats on the floor, stacked the notebooks, filled the shelves, but we can pack up and move. That's how we live.

We don't travel so light. I don't care that a *tyāgī* would criticize. They don't know what it's like. Their austerity is extreme simplicity and even bodily punishment; our austerity is being

Western. Does that make sense? Our austerity is to be complicated? To be impure? Prabhupāda understood us. He taught *vairāgya vidya nija bhakti-yoga*, but he also taught *yukta-vairāgya* —use what you have in Kṛṣṇa's service.

5

The *gopīs* are the best lovers of Kṛṣṇa, the Supreme Personality of Godhead. He tests them sometimes, or behaves contrarily with them, as when He told them to go home after they joined Him in the forest. Previously we read how the *gopīs* weren't able to join Him. They suffered the transcendental agony of separation. These same *gopīs* suffered when Kṛṣṇa told them to go home. They cried torrents of tears and felt a burning heat in their chests. They were stunned by His cruel words.

We will all have to go through trials to prove our love for Kṛṣṇa. At present, most of the trials seem to be related to the material world. When we can finally quiet our material desires by our guru's grace, then we can face the emptiness of our love. Then perhaps we will be more prepared for another kind of trial.

The fact that the *gopīs'* trials are with Kṛṣṇa doesn't make it easier for them. He bewildered them with His loud statements about religious duty to their husbands and superiors. They simply wanted to serve Him.

I am bringing this up because I want to make advancement, as do all devotees. How can we cry tears of *prema*? We have not attained Kṛṣṇa. That is our misfortune. He has not bewildered us with His strong statements of *dharma* or His *rasika* moods. Being petty creatures, we have petty difficulties.

Where did we develop such a stiff-upper-lip policy? We avoid emotion, whether spiritual or material. We will reciprocate with Kṛṣṇa, but we expect Him to be fair-minded and civil in return. Although we have heard that Kṛṣṇa will make up for what we lack—if we give ten percent of our love, He will respond with ninety percent of His—we simply expect it of Him rather than use that knowledge as an impetus to increase our own surrender. But are we ready for the *rasa* of Kṛṣṇa's reciprocation? Are we ready for His cunning words? His thievery? Are we ready to run after Him and claim back what He has stolen from us?

What kind of Kṛṣṇa do we want? Do we invite Him to our homes, tell Him where to sit, then serve Him what we want Him to eat? Do we expect Him to approve of our devotional service since we are following guru, *sādhu*, and *śāstra* like good devotees and are working within the limits of our economic means and health? Will we remember to ask Him about Himself? What kind of Kṛṣṇa do we want?

So what happened when Kṛṣṇa told the *gopīs* to go home? Did they comply?

Kṛṣṇa told them that Kṛṣṇa consciousness is not attained by physical proximity, but by chanting and hearing and doing their religious duties as wives at home. The *gopīs* were astonished to hear Him speak like that. They thought, "We have given up all sense gratification to come to Him. We don't want sense gratification. We love Him. We want to serve His lotus feet." The conjugal *rasa* is not sense gratification.

The *gopīs* cried. Then one of the bolder *gopīs* began to argue with Kṛṣṇa. Pure devotees in *rāga-bhakti* don't like to argue, but Kṛṣṇa's words were too much. She said, "You say we should go back to our husbands, but You are the supreme husband. You are the Supersoul of all *jīvas*. There is nothing wrong if we come here and surrender to You."

Kṛṣṇa tests the *gopīs*, but they prove their love for Him again and again. *We* say Kṛṣṇa is testing us too, but we are not in contact with Him. We are not even sure it is Kṛṣṇa who is handling us roughly in His embrace. For most of us, "Kṛṣṇa's embrace" is just a metaphor. We recite Śrī Caitanya Mahāprabhu's beautiful verses and we believe it applies to Him. He is the one experiencing separation from Kṛṣṇa. He is the one who will become broken-hearted if Kṛṣṇa is not present before Him. But what about our empty, lonely lives? Are they connected with Kṛṣṇa? We are not madly looking for Him, asking the trees and creepers, "Did the son of Nanda Mahārāja pass by here?" What does all this mean to us?

And if Kṛṣṇa invites us, will we even go?

6

In Vṛndāvana I can go to the Yamunā or stay in this room offering fruits and then eating them to keep up my strength. I can lie in bed, or chant, or read *Śrīmad-Bhāgavatam*. I can sit here and look for the real and immediate cool pre-dawn air in this room. Vṛndāvana is that real. Anywhere I go in Vṛndāvana, I can roam and find Kṛṣṇa. I can practice to see Him everywhere, and then I can go back to Brooklyn and remember that stretch around Govardhana. Or I can see a tree in Stroudsburg and be reminded of that tree in Rāman Retī. At least I can carry back that sensation of being in this room in the Sant Colony when I am in Ireland or Port Royal, and I can wonder, "What is the essential difference between being here right now and when I was in Vṛndāvana all those months?" It is not just the day you went to the extraordinary spots, the visit to Kṛṣṇadāsa Kavirāja's writing *kuṭir*, but the pervasiveness of Vraja-being. There is a difference between walking out onto the road in Vṛndāvana and doing the same thing in the United States. Feel that. Recall that. Come back here and live it in your mind.

What we all share when we live in Vṛndāvana is the chance to contact Kṛṣṇa. Sometimes we try to voice it when we ride together on rickshaws or discuss what Vṛndāvana means to us. But for each of us there is more, even when we don't articulate it past "I benefit from being in Vṛndāvana." Vṛndāvana is perceivable and imperceivable—it is everything together.

To understand Vṛndāvana, you have to go through the Vaiṣṇavas. You have to be under them. You have to get their permission to pray before you can go directly. Be a devotee of the devotees. This is another meaning of Vṛndāvana.

7

Pilgrimage is an ancient tradition. India does not need to advertise its holy places. Those who go there know the way. The *tīrthas* are well-guarded secrets, and yet teachers are available to those who are searching. There are many guides who can be hired for a fee who will reveal the sacred places of the *dhāma*, but to find a genuine guru who can reveal the *essence* of the *dhāma* is rare. It is even more rare to find a guru who understands the Western mentality and who has no interest in exploiting us.

We are all wandering around Vṛndāvana like beggars. Where is Kṛṣṇa? Is He in this temple? Will we feel something if we bow down here? Can I steal it from you? Will I give it to you? What do you know? Who knows? Where is the touchstone Gauḍīya Vaiṣṇava? Even when we find a person whose presence makes our Kṛṣṇa consciousness surge, we will still have to go home and face our emptiness. We *must* face it; we must accept it and we must fight it.

Early in the morning we call out to Kṛṣṇa and the Vaiṣṇavas in the holy names. That is what the Vaiṣṇava teaches—to do our *bhajana*. That is why we seek him out. He practices *bhajana*.

Śrīla Prabhupāda came to us in New York City and told us of the beauty of Vṛndāvana. He told us that he was not happy in New York City. We thought New York was the greatest city in the world. He only wished to return to Vṛndāvana. Then why did he come? He had a duty to his spiritual master to deliver the message of Vṛndāvana.

How expertly you delivered that message, Śrīla Prabhupāda. You organized your followers to stay in Vṛndāvana year round by giving them the fort of Krishna-Balaram Mandir.

8

Field Notes:

Govardhana Hill—almost purple in the sunlight; the trees are green this time of year. Rocks jut out like square chunks, reddish-yellow, stained black and other shades by the weather. We are on the inner path around Govardhana, a sand road. It is Pūrṇimā, a day when many Vrajavāsīs circumambulate on the outer, hardtop path.

My mood is all-Western, but my simple essence (spirit soul) has been directed here by my spiritual master. My American-born Godbrothers guide me. They are more acclimated to India. Before we start walking, we sit under a tree and read. Govardhana is the *tilaka* marking of Vraja. It is the place of Govinda's pastimes. "Please accept unhappy me and grant me residence near you. . . . Don't consider if I am acceptable. . . . " (Raghunātha dāsa Gosvāmī).

As we hear about the residents of Gokula, today's residents walk by. The children here are beautiful and exotic-looking. Śrīla Prabhupāda brought me to this place to hear of Kṛṣṇa's pastimes. I know to control myself and not commit offenses.

When you walk around Govardhana, your sense of self becomes small or lost. You just keep watching the man ahead. When he bows down at a sacred place you do too. I am usually self-conscious about it, and that makes it hard to pray while I lie prostrated in the sand. But I keep up the pace, walking on my tender soles over the foot-worn earth and chanting Hare Kṛṣṇa. Days like this do something for the soul.

"This is Āniyora where the huge form of Kṛṣṇa manifested as Govardhana Hill and ate all the offerings cooked by the devotees." Kṛṣṇa kept saying, "More! Give Me more!" The people offered more *capātīs*, more rice, more vegetables, but He demanded, "*More!*" Then they offered Him a *tulasī* leaf and He was satisfied.

This is a busy village. My friend says, "According to *Bhakti-ratnakāra*, anyone who sees a resident of Āniyora becomes liberated." As he says it, I see the face of an old man with drawn-in lips. I don't question it. I just keep walking.

I prefer the woods to the villages. I ask, "If the devotees like Raghunātha dāsa Gosvāmī pray for residence near Govardhana, and if you say that these little rock piles have been put together by people as prayers for residence at Govardhana, then why don't any *sādhus* live here today as we see in other places in Vṛndāvana?"

"Because there are so many *guṇḍas*. Many places in Vṛndāvana are dangerous because of that."

Innocent pilgrim.

Rādhā-kuṇḍa—Just say it simply: I offer my obeisances to Śrīla Prabhupāda. He is my sole connection. Only by his permission do I come here. I have no knowledge of or taste for Rādhā-Kṛṣṇa's pastimes. I am just a fool in a body. But I have this *praṇāma-mantra* engraved in my heart. I chant it as my heart's prayer again and again at Rādhā-kuṇḍa.

nama oṁ viṣṇu-pādāya kṛṣṇa-preṣṭhāya bhū-tale
śrīmate bhaktivedānta-svāmin iti nāmine
namas te sārasvate deve gaura-vāṇī-pracāriṇe
nirviśeṣa-śūnyavādi-pāścātya-deśa-tāriṇe

They are begging for rupees. We are drying off, wringing out our *gamchās*. It is immediately hot again. Something nice happened here.

Submerge yourself in the water. Hold onto the chain because the steps are slippery. I see what my brother does and I do it too. He cups his hands, dips them into the water, and then lifts them up to splash water on his head. It is delightful. I want to stay longer, but I don't like the turtles. They surface and look in my direction, and I hurry to finish my *gāyatrī*. Even I have to laugh at what a superficial person I am, but it is all mercy.

Devotees from Italy, America, and India sit for a short while together on a wall. We reapply our *tilaka* while a girl tries to sell us grey Rādhā-kuṇḍa *candana*. As I apply my *tilaka*, a boy watches. Then he exclaims, "Gaudiya Math! Caitanya Mahāprabhu!" This is India. In America, even the most clever boy could know only, "Oh, a Hare Kṛṣṇa." This boy sees the thin lines of our Viṣṇu *tilaka* marks, the conservative, concise "arrow" point over the nose, and happily concludes which *sampradāya* we belong to. Yes, we are followers of Bhaktisiddhānta Sarasvatī Ṭhākura and His Divine Grace A.C. Bhaktivedanta Swami Prabhupāda. Gauḍīya-sampradāya. Mahāprabhu. Prabhupāda.

An amazing sight: so many *bābājīs* inside the building on the shore of Rādhā-kuṇḍa. I don't have to judge them. I am a pink cow next to them. There is a slight camaraderie among us, but mostly we stay apart. I am afraid to write even a single descriptive word about them. When Śrīla Prabhupāda heard that Indira Gandhi, in the days of emergency rule, ordered that some Rādhā-kuṇḍa *bābājīs* be gathered and sterilized to fulfill her quota, Prabhupāda was insulted and angered to hear it. Later, he said it was the cause of her fall from power. A few days after perpetrating this act she was deposed.

As I left Rādhā-kuṇḍa I suddenly noticed that I did not have my cane with me. "My cane! I can walk without it! I'm cured!"

9

Today I walked down a lane in Rāman Retī. The man I walked with needed my attention, so I spoke to him about himself and noticed almost nothing else around us—the street, the people, the houses—I didn't even know where we were going. We could have been anywhere. I did some counseling, but I can't say that I took a walk in Rāman Retī.

Can't I remember anything? We stopped outside the gate and an old man in bright orange approached us. When he got quite close I offered him my *praṇāmas*. As I looked up, I saw he had no *tilaka* on his forehead, just an orange, circular smudge. He returned my respectful greeting. Then from behind I heard the rhythmic beat of *karatālas*. I turned and saw a man performing *kīrtana*, chanting and walking alone in the dirt lane. We turned and went into the alley toward the house we were visiting. Although I just wrote, "I noticed almost nothing," actually the impressions are there.

I saw a hog yesterday, rummaging with his pink snout along the ground. That was somewhere . . . while we traveled around Govardhana. We stopped in a village to get bananas. Three young school children stood together on the road. They seemed dazed by the sights, sounds, and odors around them.

Near our van, a man walked on foot and slightly touched another man on his motor scooter. The touch was enough to make the man lose his balance and his wife and baby fell off the back of the motor scooter onto the road. The young husband spoke angrily to the man who had touched him, but that man strongly defended himself. A crowd gathered. We watched, waiting for our Godbrother to return with the bananas. The three dazed school kids also looked on, and a man shooed flies from the *jalebis* he was selling.

At the place where they bathe Govardhana with milk all day long, the milk constantly runs down into the gutter. The dogs are fat with it. The sour milk smell thickens the air. But the priest smiles sweetly and accepts the offerings to Govardhana while conferring blessings.

10

You are in Bhauma Vṛndāvana. Crickets are like stars in the night—twinkling sounds. Things seem pretty (like the play of the antelopes in Māyāpur), but I know if I look closer, I will see savagery rather than tenderness in the animal kingdom. But there are tender moments also. Śrīla Prabhupāda notes in *The Nectar of Devotion* how even a she-tiger has affection for her cubs. I saw one monkey lying in the lap of another while the other monkey carefully and patiently removed lice with both hands.

O Keśava, Your material nature is very strange. I don't want to stare in fascination at it. I want to come gaze at Your lotus feet in the temple. But wherever I look, it is Your kingdom and Your potency. Please bring my attention to the best place, devotional service to the names, pastimes, and qualities of the Supreme Lord. Bring me to Śrīla Prabhupāda's Samādhi Mandir. Let me shuffle in the dark over to the Krishna-Balaram Mandir and bow down before Your beauty. Let me see the colors and the transcendental variegatedness. Your *tulasī* garland is thick, and the white garland in Rādhārāṇī's hand sways slightly in the breeze. . . .

It is only by the mercy of the Supreme Lord and His associates that we can gain entrance into Vṛndāvana-dhāma. Even to stand nibbling a banana in a nearby village is glorious in terms of the varieties of births available in the cosmos. But we want to enter in earnest. We have to be patient, I know, but we should make real endeavor too. Don't make offenses. Stay here for a few weeks, absorb the mood of the *dhāma*, then go back a changed person.

I keep reminding myself that I might not be able to return here. This could be my last visit. I walk the dirt lanes with this in mind. Where is Bhagatjī, Śrīla Prabhupāda's old friend of *sakhya-rasa* inclination, now? Where are so many? They have gone to join Lord Gaurāṅga, the great dancer. We will go too, but we must work hard for that visa. It will be stamped in the passport of pure devotional service.

Even if I lack that passport, I can continue thinking of Vṛndāvana. Being here helps immensely. Imbibe it. Don't waste time. Bow down to this sacred earth. Don't be concerned with what others think. That soft, enchanting sand is waiting to embrace me.

11

Traffic jams occur in the town of Vṛndāvana. I am trying to see them in a more relaxed way from the seat of my rickshaw. Today our rickshaw driver stopped because an unmanned motor rickshaw blocked half the road. The other half of the road was blocked by a large oxcart. Workers were unloading big stone slabs from the cart. A car approached from the other direction, but he couldn't get through either. Then from our direction came a dozen pack mules. They hesitated, afraid to go between the long-horned bullock and the parked motor rickshaw. By the time the motor rickshaw driver arrived, there was a traffic jam. Horns honked, bells rang, and the drivers were angry. All we needed to complete the scene were a few camels or elephants and maybe a motorcycle. Gradually, by moving aside, backing up, gesticulating wildly, and yelling back and forth—along with bystanders contributing their advice—the jam dissolved and we continued on our way. Not your average bumper to bumper grind-to-a-halt you meet in the West.

12

I discussed attraction to Kṛṣṇa's Vṛndāvana pastimes with my Godbrother inside Śrīla Prabhupāda's kitchen at Rādhā-Dāmodara temple. Prabhupāda, like Lord Kṛṣṇa, is *sarva-jña*, all-knowing, and he guides us now, even after his disappearance. We were bereft of spiritual life before Prabhupāda came to the West. Kṛṣṇa knew this and sent us Śrīla Prabhupāda. Now Prabhupāda continues to know our needs. He will instruct us what to do further. Let us pray to him and consult his books. What next, Śrīla Prabhupāda? I just heard you speaking the *Kṛṣṇa* book on the section where Vasudeva preached to Kaṁsa. He said just as one walks on the street by putting one foot down securely and following it with the next, so we move securely from one life to the next as ordained by Providence. And just as the caterpillar moves from his stem to the leaf, we will know our sure passage—from this life to the next, from *vaidhī-bhakti* to spontaneous love. We want to know what we should do, what is the required work.

I am also consulting our friend, the Supersoul. Please tell me what to do, inner guide and guru. What is best for a particular follower of Śrīla Prabhupāda? The seas are not always clearly charted for each individual. Even though the seas have been traversed thousands of times, every voyage is unique.

Emerging from the Rādhā-Dāmodara temple, I looked for my Birki shoes. Suddenly, one shoe came flying through the air and landed nearby. A cleaning lady with an unfocused eye who was gathering sticks into bundles had thrown my shoe. But where was the other? We can assume the monkeys stole it. A temple authority came along and calmly suggested I try coming back in a day or two to see if it turns up. Okay.

Out onto the street, our rickshaw driver is sound asleep, his body curled in an awkward position on the rickshaw seat. Madhu and I don't have to talk about our visit to Prabhupāda's rooms. Better we chant our *japa*. We silently observe the fantastic panorama of human and divine consciousness all the way from the bazaars to Rāman Retī and our ISKCON temple. There is that graffiti again that spells Rādhā. Kṛṣṇa is in every temple. "*Jaya* Rādhe. Hare Kṛṣṇa. *Haribol.*"

Back at the guesthouse I opened *Caitanya-caritāmṛta* at random and found this verse: "All the inhabitants of Vṛndāvana are Vaiṣṇavas. . . . Even though some of them do not strictly follow the rules and regulations of devotional service, on the whole they are devotees of Kṛṣṇa and chant His name directly or indirectly. Purposely or without purpose, even when they pass on the street they are fortunate enough to exchange greetings by saying the name of Rādhā or Kṛṣṇa. Thus directly or indirectly they are auspicious" (Cc. *Ādi*, 5.232, purport).

13

I recounted a little story of how Śrīla Prabhupāda told us the people in Vṛndāvana call out, "*Jaya* Rādhe." My Godbrother said that the benefit of writing is to preserve these stories. Yes, I count on that. Get it down. The sweat on the back of my neck.

Socks and earplugs lying on a cot, mine. But what did I see in Śrīla Prabhupāda's room? His cot, his picture, a *daṇḍa*, details of the room he used. We sat there *now* and talked. Now we are moving on in time, we are further down the stream. Everyone alive is floating downstream approaching the waterfalls of death. No one knows exactly how far away they are, but the falls are somewhere ahead. Some can hear them roaring, others are oblivious. But the river sweeps all of us along. We hear rumors. Suddenly something is ahead, a rock or a chance respite on the shore, or the waterfalls. During the brief respites, you congratulate yourself and think, "I will stay here always." But then you are plunged back into the river.

Can you really preserve anything by writing it in books? Won't they too be floated downstream after you? You see the trees on shore and cry out Lord Hari's names. I cannot be shy or wait for the exact feeling of heart that I desire. Śrīla Prabhupāda writes, "Even if one has not developed this consciousness, one should accept it theoretically from the instructions of the spiritual master and should worship the *arcā-mūrti*, or form of the Lord in the temple, as nondifferent from the Lord" (Cc. *Ādi*, 5.226, purport).

Prayer and devotional service are labor, but they carry the best reward. One time Śrīla Prabhupāda noticed one of his devotees looking tired and thin. Śrīla Prabhupāda commented, "Heavy *bhajana*." It can be like that.

The three necessities for entering Vṛndāvana according to Narottama dāsa Ṭhākura: give up material desires for satisfying the senses and bodily needs; enter through the six Gosvāmīs' line; receive Lord Nityānanda's mercy.

How can I expect to eliminate sense gratification? At least I can be simple. I don't have to hanker for special foods and drinks. I can accept whatever comes. I can follow Śrīla Prabhupāda, the six Gosvāmīs, Lord Nityānanda, and the authorized teachings coming down through our *sampradāya*. Achieve

Kṛṣṇa's blessing by always being willing to contribute to His movement. I cannot come here only to take something away for myself. Śrīla Prabhupāda wants us to become *cintāmaṇi* (touchstone). That will be proved not by our promises, but by our actions—can we give Kṛṣṇa consciousness to others?

Just imagine such a motivation: become strong and help others. Yes, that will be the automatic result of becoming strong, as long as we live in the fellowship of devotees.

14

These ruminations in the middle of the night: "Give us this day our daily bread" of devotional service. Praying to Kṛṣṇa, "Please let me execute devotional service. Please let me realize myself as a servant of all others. Let me carry out my service to them with enthusiasm, energy, and self-satisfaction. Devotional service is *yayātmā-suprasīdati*, satisfying to the deepest sense of self.

The sun rises. I notice it suddenly in its entirety, a ball like the moon, not yet blazing intolerably like fire. When it is fully risen, the sunshine pervades everything. It is hot, too hot. That first sight of the moon-like sphere is deceiving. It makes me think it will be cooling or that it will be subdued by the cloudy covering. But it is always ablaze. The majestic sun.

Everyone is a servant of Kṛṣṇa in Vṛndāvana, even the sun. When Lord Indra attempted to revolt, he was humiliated. Lord Brahmā too. Residing in Vṛndāvana helps us to see things from that perspective, how the pleasure pastimes of Kṛṣṇa and Rādhā come before the natural manifestations of the universe. Kṛṣṇa is the *most* beautiful; He is all-attractive. His beauty and *līlā* in Vṛndāvana's *kuñjas* are more important than His activities as the first cause of the material world.

15

Sometimes I doubt everything. You mean nothingness? No ...

Do you doubt the experience of sitting on this bouncing rickshaw while Vṛndāvana life flows at you and then past? Do you doubt the experience of seeing the hog swallowing water from the big puddle of muck he stands in? Or the many-colored electric lights and shops selling pictures of Kṛṣṇa? Do you doubt the existence of the shopkeepers who sit out and offer their wares? What about the call you sometimes hear, "*Haribol, Jaya* Rādhe"?

No, I know I exist in some form, just as everything exists in some form. I know that I am an aspiring devotee of Śrīla Prabhupāda. For example, when a Godbrother started describing how Prabhupāda acted as a personal guru to his disciples, especially in the early years at 26 Second Avenue, I certainly had no doubt about that. I wanted to remember it more—the guru who stayed with us, taught us, captured our hearts, engaged us in service.

This is an example of something I believe. I also believe I was a nondevotee of Kṛṣṇa in a world too big and alien for me. I couldn't cope. Then I met my spiritual master and entered the Kṛṣṇa conscious world. I will not leave this world of loving service—that is my spiritual master's gift to me. My effort to stay with him is called *guru-dakṣiṇā*. I render service and keep that connection of *guru-sevā* alive. Everything else will develop from that relationship.

We stopped. The rickshaw driver said he had to do something for a minute. He left his new shoes on the road and walked off. Then a motorized rickshaw honked that we were in the way. Someone pushed our rickshaw back so the motorized rickshaw could pass. Then a car ran over our rickshaw driver's shoes. Finally he came back. During this time, my Godbrother and I spoke confidentially about our hopes to attain spiritual life. Yes, I will keep reading *kṛṣṇa-kathā* and aspiring. I don't mean at all to say that I am hopeless. I just wanted to report, however, that usually when I reach a holy place or temple and I have the opportunity to pray, I go blank. Not blank exactly, but I get stripped of flowery words or higher aspirations connected with that holy place. All I have left to say is, "Prabhupāda, I am here. I am nothing but your disciple and I am glad that I am some kind of devotee. Please help me to do better. *Nama oṁ* . . . Hare Kṛṣṇa Hare Kṛṣṇa . . . " Nothing more than that. And after a few minutes, I am ready to go back.

I have heard that prayer deepens in concentric circles. There is the verbal level where the mind is uncontrolled. That is no prayer at all. Then there is prayer engaging the mind and voice. Deeper still there is prayer with mind, voice, and heart, and then prayer of the heart, the whole self. Some Godbrothers who live in Vṛndāvana do *daṇḍavat parikramas*, continually prostrating themselves in the dust of Vṛndāvana. It is difficult, but after a while your bodily concerns become inconsequential, your mind surrenders, and your prayer becomes wholehearted. That's the state I want to achieve.

16

A man intones his *śāstra* all night. He wants the world to witness the fulfillment of his vow, so he broadcasts into the cricket-chirping, pigeon-roosting night. The distant stars are cold witnesses. Some of us complain, "Why is he keeping us from sleep just because *he* has a vow?" But in Vṛndāvana, you just have to learn how to adjust. You cannot call the police and complain, "Some guy is broadcasting his prayers over a loud speaker and keeping us awake." No policeman would think of stopping the *sādhu* in his *āśrama* any more than he would consider rounding up the dogs or hogs or monkeys. Vṛndāvana means live and let live. All these creatures have somehow gained shelter in Rādhārāṇī's earthly Vṛndāvana. It is we Westerners, with our ambitious, hurried natures, who need to learn to adjust to Vṛndāvana's Kṛṣṇa consciousness. We have to learn to live humbly in the land where everyone is given mercy. We are not better.

Another *sādhu* has begun to recite. His voice is hoarse and sometimes bawling. He is earnest. I cannot make out what he is saying, but sometimes I catch the words, "Rādhe, Rādhe," "Patīta," "Kumarī." Who am I to judge?

There is also a line of beggars who sit just outside the wall of Krishna-Balaram Mandir. I think they do well there, and that is why they regularly line up. We on the other side of the wall are also beggars, but we have money and airline tickets in belts strapped to our chests. We beg for Śrīmatī Rādhārāṇī's mercy, beg for faith (which even poor Vrajavāsīs have), and beg to live in the dust of Vṛndāvana.

The bell strikes 12:30 A.M. Kṛṣṇa knows—He is in my heart. Śrīla Prabhupāda encourages me, but he also knows my plight. Śrīla Prabhupāda is happy to say, "My sons are trying to improve." I blank out with sleepiness.

17

The Kārttika festival is in full swing. There are colored lights with bright green fluorescent tubes on top of the temple domes. Some devotees enjoy the crowds and socializing, but I mostly wait for it to pass. Yesterday I answered quite a few letters.

It's cold here now. Devotees are starting to get sick with sore throats and congestion. The monkeys are bolder, stealing right from the devotees' hands and striking aggressive poses when threatened.

In the temple room, Rādhā-Śyāmasundara seem to grow more lustrous and attractive. Śyāmasundara is full of pleasing curves, a graceful youth. Rādhā is lovely, blessing all who come to worship Her Lord. We need to take Their *darśana* again and again, even if we don't have the edge of awareness. We will miss Them when we are away. We will miss Vṛndāvana-dhāma. When we remember Vṛndāvana in separation, that will be our perfection. Wherever we are, the *śāstras* and the gurus will always be the keys to open our spiritual awareness. Our own simple faith will always be the most precious commodity we can bring to this encounter.

18

The bell is ringing. Noon *ārati* is going on in the temple. I imagine myself five months from now in the back of my Renault van, sitting on the bunk. I have a six-hundred page manuscript typed and bound and I am reading an excerpt aloud to Madhu and another devotee. Maybe we are parked in South France on the way to Barcelona. Reading the manuscript, we get a glimpse of Vṛndāvana and the goal we hope to always keep in mind. Cars and trucks whiz by on the European highway. I read something about the chirping of the squirrels at noontime while the temple bell rings slowly, tolling . . . tolling . . . and everyone is busy in his existence—workers hammering and sawing, *brāhmaṇas* busy on the altar, and the animal kingdom, sleeping, defending, climbing walls, cawing. Then the sound of the conch resonating through the air.

It is ironic how we keep thinking of going somewhere else. When in County Kerry, I think of Vṛndāvana, and in Vṛndāvana, I think of County Kerry. There is a little bird on the *gurukula* wall. I don't imagine he is thinking of any faraway place or future time better than the present. He is not waiting for his secretary to return from New Delhi to tell him whether plane tickets are available during the Christmas rush. The bird stands on his spindly legs for just a few moments before his instincts take hold and he soars off to catch an air current.

Everything in Vṛndāvana is sweet and meaningful. I would like to write down at least one millionth of what is going on here. The earthiness of the *parikrama* trail, the people who say, "Rādhe, Rādhe." One millionth. Keep at it.

Tonight I will give a talk to disciples. The group gets smaller as Kārttika draws to a close. I plan to read from Uddhava's remembrance of Kṛṣṇa in Vṛndāvana in the Third Canto. Uddhava went deeply into trance remembering Kṛṣṇa.

Earlier, I read the talks of Lord Caitanya and Rāmānanda Rāya. Prabhupāda states that we have to hear with pure faith, not like the impersonalist logicians or scholars, and definitely not like the *sahajiyās* who hear from a guru outside the authorized *paramparā*. As I read *Caitanya-caritāmṛta*, the monkeys in the courtyard jabbered and screamed. I ignored them. I stayed with *Caitanya-caritāmṛta*.

19

Yesterday I was invited to travel by jeep out to the Vraja Maṇḍala *parikrama*. Fifty or so devotees have been walking all month around Vṛndāvana. Yesterday they were at Brahmāṇḍa Ghāṭa, the place where Kṛṣṇa ate dirt. I was prepared to read and lecture. Anyone can speak by faithfully selecting passages and interesting points from Prabhupāda's purports and then elaborating on them by applying relevant lessons from ISKCON life.

In one purport, Prabhupāda explains that when mother Yaśodā couldn't understand the cause of the universal form appearing in Kṛṣṇa's mouth, she surrendered to the will of the

Supreme. We should do the same when we are bound by events. Then *yoga-māyā* intervened and mother Yaśodā regained her simple, profound affection for Kṛṣṇa. We should have a simple affection for our particular service in Kṛṣṇa consciousness. So many things may occur as upheavals, politics or other worldly disturbances, disturbances within ISKCON, or disturbances within our own minds, but we must be able to return to a simple affection and attachment to the daily devotional activities.

Mother Yaśodā was beyond Brahman realization. She was beyond Paramātmā realization, and even beyond Bhagavān realization. Bhagavān became her son and sat on her lap. Kṛṣṇa doesn't want His devotees in Vraja to worship Him with awe and reverence as the Supreme Personality of Godhead. Of course, we have to cultivate a sense of God's greatness, especially in the beginning. If we don't recognize Kṛṣṇa's greatness, we may take Him cheaply, as *sahajiyās* do, or fear Him, or misunderstand His pastimes. When we attain love beyond Bhagavān realization, Bhagavān will become our friend, child, or lover.

It was nice speaking *kṛṣṇa-līlā* to the devotees on the Vraja Maṇḍala *parikrama*. Later we sat parked at a train crossing, waiting for the train to pass while our senses and minds were bombarded by the noisy traffic. A sign on the road: "Be kind to birds and animals. Notice their pains." I noticed a skinny female dog being harassed by eight puppies. They demanded her milk and eventually she couldn't refuse them. In another village, I saw a dog with a bone sticking out of its mouth.

The ancient locomotive finally chugged by. Backward India. But only here can we find the dust of Vraja. I ate some dirt from the same place where Kṛṣṇa ate dirt. Then I drank a few drops of Yamunā water.

"*Oṁ*" sign on a bus. Water chestnuts for sale. We pass a roadside chapel with orange Hanumān inside.

With the *parikrama* devotees, we discussed the riches available in Vṛndāvana. Some verses declare that there are jewels to be found everywhere and that the associates of Kṛṣṇa live in great palaces. "In a temple of jewels in Vṛndāvana, underneath a desire tree, Śrī Śrī Rādhā-Govinda, served by Their most confidential associates, sit upon an effulgent throne." Devotees gave different views of what this means. Vṛndāvana is usually simple and rural, but it can manifest any opulence desired by the Lord and His devotees for Their pastimes. But there is an inner meaning—the true wealth of Vraja is not gold or marble, but the pure affection exchanged between Kṛṣṇa and His devotees. We look for flashes of that opulence as we traverse the land of Vraja.

I knew that I was supposed to walk yesterday morning. I wondered whether I would be able to make it barefoot. The most important thing is to be humble as we walk on the same earth Rādhā and Kṛṣṇa walked on. This earth is more fortunate than we are.

Today, my disciples and I walked around Vṛndāvana together. Someone photographed us walking in the cold, dark 6 A.M. As the sky grew lighter, we stopped and read from *Kṛṣṇa* book about Kṛṣṇa praising Vṛndāvana. Later we stopped again to read of the *gopīs'* praise of Kṛṣṇa's flute. It had begun to warm up, but my feet tingled with cold, electric energy and the pinches from the pebbles. This earth is not so hard. It has been trod upon by millions of people before us.

"Did you ever go on *parikrama* with Śrīla Prabhupāda?" a disciple asked me.

"No, but I took some walks with him in Vṛndāvana." It was such a rare opportunity, to be with Śrīla Prabhupāda in Vṛndāvana.

We continued to stop and read and speak little purports. I told them we should regularly make stops in our rush through life to read *Kṛṣṇa* book. I told them the *gopīs* were not full of malice toward Kṛṣṇa's flute, but they admired the flute's ability to please Kṛṣṇa. The *gopīs* simply wanted to please Kṛṣṇa.

Kṛṣṇa, let me walk with no headache or ankle collapse. I told them Lokanātha Mahārāja invited me to go on Vraja Maṇḍala *parikrama* in future years; he said I don't have to walk, they will "carry" me.

"Oh, do it," my disciples said.

"I'll cook for you on Vraja Maṇḍala *parikrama.*"

"I'll type."

"And I'll write," I said, "although many have already written diaries on *parikrama.*"

"But not like your diary."

It is a great responsibility to guide these disciples, and it is wonderful to see how happy they were to walk in our spiritual family relationship. I thought of how Prabhupāda nourished me like this. Now it is my turn to nourish others.

When we got back to the guesthouse I could hear the twenty-four-hour *kīrtana* from my room. The lead singer was a Westerner, singing like a cowboy crooner. I could also hear women's voices in the chorus, repeating the *mahā-mantra* over and over again.

The sky is clear today. The air carries a pleasant November chill. The sparrows chirp and the parrots screech. Vṛndāvana is such a nice place. You can *feel* its specialness. All of this is possible because Śrīla Prabhupāda left Vṛndāvana to bring Vṛndāvana to us, and to bring us here.

A disciple reminded me that one time while walking on a California beach, Śrīla Prabhupāda said that the sound of the crashing surf was the beating of the *gopīs'* hearts in separation from Kṛṣṇa. Wherever Prabhupāda is, that is Vṛndāvana.

20

Some Māyāvādīs passing on the road glance up at me. They are dark-skinned in bright orange cloth. They look like Buddhists. After them come tall, thin men in white, each balancing a bundle on his head. Now no one. But I don't face myself.

I am preoccupied, as we say, occupied with surface matters, and can't go to my own heart because it feels empty. There is a sense of well-being and patience. I am okay, but when I desire to write something vital by this method, then I face a lack of depth, a lack of devotion. I have no access to emotions of *bhāva* for Rādhā-Kṛṣṇa.

A young boy who looks about eight years old, is smoking. He squats, puffs, then gets up and walks away from the blue cloud that forms over his head. I have nothing to say about it. His equally small friend has joined him and they walk out of my sight.

Are you trying to escape these outer sights or are you trying to weave them in? I am trying to write Kṛṣṇa consciousness in Vṛndāvana. I write what I perceive and think. I am not attempting to make it into a neat package. I think and see in Vṛndāvana, and I write it down as if it is all that I need at the moment. What can the ringing of a bicycle bell mean at this exact moment? How can it remind me of *vraja-līlā*?

Kṛṣṇa consciousness means to meditate on the nectarean pastimes of Kṛṣṇa and the Vrajavāsīs. It also means appreciating them. When will I enter Kṛṣṇa conscious meditation day and night? Raghunātha dāsa Gosvāmī called out "Rādhā! Kṛṣṇa!" in madness. He ran on the bank of the Yamunā and rolled in the dust at Rādhā-kuṇḍa. He wrote books and chanted the holy name with love. He had no time for sleeping and eating.

I meditate a little at a time, fifteen minutes or so. Then I hear the sounds of Vṛndāvana today and see the well-dressed pilgrim in the blue *sārī* or hear the lone man playing whompers and singing the holy name. I look down and see the earth again, hear the pigeons coo. A tractor putt-putts in the field and the breeze is warm at my back.

Be serious. What am I studying? Am I making the best use of my time? Can I chant Hare Kṛṣṇa with a little more feeling? Better I write that I see a dog trotting across the field than that I remember Burt Lancaster in his leading role in *From Here to Eternity*. I have that choice. I also have a choice to prefer *śāstra* over the dog. But some choices are not immediately mine because they are based on qualification. For example, I cannot choose to feel ecstasy at any moment. I cannot choose to know and understand my place in Rādhā-Kṛṣṇa's pastimes. I can choose to act humbly and to pray and serve and hear. I can choose to work in whatever way is auspicious for my Kṛṣṇa conscious development.

I see a male donkey tied with two ropes. One joins his right front leg to his right rear leg, and the other joins his left front leg to his left hind leg. There is enough play in the rope that he can walk, but he can't run. They didn't tie the female donkey. The male approaches her from behind, desiring to mount her. She kicks, aiming for his face. She strikes him again and again, just like Śrīla Prabhupāda describes. He keeps trying and she keeps running away. I sympathize with her. They run around and around while a little boy with a stick runs after them, trying to get them to go docilely with him.

A genuine Vraja *sādhu* would laugh at these notes. He will see me as a refined Britisher of the imperial age, recording impressions of India for people to read in London. No, I am not that. The donkeys mean something to me.

My spiritual master will help me. He will redeem my efforts and allow me to serve Rādhā-Kṛṣṇa when I show more surrender. Someone is calling out. It sounds like she is hawking goods in the street. "People of Vṛndāvana, if you want fruits, come and get them from me!" called the fruit vendor. Kṛṣṇa went to meet her, carrying grains for barter. They spilled from His little hands. The fruit vendor gave Him plenty in exchange and her basket filled up with jewels.

Wake up. Every inch is Vṛndāvana, the bricks and dirt and grime . . .

21

I am writing at Baladeva's house. A turtle is trampling down the blades of grass on his path. His chassis is low-slung. He stops and stretches his long yellow neck upward—it bulges like a frog's. He gets around.

This yard has nice shade, but I think of reasons to leave soon. The neighbors are suddenly noisy as they clean their pots on the other side of the wall. The flies are merciless, as is the heat.

O Rādhā and Kṛṣṇa, all universes emanate from You. You are the best persons of all. You reside in the *aprakaṭ* Vraja and in the hearts of pure devotees. I know how to form the letters of the English alphabet and how to make sentences. Therefore I can record the things I have heard in *śāstra*. Is it all right if I do so? Will it be a consolation? Will it be pleasing to You? I cannot sing or write poems like Tulasī-mañjarī or Tuṅgavidyā-gopī.

Rādhā and Kṛṣṇa love blissful Vraja. Sometimes Kṛṣṇa points out to Rādhā, "Just see the moon, the lotuses, and the Yamunā. They are all praising You." Vraja's nature serves

Rādhā and Kṛṣṇa. They please all who are pure in heart. He is God and She is His eternal consort. To the Vrajavāsīs, They are even dearer than that.

I heard that when Ganges water mixes with any water, even water in a drain, that water becomes Ganges. I beg that the genius of this place, Vṛndāvana, will mix with any streams of words I write and they will become Vṛndāvana writing.

Dear Gurudeva, I mean no harm. I am a jester, a caretaker of spiritual children and uneasy *bhaktas*. I am one myself. I amuse myself. But I want to be serious too. I keep insisting you take me as I am, but I know that the final choice is yours. You can allow me to follow my whimsy and it will leave me stranded. Please do not kick me away. I hope to learn to love Vṛndāvana on this visit. I hope not to offend. I am working at this for you and the *bhaktas*.

22

"O King, when the young ladies in Vraja heard the sound of Kṛṣṇa's flute, which captivates the mind of all living beings, they all embraced one another and began describing it." Is it that the flute song reminds them of Kṛṣṇa? Although we cannot hear it now, can we say it produces overwhelming feelings of Kṛṣṇa's sweet presence? The verse says they "began describing it." But in the verses that follow, they don't attempt to describe a melody, but a person, Kṛṣṇa—and the *effect* His flute has upon those who hear its song. For us, if we want to know the flute, is it a process of *neti-neti,* not this, not that?

How can a *sādhaka* become eligible to hear Kṛṣṇa's flute? Should he try to imagine it? No, no imagination. What about those who play the flute in this world? Especially in India, people are fond of the flute. There are many expert flutists, and it is even sometimes played in *bhajanas*. Does a devotee "spit on" such noise, taking it as irrelevant to Kṛṣṇa's flute? Or does it remind advanced devotees of Kṛṣṇa? I seem to remember that in *Caitanya-caritāmṛta*, *Antya-līlā*, Lord Caitanya once heard a cowherd playing a flute and it sent Him into ecstatic trance.

The words *veṇu-ravam* in this verse indicate "the vibration of the flute." This reminds us that the chanting of the Hare Kṛṣṇa mantra is also a sound vibration. Sometimes it is said that the *gāyatrī* mantra has a connection to the flute song—what is it? Brahmā heard the flute of Kṛṣṇa and spoke it in the form of *gāyatrī*. What does that mean?

This is a sort of scholarship of the intellect. Do I think I can probe Prabhupāda's heart by intellectual inquiries so that he will reveal his devotional gems to me? I just want to continue hearing Prabhupāda's descriptions in the *Kṛṣṇa* book and learn to appreciate what he is giving. It cannot be gained by intellectual exchange. I have to hear with submission.

23

The night is dark, but I have an electric lamp lit. The *choukīdār* blows his whistle somewhere out there. A storm came last night as I tried to sleep, and I had to climb up the shelves to shut the windows. Lightning and thunder kept us awake for awhile, but the rainfall is auspicious. I write to the music of the Indian air cooler and the crickets. I hope today will be a peaceful Ekādaśī and that I will be able to stay home and read and write.

When I came up to this roof to write, I had to wipe last night's rain off my desk. I am determined not to look at people passing stool in the field across the road, and not to be concerned with what our rooftop neighbors are doing. I have covered my arms and head with a *gamchā* to protect myself from mosquitoes and flies—these last two obstacles are the real test of my determination to write this morning.

The sky is lightening. The Oriental Institute field is soaked, and the trees and shrubbery are green and leafy. Here comes a file of elderly, wizened pilgrims down a windy foot path.

O Vṛndāvana, even I . . .

Every place on earth, especially rural places, can be divine at this time of day. A dawn sky streaked with blue clouds, birds flying. Maybe I will be able to think more of Vṛndāvana when I am in those other places. Let a bell anywhere remind me of the bell at Krishna-Balaram Mandir. Let me not forget this most special place.

"All directions are filled with glory! The world is full of bliss! Oh! Oh! I do not see anything except Vṛndāvana" (*Vṛndāvana-mahimāmṛta*, *Śataka* 4.32).

A bird formation flying across the sky in Vṛndāvana is special, because while seeing them, I hear someone intoning Vaiṣṇava chants, and I know I am in Vṛndāvana in the morning. It is not the same as being in Guyana or Pennsylvania. I am not entirely sure what the difference is, but I cherish that difference anyway and I pray to return to Vraja.

"If fools see defects in this inconceivably glorious earthly Vṛndāvana, where everything is effulgent . . . then what can the wise, who have the eyes to see, say to enlighten them?" (*Vṛndāvana-mahimāmṛta*, *Śataka* 4.51).

"O dearmost, supremely blissful Vṛndāvana, if I could see the splendor of your moving and nonmoving residents with millions of transcendental eyes, if I could smell your sweet fragrance with millions of nostrils, if I could hear about your noble virtues with millions of ears, if I could wander through you with millions of feet, and if I could bow down to offer respects to you with many millions of heads and hands, I would still not be satisfied" (*Vṛndāvana-mahimāmṛta*, *Śataka* 4.53).

Vṛndāvana is glorious because it is Rādhā and Kṛṣṇa's playground. Śrīla Prabhupāda was eager to bring his Western disciples here, so he constructed the Krishna-Balaram Mandir. He wanted us to live here carefully, avoiding offenses, chanting, hearing, and becoming purified by the spiritual atmosphere. Then he wanted us to go out and preach.

24

From hundreds of yards away I see a monkey walking on all fours across the *gurukula* roof. If they came to this roof, it would be too distracting. That's another opulence of the Sant Colony—no monkeys.

Yes, I know, this is surface stuff. I should know better. But I cannot expect to be one of those *vairāgī* mendicants, mentioned by Prabodhānanda Sarasvatī, in this lifetime. They wear only a torn cloth and wander homeless in Vraja, always crying in *gopī-bhāva*. That form of worship is not even recommended by our spiritual master. At least I aspire to read verses like this:

"I think the ultimate goal of life is to attain even a small amount of love for the land of Vṛndāvana, which is opulent with the splendid pastimes of Śrī Rādhā-Muralī-manohara's feet" (*Vṛndāvana-mahimāmṛta*, *Śataka* 4.65).

"O Śrī Vṛndāvana, I am now very fortunate. I have become the object of your very, very great mercy. You have given me the right to reside within your boundaries, a right that is prayed for by Lord Brahmā, Śukadeva Gosvāmī, Sanaka Kumāra, and other great souls. This gift gives me hope that some day I will directly serve the splendid, charming, eternally youthful, eternally amorous fair and dark divine couple" (*Vṛndāvana-mahimāmṛta*, *Śataka* 4.80).

It's humid. I can't get inspiring dictation from my own skin, and right now, the sight of four young Vrajavāsī boys loitering along the path doesn't direct me to Kṛṣṇa consciousness. Pray for mercy. You say you are what you are, but you pray, "Dear Lord, please forgive me and improve me." Prabodhānanda Sarasvatī prays directly to Śrī Vṛndāvana: ". . . If you have granted me residence within your boundaries . . . then why do you now hesitate to allow me to serve the great souls that live within you?" (*Vṛndāvana-mahimāmṛta*, *Śataka* 4.81).

I can also pray to Vṛndāvana-dhāma by Śrīla Prabhupāda's mercy. Let me beg for attachment to the *dhāma*; let me travel to its holy sites. Let me one day aspire to live here all the time.

Recently, I read references to retiring to Vṛndāvana in your fifties as a *vānaprastha* (Prahlāda recommended it to his father as "the best thing" he had learned.) But I am not a *vānaprastha*. Śrīla Prabhupāda once said to one of his disciples, "Preach while you are young. When you are old, retire to Vṛndāvana and chant Hare Kṛṣṇa. . . . But you cannot retire unless you have preached sufficiently. The mind will agitate. If you have preached, you can retire and chant Hare Kṛṣṇa—so preach as much as possible" (*Śrīla Prabhupāda-līlāmṛta*, Vol. 5, p. 94).

What is young? What is a devotee's retirement age? It varies. Retiring in the spiritual sense is for the very advanced. Mahānidhi Swami makes the point that Śrīla Prabhupāda approves our living in Vṛndāvana if we continue preaching here (as I might do by writing—or if I could improve myself, as befits one who accepts disciples).

"Although Śrīla Prabhupāda rejected Subala's idea for solitary *bhajana*, he did accept that one could continue living in Vṛndāvana provided he preached vigorously. Śrīla Prabhupāda told Subala: 'Better we spend our whole life and die just to make one person Kṛṣṇa conscious. That is our line, to become so absorbed in preaching Kṛṣṇa consciousness, whether in Vṛndāvana or anywhere" (*Appreciating Śrī Vṛndāvana-dhāma*, p. 247).

That is a good point—that one may also preach in Vṛndāvana. When a brother hears that someone is residing in Vṛndāvana he says, "Oh, but Śrīla Prabhupāda wanted us to preach." The six Gosvāmīs came here *just to preach.*

Thoughts on a humid afternoon.

25

A person in Vṛndāvana bows down. He is proud, foolish, but he worships the *dhāma* and the holy name. His writing is *bhajana.*

A bird like the whippoorwill . . . Now I will quit writing, he says, but no, go on.

I am a little nuts and this isn't a perfect pen. In Vṛndāvana, *in Vṛndāvana.* I keep saying it like a magic formula. I keep begging. But what do I want? I think I will be satisfied if I can write a pleasing, flowing record of my experiences.

Commendable, commendable.

I am not being sarcastic, but why not go deeper?

The writing should be the by-product of my prayer.

Okay, okay.

And you ought to know by now that writing is your *dharma,* so stop criticizing yourself for it. You may desire to go deeper, but writing isn't exactly a "by-product." It *is* your head on the earth and all parts of your body in *daṇḍavats.*

My prayers to Vṛndāvana are for simple things like, "Please let me chant with attention and love in the morning. Or let me feel unworthy that I cannot do it—but not in a neurotic way. *Let me cry.* Let me improve. Teach me how to chant."

Yes, Lord, I would like to write sweet love songs to You, but I am not qualified. So what does a guy do who wants to write in Vṛndāvana, who has come to Vṛndāvana just to write? He can write Prabhupāda's biography and purports to the "Prayers of

King Kulaśekhara," and he can do this—the simple days and nights in a house of old bricks and cement in Rāman Retī. It is the best situation I have ever had in Vṛndāvana, and I thank You for it.

I am just stressing and digging a little here to look for more. My wish-blessing: may you continue to hear in good consciousness. May Prabhupāda's words penetrate your thick skull and your dry heart.

O Vṛndāvana-dhāma, I need to quiet down.

26

Certainly the trees will see you come and go from Vṛndāvana. They don't write books trying to average a hundred pages a week, and they don't make photocopies so it doesn't get lost.

If we don't have lights by this evening, we will still get by.

"Although I am very wretched and fallen I still yearn to attain the wonderful state that even Lakṣmī, Śiva, and all the demigods cannot attain. Because I have offended you I cannot attain even a single drop of your transcendental nectar. I do not make even the slightest attempt to renounce the objects of sense gratification, which make one forget the path of religion. I am filled with bewilderment, grief, fear, and shame. O Vṛndāvana please protect me" (*Vṛndāvana-mahimāmṛta*, *Śataka* 6.3).

How do I relate to this verse? I lack the intensity to feel myself wretched and fallen or to be filled with shame. But when he says, "I have offended Vṛndāvana," I think that is why I cannot attain the nectar for which I am anxious. And when he says, "I don't make even the slightest effort to renounce sense gratification," I think, "What does he mean?" Does he mean illicit sense gratification, heavy stuff like the *karmīs* do? I have renounced all that, smoking, drinking, going out for entertainment. But if he means the regulated sense gratification which is allowable, then it is true: I make no effort to reduce it. I am attached to my bodily comfort. Then if I am guilty of *aparādha* and sense gratification, why don't I admit it and feel low and ashamed? I don't know why.

Berating my complacency. But let me be peaceful, I say. I want to hear the flapping of the laundry in the wind, see the play of shadows as the clothes line sways in the evening sunlight. Don't tear me away from this peaceful vision. I am here on an assignment, so why are you distracting me by telling me I am so unworthy?

Vṛndāvana is rural and religious, even today. More *dhotīs* than pants. When you see a young man in a gold and black striped shirt, gray pants, and sandals, it looks out of place. Your eyes are used to the old *dhotīs* and informal religious garb of mendicants or poor people—Indian cowherd garb.

If I lived here all the time, I wouldn't try so hard. I would settle for a regular, long-term service. I would read calmly. But I have other places I need to go. I have to preach in the West and guide disciples. So I am here like any Western-based devotee, soaking up the nectar. I want to go back with something to share. This is my slide show, my gift for my friends.

27

"O mother, in this forest all the birds have risen onto the beautiful branches of the trees to see Kṛṣṇa. With closed eyes they are simply listening in silence to the sweet vibrations of His flute, and they are not attracted by any other sound. Surely these birds are on the same level as great sages" (*Bhāg.* 10.21.14).

If we hear Prabhupāda's purports to the *Bhāgavatam*, then we will remember what he says and develop faith. We are faithful to the *līlās* because Prabhupāda has explained them to us. If we had read *Śrīmad-Bhāgavatam*, even with Viśvanātha Cakravartī Ṭhākura's commentaries, we would still not have become devotees. We would still have needed a guru's favor. We receive the guru's favor by "submissive aural reception." It's hard to understand, but it's true.

If my own speaking has any potency, it's because I repeat what Śrīla Prabhupāda says. I say it in faith and someone can hear it with faith. That is *paramparā*. I cannot speak it on my own; I have to be linked to the disciplic succession. I stay linked by repeating the words of my spiritual master. Therefore, although I don't *see* Kṛṣṇa's pastimes or realize them, I pass on the *śraddhā* and the pleasure and conviction that comes when you hear from the pure devotee.

In this verse, the birds are compared to sages. They close their eyes in ecstasy when they hear the flute. The branches of the trees are also transformed in ecstasy. In *Kṛṣṇa* book, Śrīla Prabhupāda writes, "From the behavior of these birds, it appeared that they were great scholars in Vedic knowledge and that they took to Kṛṣṇa's transcendental vibration and rejected all branches of Vedic knowledge." They rejected other Vedic branches and preferred the branches of an ecstatic tree that was struck with the vibration of Kṛṣṇa's flute.

The birds hear the flute. Don't ask, "How can there be such birds?" Don't ask, "Why is there anything?" Śrīla Prabhupāda explains that there is a ball dance in this world because it comes from Kṛṣṇa's original *rāsa* dance. Everything here has its origin in the Supreme. This is stated in the Vedānta aphorism, *janmādy asya yataḥ*—everything emanates from the Supreme Personality of Godhead.

That is why there are birds. In this world, the birds are an expression of His artistic nature. Various species exist to fulfill the desires of conditioned souls to have certain types of bodies with a certain set of senses. It is *māyā's* arrangement. It is a punishment or an awarding of karma. We wanted the human form of life, thinking it could satisfy our desires for happiness. But it is defective—*asat, acit, nirānanda*. In human life, we can learn of our big mistake and learn of the terrible system we have bought into. We can desire to get out of the cycle of birth and death. This awakening comes from hearing the spiritual master. The one who awakens our devotion to Kṛṣṇa consciousness is the spiritual master.

Vedic science is passed down from guru to disciple. By the same system that teaches us the transcendental ABCs ("You are not this body"), we can also learn of Kṛṣṇa's flute and the bliss it gives the birds who hear it in Vraja. The birds are not symbolic. They are birds. But to understand anything about these Vrajavāsī birds, we have to hear from the Vedic literature. We can do this not only in sessions where we sit at the guru's lotus feet and hear him speak, but we can read the commentaries and verses of scripture. By hearing from the guru in person, and by serving him, we can hear him speak in *paramparā* in his books. The books are enhanced by hearing—the books are opened by the explanations of the spiritual master. We should be in the mood of Mahārāja Parīkṣit, who heard his spiritual master speak with great urgency. Impending death should make us inquisitive, learned, and faithful.

28

We went out today. There was the usual rapid-fire bombardment of sights and sounds. I want to record a few things here that seemed worth saving.

I saw a cow nosing its way into a travel bag that someone had left on a motor scooter. The cow was actually opening the pack and getting into whatever was in it. Then on the way back, I saw another cow stealing grass from a horse-drawn cart.

These carts have a space underneath where they store grass to feed the horse. This cart was unattended and a cow was pulling the grass out from under it.

Westerners sometimes talk about the cows in India's city streets. They think it is a sign of neglect. They say that if India is supposed to protect cows, why are so many starving cows roaming the streets? But when you come to India and see how the humans struggle in the cities, it doesn't seem that the cows are at a particular disadvantage. People can't give cows some extraordinary preference over themselves. If the humans are struggling to get by, then the cows are partners in the same poor existence. Prabhupāda used to say that outsiders advertise the starving and dying people of India, but he never saw them himself. The people may be skinny, the cows too, but they are getting by.

I also saw a big white and tan goat sitting on a rope cot. These cots are for people, but the goat was acting like he owned it. Although you repeatedly see certain things, they can still be amazing.

Today we saw a big, fat water buffalo, soaking wet, walking down the street with a young boy behind it and another in front of it. The buffalo cow seemed to have a special value—she had big udders and was being attended by two boys. Buffalo cows are grotesque. They look like big rubber boats.

We also saw *sādhus*, ladies, merchants, *śūdras*, Muslims—so many sights and sounds flashed by that it's bewildering to even remember them all. It's good to be back in our quiet *āśrama* with a peaceful day ahead and then another.

29

"Eager to claim this body and house as my own, I am very pathetic. Pleased by worship from the people, I am pathetic. Blossoming with happiness to hear a few words of faint praise, I am pathetic. Even though in my hand rests the eternally splendid fruit named Vṛndāvana, which even goddess Lakṣmī and the great demigod Śiva cannot attain, I still refuse to taste it" (*Vṛndāvana-mahimāmṛta, Śataka* 12.12).

I am pathetic. I can't enter Vṛndāvana.

I want to say, "Accept Vṛndāvana as it is," but I'm not qualified to do that. Actual Vraja means Rādhā and Kṛṣṇa sporting on a swing, in the river, at a game of dice. When I say "Vṛndāvana as it is," I translate it into Vṛndāvana as I perceive it in my extremely limited way; the place where day after day there is no electricity; the place where my body is always sweaty and the bath water brown and salty.

Don't deny your good fortune in the name of modesty or the cynical habit of chopping down all good things. Don't cut down this auspicious young tree of hope of living in Vṛndāvana.

"Take me to Vṛndāvana. I will pass my entire life there placing myself at the feet of the great souls who are the crest jewels of all saints, and from whose mouths flows the nectar stream of the sweet transcendental pastimes of the dear lover of Śrī Rādhā" (*Vṛndāvana-mahimāmṛta, Śataka* 12.55).

The following is a verse from *Vṛndāvana-mahimāmṛta* that catalogues the poet's disqualifications. He means it. But despite all his shortcomings, he will take shelter in Vṛndāvana. Some wonder why spiritual persons still have so many faults. They prefer to go to *sādhus* who claim they have a deep taste for *rasa*. But the fact is, a holy man sees his own faults; he's good at that. It saves him at death. He takes shelter of the all-forgiving Lord. At least those *sādhakas* who still have faults need to admit them. Those who are completely pure admit faults they don't have. They are trying to teach others.

"I, who am a great palatial mansion where the most painful sufferings of hell reside, who am arrogant, deceptive, and shameless, who am bitten by the serpent named woman, who am not peaceful, who deep in my heart have love neither for Lord Mādhava nor His devotees, who am dull and stunted, who have no power to understand the land of Vṛndāvana . . . who is not firmly situated in celibacy, whose host of sins make it difficult for me to obtain the mercy of saintly persons, and who have no other shelter, shall now take shelter of Śrī Vṛndāvana" (*Vṛndāvana-mahimāmṛta*, *Śataka* 12.67–8).

When Lord Caitanya wandered in the forests of Vṛndāvana, a male and female parrot appeared on a tree and began to speak. They spoke with intense *rasa*, the male praising Kṛṣṇa and the female praising Rādhā. When the Lord saw the bluish necks of some peacocks, His remembrance of Kṛṣṇa awakened and He fell to the ground in ecstatic love. Balabhadra, the Lord's servant, sprinkled Him with water, fanned Him, and chanted the holy names. The Lord then gained outer consciousness and began rolling on the ground. He then ordered His friends, "*Bol! Bol!*" and they chanted Kṛṣṇa's names. The Lord's friends became anxious to protect Him because He was in uncontrollable ecstasy from one moment to the next. This is Vṛndāvana as it is, experienced by Śrī Caitanya Mahāprabhu.

"When Śrī Caitanya Mahāprabhu was elsewhere, the very name of Vṛndāvana was sufficient to increase His ecstatic love. Now, when He was actually traveling in the Vṛndāvana forest, His mind was absorbed in great ecstatic love day and night. He ate and bathed simply out of habit" (Cc., *Madhya* 17.228–9).

Kṛṣṇadāsa Kavirāja Gosvāmī says it is impossible to fully describe Lord Caitanya's ecstatic manifestations while He walked through the forests of Vṛndāvana. We read it today and store it somewhere in our empty hearts for future reference. Don't say I have no taste. I have very little taste. Lord Caitanya has all taste. But what does it matter who *I* am? Let us hear together of Lord Caitanya and Raghunātha dāsa Gosvāmī and those great saints to whom Vṛndāvana revealed all her secrets. They are our solace.

Prabodhānanda Sarasvatī says the great souls who drink the nectar flowing in Vṛndāvana have left us. "Now we are dead and can associate only with their names." He says they who became overwhelmed with *prema* when they saw the *guñja* berries in Vṛndāvana, "who muddied the ground with their tears . . . have now abandoned this world bitten by the poisonous snake of Kali-yuga and have attained Śrī Śrī Rādhā-Kṛṣṇa's lotus feet. Now we are left only with persons like ourselves. Now our hearts have become withered and dry and we are no longer able to maintain our lives" (*Vṛndāvana-mahimāmṛta*, *Śataka* 12.59–61).

30

When I notice a frog on my pillow, I am startled and my heart jumps. Is this fear? Such a lively emotion! Can't you transform it into Kṛṣṇa consciousness?

As I write, a monkey jumps on our roof. Action! My adrenaline flows. I wish Baladeva or Madhu were here to chase him away. He's up on the *paṇḍāl* beams over my head. I rap the stick sharply on the cement and he responds, but then reconsiders. He jumps back a foot or so and then decides to go about his business regardless of my stick. The friendly sparrows are also up there with their light-footed hops. But the monkey is like a Śaraṇāgati bear—go away! I'm not going make a big effort to search him out and chase him. It's not worth it. I came up here to write.

Śrīla Prabhupāda writes in his Tenth Canto purports that sometimes people find the Vṛndāvana monkeys to be a nuisance, but Kṛṣṇa distributed butter to them, showing us that all food is God's mercy and everyone is entitled to a share. I'm not so generous and I don't regard these monkeys as the "celebrated monkeys of Vṛndāvana" who take butter from Kṛṣṇa's hand.

The sun is orange only for a little while. It's beautiful. Then it rises higher and turns to a hot white-yellow. You can watch the transformation moment by moment.

"O Śrī Vṛndāvana, may your splendid handsomeness, which is increased by the two rivaling handsomenesses of the youthful transcendental forms of Śrī Śrī Rādhā and Kṛṣṇa, who are . . . enjoying a festival of passionate amorous pastimes, arouse spiritual desires within me" (*Vṛndāvana-mahimāmṛta*, *Śataka* 12.79).

(The sun is blazing now and the neighbor has increased the tempo of his prayers—his tongue is almost tripping over the Sanskrit as he ends each line in "*aha.*")

Prabodhānanda Sarasvatī states that his heart doesn't consider anything except Vṛndāvana to be real or important. He also says his desires are difficult to fulfill, but he prays to the dust of Vṛndāvana to fulfill his wish to do direct service for Rādhā and Kṛṣṇa. That's my goal too. But it's so far away that I can't claim it as part of my heart. I don't dream of it. I don't tremble with joy because of it. I don't feel miserable when the vision is removed from my attention. I don't jump to my feet when I see it again as I do when the monkey (or the frog) reappears in the pathway of my eyes. I'm pathetic.

You ask for the moon but then don't show ambition to attain it. They laugh. Yet Prabodhānanda Sarasvatī has written his prayers for people like me. We can ask for what we don't deserve and depend on Vṛndāvana to be merciful. But to make a prayer like his is not as easy as it seems. It appears to be a list of disqualifications and a statement of hope that Vṛndāvana will be liberal and overlook everything. It only works when we have faith in the power of Vṛndāvana. I pray for that.

"O forest of Vṛndāvana, it is not proper for you to ignore me, who has fallen into the blind well of hellish life and who has now taken shelter of you. In the three worlds no one else is willing to protect me, whose intelligence has been destroyed by a host of sins, who disobeys all the orders of the Supreme Lord, and who, although he thinks himself very intelligent, is in reality the greatest of fools" (*Vṛndāvana-mahimāmṛta*, *Śataka* 12.91).

31

"If one hears the singing of the birds of Vṛndāvana, then what is the use to him of all the *Vedas*? If one recites the names of the trees and other living entities in Vṛndāvana, then what is the use to him of a host of prayers and mantras? (*Vṛndāvana-mahimāmṛta*, *Śataka* 13.13).

That blue-topped bird is back today at the end of the bamboo beam. I'm glad they like to perch here. He turns his head almost completely around like an owl, looking all around, his body and feathers trembling in the breeze. Even if it doesn't rain, there is relief in the air.

A squirrel is chirping loudly and running on the wall. What's he afraid of? No one is chasing him, but he's chirping like a bird. A dozen or so goats walk the path in the direction of ISKCON. Little ones run to catch up. Two boys in short pants walk behind them. The goats are wandering out into the field, so the boys run after them and yell until they turn back.

I don't know what I desire. *Na dhanaṁ, na janaṁ, na sundarīṁ*. I don't want money or a beautiful wife or the pleasure of beautiful (mundane) poetry or followers. Then what do you want? Please don't say, "I only want to say a few bold, fluffy, birds have arrived on the roof." Say, "I only want Your causeless devotional service life after life." Yet Prabodhānanda Sarasvatī says if I recite the birds' names, it's like praying. They peck at the ropes, they hop on the canvas roof. They are all over the place. A blue-headed rough-breast has been sitting on the same perch for twenty-five minutes.

"Fools think the moving and nonmoving creatures in blissful, spiritual Vṛndāvana are conditioned souls bound by the modes of nature. We say they are worshipable for everyone and they are the two sources of the nectar treasure of pure devotional service to Śrī Rādhā-Muralīdhara" (*Vṛndāvana-mahimāmṛta, Śataka* 13.22).

Are these verses exaggerated to enthuse neophytes? It would be offensive to think so. Are these statements understandable only to liberated souls? I don't know. I want to think like the *sādhus* think, although I have no realization and there are no commentaries to unlock their inner meanings for me. I take them for what they are. If I can appreciate Vṛndāvana's trees and creatures, it will be a great gain for me and an asset in approaching Rādhā-Kṛṣṇa.

"Continually gazing at the intense sweetness of Vṛndāvana, Śrī Śrī Rādhā-Kṛṣṇa smile and laugh with unrestrained happiness. . . . and They melodiously sing the names of Vṛndāvana, saying: 'Beautiful Vṛndāvana,' 'All glories to Vṛndāvana,' and 'O Vṛndāvana!' What cannot be obtained by they whose tongues speak in this way?" (*Vṛndāvana-mahimāmṛta, Śataka* 13.18).

32

"Digest, digest," I tell my innards, and they grump back, "Eat less, eat less." But I can't starve. Everyone can see how skinny I am.

A bird raises its foot and scratches its head. One coos. The crow caws. Others whistle. The *mayūras* (peacocks) call from the fields. The sun ball is now clear of that low building, round and orange in the rare moment before it turns to fire. Make your wish now as the moment passes: May I worship Govinda and transcend the lethargic and troublesome body. May I relate to others without regret and anxiety, being myself and trying to serve devotees and the Lord.

Loving God is not a process of denial but of affirmation. The sunrise is part of God's artistry. The eternal adventure is to respond to Kṛṣṇa's call, "Come home."

"Cut the great ropes of misplaced hope, leave the poison forest of sense gratification, and fly, O bird of my heart, to the nectar forest of Vṛndāvana" (*Vṛndāvana-mahimāmṛta, Śataka* 14.3).

I was thinking this morning of Prabhupāda's Vṛndāvana poem: "All that is left is a list of names." My mother rejected me; my father too. It is all a fruitless glory. No wife, sister, material career, few friends. Even my position as initiating guru and author—what are these? Their essence is only service to others. Without that essence, they are illusions, meaningless. It's funny, actually.

33

Someone is playing a flute (not Kṛṣṇa)—a primitive, funky tune. I am sitting under a tree in a field where a few weeks ago, pilgrims had a city of tents. Madhu and I are on our way to Rāman Retī. I am not in the best mood. It is better to start out early in the morning. My head is already filled with letter exchanges and I have to give a lecture in the afternoon and another tomorrow morning.

Bicycle bell. Water buffalo grunting, headed my way. I am on the edge of the *parikrama* trail. Some people use this trail as a thoroughfare, but there are others too, in the exuberant mood of *parikrama: "Jaya* Rādhe!" I am somewhere between these moods.

The air is still nice, not too hot yet. The unmelodic flute goes on.

I would like to stay in Vṛndāvana. ISKCON devotees are starting to go back to Sweden and England and wherever else they are from. Some are writing me a last note: "I leave with mixed feelings," or, "I'm full of inspiration and hope that I can keep a little of it, like in a bottle I can sip from when I'm out on book distribution in London."

Rāman Retī: Nearby, there is a black cow with one white patch on her side. She lifts her hooves to shake off the flies. Lots of turds in this field from cows and others. The cows are frisky, fighting each other by butting their heads. One black calf approached me and I patted her, but now she is interfering with my writing. A white female dog wags her tail. The cows and calves surround me. Madhu is keeping them from getting too cozy. One brown and white speckled cow is picking fights with other cows and even with the dog.

Rāman Retī is right out of *Kṛṣṇa* book. Parrots screech and fly from one tree to the next. But now it is a desert despite the rains. Still, I can imagine Kṛṣṇa coming here and leaving the cows to pasture while He and His friends have a game of *kit-kit* in the field.

A well-dressed lady stops at the sacred well and pays her respects. Indian men and women sitting near the Kṛṣṇa-Balarāma tree draw designs in the sand. A firecracker explodes and peacocks cry out in protest. Parikramers with beadbags walk the trail.

I'm like a calf, ready to jump at any loud sound. I look up at a passing tractor and strain my ears to catch the sound of a bicycle bell. Mourning doves, parrots—I can't think much or sort it out, but I want to collect as much as I can before it's over.

I started out with shoes, but then I took them off and felt smaller and electrically connected to the earth. Shoes give you material confidence; parikramers don't wear shoes.

34

I remember in the West, I would see a hawk and be aware that I was not in Vṛndāvana. I would hanker to be in that place where your senses' reports are connected to *kṛṣṇa-līlā*. A tree in Vṛndāvana is much different than a tree in Ireland. But I also knew that when I came here, face to face with trees and bushes and birds—I would not be able to enter the mystery.

Kṛṣṇa, I do love to be a devotee. I want to be a devotee, although I am not ready to pay the full price. I have no desire to be something other than a devotee. I want to go on *parikrama* and bow at the roots of the *kalpa-vṛkṣa* trees. I want to hear from the Vaiṣṇavas and serve them. And I want to please Śrīla Prabhupāda by my actions.

35

I saw Yadubara Prabhu in the crowd yesterday. Heard he is making a film in Calcutta on the life of Lord Caitanya Mahāprabhu. Saw Santosh. He is now a professor in an American university. Heard he is doing a translation of *Prārthanā*. Saw others I won't mention and don't know what they are doing.

You have been indoors all morning, but not inside yourself.

What does it mean that I am on the surface of Vṛndāvana? Sounds like landing on the moon and walking over the crust. You don't get to see the people or the culture of the moon, just a desolate view of the crust, the craters, and outer space.

And what is the unconscious? Materially, it is the storehouse for impressions from many lives—animal drives, spiritual feelings, fear—mixed and unclear, spewing out in the life of dreams.

What good will remembering your dreams do? It's not like I am dreaming of Nanda-nandana herding His cows or of the exchange of sidelong glances between Kṛṣṇa and the *gopīs*. But it may help anyway. The person inside me is trying to express himself. He shouldn't be repressed. Let me hear the cues so I can attend to him. If we know better who we are, then we will stop clamoring to be heard and we will be able to chant with attention.

36

Someone said ISKCON devotees tend to be arrogant and to not respect the saints of other *sampradāyas* or other religions. Granted, we neophytes tend to be arrogant. We should be as humble as a blade of grass. We should think we know very little or nothing of love of God. We should respect all living entities—no *sādhu-nindā*, no *nindā* at all.

But I suspect a hidden agenda in my friend who says we should respect all saints. What if I say to him, "I respect all saints from afar, but I am fully satisfied to follow the *ācāryas* of the *rūpānuga-sampradāya*. And within that channel, I want to follow the line of Bhaktisiddhānta Sarasvatī and His Divine Grace A.C. Bhaktivedanta Swami Prabhupāda. I am such an ignorant child in spiritual life. That's why I don't trust myself to go to so many saints from different paths. I may get bewildered. The teachings and examples of the six Gosvāmīs, and the way their *śikṣā* has been presented by Viśvanātha Cakravartī Ṭhākura, Bhaktivinoda Ṭhākura, Bhaktisiddhānta Sarasvatī Ṭhākura, and Śrīla Prabhupāda, is fully satisfying and the safest for me?"

Before I met Śrīla Prabhupāda, although the saints of many religions were existing and in a sense available to me, they could not help me. Even the many incarnations of Lord Viṣṇu who appeared while I was wandering from birth to birth did not deliver me. But Śrīla Prabhupāda has saved me.

He is teaching that Lord Kṛṣṇa is the Supreme Personality of Godhead. Lord Caitanya is teaching the same thing, liberally giving *harināma-saṅkīrtana* and the *ujjvala-rasa* of Rādhā and Kṛṣṇa's pastimes. There is nothing to equal this.

As for contemporary practitioners in other faiths or *sampradāyas*, they may be more adept than ISKCON devotees in performing austerity, in study, in purity, even in surrender by devotion. I respect them. But it is not just a dogmatic attitude that keeps me from studying their books or going to talk intimately with them. I am too intent on the work of assimilating my own *sampradāya's* gift, the mercy of Lord Caitanya. And despite my disqualifications, I am stuck like a bee in the honey of the flower that is *vraja-līlā*. I don't want to leave. For friends, I seek those persons, whether householders or *sannyāsīs*, who cry when they sing, "*He* Gaurāṅga!"

Am I being sentimental? Narrow-minded? Hypocritical? Maybe. Although I want to be free of *sādhu-nindā* and I don't want to slight others, I want to keep my simple faith and interest reposed at the lotus feet of my spiritual master.

37

In Vṛndāvana, my mantra, my life-beat, my claim is plainness. It doesn't mean, "Leave me alone. Whatever I do is perfect." It doesn't mean you let the spider bite you. You can't give up your phobias and bad habits just because you have come here. You don't suddenly become a spiritual giant. But you are here. There's a special quality, a simplicity to Vṛndāvana life.

The nice thing about pre-dawn is that there is no cricket match. There could be loud music, but as yet there isn't any. It's quiet and you talk to yourself about the unseen mystery of Vṛndāvana. That seems so much more possible this early in the day. You look down into a mental well and seek.

38

I got up at 10:30 last night to answer the call of nature. Then back to bed, wondering what I want to do. Couldn't sleep well. Wanted to think things out. Kṛṣṇa, mercy will descend from You. There is no other way to achieve it. If I say one thing honestly, then another honest thing may come. But even if I am released from all obstruction, my own deepest, clearest thoughts can't reach far. I'm like the astronomer looking through his telescope. The human eye is limited, the brain defective. Spiritual truth descends. So I write, hoping to catch the rain, waiting (and singing) like a *cakora* bird waiting for a moonbeam.

39

Out of the house. As yet gentle sunshine. We walk the opposite way on the *parikrama* trail. Cows with decorations around their necks. No way I can describe the external phenomena of even a quiet ten-minute walk in the back section of Vṛndāvana. Don't try. We've just crossed the railroad tracks and we're sitting on a stone ledge under a tree near a small temple. One plaque in the temple portrays Hanumān carrying the mountain. At first I thought it was Lord Caitanya dancing.

We could go to famous, meaningful Gauḍīya Vaiṣṇava stops. I hope we will do that before we leave India. But I don't like having to deal so much with priests and whether we bow down in the right way with the right etiquette, the donation, trying to communicate, etc. So today we walk and stop and see and feel what we can. We are quiet; the sights and sounds are fresh—even the squeaking of a bicycle as it goes past, the slopping sound of water dripping from a pipe to the ground, the shrill cries of a group of bold-fluffy birds nearby.

Some people greet us, "Hare Kṛṣṇa, *Jaya* Rādhe." We don't imitate their greetings. But they call out from their homes, or a *sādhu* with big red and white Vaiṣṇava *tilaka* loudly insists, "*Jaya* Rādhe!" and we reply, "*Jaya* Rādhe."

Some smart-aleck kids are curious. They've stopped their bicycles and are making sounds with their mouths. Now, "Where are you from?"

"Ireland."

"How long are you staying?" The others are looking at me. One holds a tape measure. I'm ignoring them, but can't keep it up. They're about to outlast me (the crazy writer). But there is no tension—just enough distraction to destroy my composure for writing.

I am writing in a script that is mysterious to them. The two boys say, "Hare Kṛṣṇa," to dislodge me. We happen to be sitting by a tree where pilgrims circumambulate. I could try to outlast the curious boys, but I think I'll go now.

Now we're a little further down and have stopped again. There is a clearing off the road with a Śiva-liṅga on a platform. Squirrels are running around. To climb up, I reached for a tree trunk, but it was a cactus and pierced my finger. The squirrels are coming close to check me out. They are a little like the boys, distracting. If there were no distractions, what would I write?

Kṛṣṇa, You are here in these sacred places. We have no guide; we can't find You. We don't know what pastimes You performed in this place. All of Vraja is filled with the places of Your *līlā*. You walked and played here, no doubt. Now it's covered over. We are walking and chanting Hare Kṛṣṇa here, hoping that something will be conveyed to us by the earth, trees, air, animals, and temples, and even by the seemingly ordinary people riding by on their ox-drawn carts or on their bicycles.

I'm nursing the wound I got from the thorn bush. Sitting in a writer's *āsana*. Yes, it would be nice to hear the Lord's pastimes in Vraja. That's what makes an outing a significant spiritual experience. But if you chant and walk and see even ordinary sights in a receptive mood—a peacock, a pilgrim, the *parikrama* trail—so much can be understood.

40

Memories float across my mind: the "Signs of Life" train-crossing film shown to fourth graders at Public School No. 8. The wooden chairs with hinges in the auditorium. Teacher rehearsing us. She plays the piano, wet sweat under her armpits stains her blouse. Kids, Levi's, sighs—get out of Staten Island, please. But why this Vṛndāvana instead? Why? I'll tell you why. You go back to Staten Island and it's so much teenage vice and the crap of Dad's Republican party cigars and Mom's brainwashed hanging on to middle-class 1950s happiness and Catholic hypocrisy. I couldn't take any more even then, so why go back now and look at that sad self who didn't know anything? What else was there but playing basketball with Phil Backoff? How many things did I not understand then?

Whereas in Vṛndāvana, there's hope for *much* more. God is revealed as a cowherd boy. And the long, gradual, realistic road to reach Him over many lifetimes. The transmigration of the soul. The grounding in all these subjects as given to us by Prabhupāda. The inner meaning hidden for us, waiting for us to be ready for more. Yes, Vṛndāvana in any spiritual depth is where I want to be. That's why when you spew out images like "Signs of Life" train-crossing films and wind up in your teenage years, I say halt. I want to get down to the marrow of my spirit; I want to see the beauty of *this* day.

41

I'm used to the surface of Vṛndāvana. It doesn't disturb me much. Last night we got stopped in traffic jams one after the other. One was at the railroad crossing. We waited. People kept crossing with their scooters and on foot, ducking under the barriers until the last minute when the locomotive came wheezing by with its big headlight. They lifted the barriers and cars came forward on both sides with no organization or control. Then we got caught in a wedding procession. People held up dozens of long fluorescent bulbs, and carts were decorated with ornate flashing lights. We took to a side street, but we couldn't get the cows to move. Then there was a bus that couldn't move. I didn't mind so much. We went on talking.

People on foot make fun of us. Let them. It's mild. We don't get upset by the people we see here. It's better than you-know-where.

In India, many people treat us as *sādhus*, priests. Not in the West. Some brothers said it's good to get out of India and that role of seeing yourself as an honorable, brahminically superior person. Who touches a *sannyāsī's* feet in America?

42

Don't pride yourself that you are free of the frantic rush of the West. "I have no heater except the sun. The electricity goes off sometimes." So what? It can be just as much sense gratification to be living in the mode of goodness (*sattva-guṇa*) while living on the surface of Vṛndāvana without the anxiety of separation.

The old man on the next roof over comes out shouting, "Hut!" I look to see if it's a monkey he's chasing, but it's only a squirrel. The old man gathers up a small rug. His sunning on the roof is done for the day. Soon it will be cold again. That's the cycle. To live just for the cycle of nature—sun, dark, moon, cold, under quilts, rise in pre-dawn, mechanical *japa*, bathe, walk to *mandira*, greet the sun again, etc.—is not enough.

Sweet water here is a luxury. In the West it would be something else. This standard is simpler and closer to religious life. But in a sense, it's a greater waste. You come all the way to Vṛndāvana, but invest your being in savoring water, proud that you can drink it without touching your mouth to the cup. That means you are gradually becoming a Hindu *sādhu*, that's all. Where will that lead you in the next life? It's not enough, friend.

The reality of living here is taking hold. I have been able to come here two years in a row and spend two or three seasons (this year I came at the end of monsoon, then went through autumn and winter). So my writing here is no longer an enchanted daydream. I must face the fact of my existence in Vṛndāvana. I used to think *any* writing while here would be divine—superior to impressions in the West. Devotees used to write to me, "Come to Vṛndāvana. You never visit. Why? You are a writer. This is the place where the six Gosvāmīs wrote. Come on." I had an idealized picture in my mind that I would come here and what?—crouch under a *kadamba* tree and write? Did I think Rādhā would personally deliver me milk? Not exactly, but something like that.

Instead, I have reality. My reality is wonderful, but it is also limiting. It's just me and my writing methods, my old *karmī* impressions, sitting on the roof. I don't go out to sacred places much. But on days like yesterday, I associate with my Vaiṣṇava friends. I will have to gradually improve my Vṛndāvana reality and then the writing in Vṛndāvana will automatically improve.

43

Before I leave Vṛndāvana, I want to ask someone why the air and sky is so hazy. I want technical terms and a reasonable explanation. Fog, or smoke from fires, a reason like that. A poet can't just talk of effects without dealing with causes. It's the density of the haze that attracts me, and the fact that directly overhead—as I hold my head back to see it—the sky is clear blue.

It's not perfectly clear today. I don't think this is industrial smog or carbon monoxide from cars Los Angeles style. It's something natural, and it's getting thicker. Even the sun is covered. It's definitely a Vṛndāvana phenomenon.

Everything happening here has a unique flavor, like the striped sweaters they knit. The way the dirt is—sand-dirt. The combination of birds. Again I lack the science (ornithology) to tell you their names, but they are unique. Vṛndāvana is the coming together of ancient and contemporary. It's neither old nor new. It's *prakaṭ* and *aprakaṭ* in the same locality.

44

M. said I don't have to write utterly from the heart. It's not possible and many don't want to hear the details. I'm telling a tellable story in spurts. At least I'm not a hack trying to satisfy the editors of *Woman's Day* or *The Saturday Evening Post*. I write what I know and do, but I can't always go all the way with it.

Workers have completed a low brick wall on the "secret" construction next to this building. They get sand for mixing with cement by digging a hole in the ground. They get water by coming into our yard and using our pump.

I smell the earth and some odd smells when we go out the gate in the morning. We saw a new store or structure—what to call it? Someone had piled up some bricks without cement and used wooden soda crates to make a four-walled room right on the road near the temple. Overnight they covered it with an old cloth for privacy. When we passed it at 4 A.M., there was a light on inside and pop music on cassette. I suppose it's some commercial shop. No license, no building codes, no nothing.

That's a level of Vṛndāvana—what I see. A dog came up to me. He had cuts on his leg and he limped. What did he want from me? These miserable curs fight and maul each other. Rugged, destitute creatures like no dogs I've seen in America.

How they survive like weeds is amazing to me, but they always look defeated and barely alive. They are desperately feisty, yet cowardly, mean. That's past bad karma.

Another level is what I have heard from *sādhu* and *śāstra*. This is transcendental to the senses. In our *sampradāya*, we have the most learned and refined understanding of the goal and purpose of life, the soul, and God. Yet it usually exists in the context of simple material life, even poverty. But it's not degraded poverty. And since Bhaktisiddhānta Sarasvatī and Śrīla Prabhupāda, material poverty is not a requisite. But we do have to be renounced, using whatever we have in the service of Kṛṣṇa.

What do they tell me? When my mind is purified and I am free from anxiety and lust, then I will be able to understand Vṛndāvana and the love of Rādhā and Kṛṣṇa. When I am eager to study the books of Rūpa and Raghunātha Gosvāmīs, then only will I be able to understand the *yugala-pīriti*.

"O Lord Hari, Lord Hari, how wicked I am! I did not worship the lotus feet of Rādhā and Kṛṣṇa in Vrajabhūmi even for half a moment, and I am completely unable to understand the mellows of transcendental love" (*Prārthanā* 3.1).

The *ācāryas* know the fallen *sādhaka*'s state of mind. They address us as if they too cannot practice *bhajana*. Today's *Śrīmad-Bhāgavatam* lecturer said it's not enough to work hard. You also have to hear *śāstra*. Then you will realize it's Kṛṣṇa you are working for. I know this lecturer and am inspired to sit with him and hear his realizations. But in order to lecture to a large group, he raised his voice and made dramatic emphasis quite different than his ordinary talk. I found it hard to take. There is something artificial about the lecturing communication. But it has its place. Write him a note and say some of this?

45

Abhaya dāsa wrote me that after twenty-eight years in power, the PNC party in Guyana has been replaced by the PPP. He wonders if this will have an adverse effect on ISKCON. Multiply that by twenty and thirty different reports. Someone wants to know what he should do with a piece of land his father gave him in Trinidad. What is my opinion about entering contests that appear on the back of juice cartons in Ireland? A lady wants to know, "Now that the man I married has become inimical to Vaiṣṇavas and doesn't support his wife and children, should I still follow him?" Another asks, "Would having a child solve the problem of my husband's falling down and his coldness toward me?" I don't mean to heartlessly expose these confidential inquiries. I'm just explaining to myself why I may be pausing and looking around rather than taking earnest last stabs at being in Vṛndāvana.

Just below me they are digging in their garden and talking. The Hindi "talk show" radio is being broadcast as usual at this hour; I don't know what they are saying. A man and his wife walking on the path. I feel as if I'm an owl revolving his head around 360 degrees, looking . . . for what?

Flags are mostly limp. Domes saying to me, "Take your last chance and see us and speak. Do you know what temple domes are saying in Vṛndāvana?" The ISKCON temple bell says, "Do you think you will always be able to hear me ring 4:00 P.M. in Vṛndāvana?"

"Although I sometimes hear the nectarean message of Godhead from the mouths of devotees, because I commit so many offenses, I do not become purified. . . . What will I do when death comes?

"Although again and again I heard the *śruti* and *smṛti* scriptures' declaration that one should take shelter of Lord Hari's lotus feet in order to become fearless, I did not chant Lord Kṛṣṇa's name, and I did not meditate on His transcendental form" (*Prārthanā* 8.4).

46

I can remember golden Śrīla Prabhupāda in his gray *cādar* wherever I am. I will be able to visualize the stout marble pillars and ornate ceiling work of the noble Samādhi Mandir and a band of devotees standing at the open Deity doors. The whole terrain will be so familiar to me that I will be able to remember it in my mind or in my sleep. After the *ārati kīrtana*, while on your knees, take one last look at Śrīla Prabhupāda. Then start for the door, not speaking, even though surrounded by devotees. Put on your sandals, go carefully down the steps—and watch out you don't trip on the low-lying pole. Hear the almost eerie sound of the all-night harmonium being played in the temple and the voice of the one man singing there. Bow down to Śrīla Prabhupāda again, on the rug. Go forward and touch his foot. Take your place. Wait for the big doors to open, conches to blow . . .

You are so distracted you catch only a fraction of it every day. That's why there is value in the accumulated experience of attending the programs daily. Even a little devotional service will never suffer loss or diminution, and it can save you from the greatest fear.

As for *japa* . . . By walking the ground in Vṛndāvana while chanting, maybe something will stick. You will have the tendency to romanticize it when you think back. You may recall only some good details—imagining yourself alone at any early hour in the *bhajana-kuṭir* by candlelight. It will help sustain you in less ideal situations. You may tend to forget how inattentive you were, how concerned you were with the body. I don't say it's good to create a rosy picture of Vṛndāvana memories, but whatever you can do honestly, now and later, is worth the endeavor. You have no choice but to chant and go to the temple, even if you can't attract Kṛṣṇa by your activities. Then add the plea to it.

O Gopīnātha, I have fallen into the deep rut of mechanical "*bhakti*" performances. My faultfinding mind gives me no rest. I hold on to my false ego as if it were my most precious possession. How will You extricate me from this position? I beg You to give me special mercy, for then I will be able to tell the devotees how nice Kṛṣṇa consciousness is and what we all have to look forward to. I will remain humble. It's up to You.

47

Last day. A bird repeating a cry, but it's too early for dawn. His voice sounds like a hoarse whippoorwill. Maybe he's crying because it's so cold. But who knows? This is the land of Śrīmatī Rādhikā. He could be crying for any reason.

Why do I cry? I am hungry to make advancement. Please don't take Vṛndāvana for granted. I blocked out the night noises with earplugs, but now I hear an *āśrama* broadcast and peacocks off in the distance. Certainly when I leave here, it will be impossible to hear these things. Then I will experience a shadow (*abhasa*) of separation from Vṛndāvana. Maybe I will appreciate it even more than I do at present.

Why am I afraid of the crunch of loving emotions? I always try to prepare myself to soften the blow. I try to think what it will be like sitting in the airport waiting room in Delhi, thinking about Vṛndāvana, feeling bereft. Then when I enter the Western world of material efficiency, I will wonder where my

Vṛndāvana life is, my quiet, homespun *bhajana*. Will it be washed off? Is this what will happen? How can I live with that?

I won't be wearing a *bandhī* in the West. I won't be walking the sandy lane spotted with the dung of animals. I won't be seeing the darkness lit by the light atop the white temple dome. I won't be seeing the gorgeous architecture of Prabhupāda's Samādhi Mandir.

I will be preaching. I will be serving my spiritual master. I will also be remembering Vṛndāvana. But I won't be hearing the temple bell on the hour and the half hour, although if I'm lucky, I will hear it inside my head.

When I get back, I will start the process of looking at the calendar all over again, wondering if I will ever return from the world of calamity and war—whether that world will prevent me from getting back to Vṛndāvana. Or whether my body will completely break down. Whether I will be dependent on what I have stocked up so far . . .

Therefore I wrote in Vṛndāvana. For later, just in case.

Other Places

Māyāpur

1

I was chanting on the roof at 3:30 A.M. The near-full moon was covered in long blankets of clouds. Eventually, the clouds blew past and the moon shone brightly. So many blessings are coming to me, but not the blessings of pure love of God. Kṛṣṇa reciprocates with us, so I must be indicating to Him that I want a shelf full of medicines, a mattress and bolster pillows, Bisleri drinking water, my own house to live in—and Kṛṣṇa is saying yes easily enough, since He can grant anything and everything. I have requested pure love, but He hasn't heard that request because I don't ask deeply enough.

It is a sad fact. D. H. Lawrence said, "Ours is a tragic age and therefore we refuse to take it seriously." If I took it seriously—that I am opting for less than pure love of Kṛṣṇa—it would be more than uncomfortable. It would be unbearable. But I don't take it seriously. Śrīla Prabhupāda said the asuric sinners would shudder if they accepted the facts of transmigration of the soul; therefore they refuse to consider it.

It is not just a matter of giving up amenities, but we have to give up everything, including our sense of identity. I don't seem to be able to do this. This is what is so tragic, but even as I say it, it doesn't mean much.

All *jīvas* participate in the universal conditions of birth and death. Kṛṣṇa preaches to all *jīvas* when He instructs Arjuna in the *Bhagavad-gītā*. Yet each individual has to realize it alone. A Godbrother just wrote me and said how he has been suffering from family attachment. He is married, but is now separated from his wife and children. He writes, "Now the words 'family attachment' have taken on a new depth of color and power to me. I have been there and it is not at all an abstract idea. It is a tight, tight bond, and breaking it is like having Godzilla pound on your heart. Maybe even worse."

I have to realize my predicament. It is still an abstract idea—that I don't love Kṛṣṇa. No one can do it for me. They can point out the urgency—but I have to feel it for myself and do the needful.

2

Praise Śrī Kṛṣṇa who performs the *rāsa* dance and who lives in the *dhāma*. There are peacocks here in Māyāpur, and a steady din of crickets (and a million other insect species) in the night. They are background music. Poets hear them as asking a question: "What are you going to do to attain Kṛṣṇa consciousness in your brief lifetime?"

Soon devotees will start rising, scraping chairs, clearing their throats in the bathroom. The sounds will get louder. Then we all gather for *darśana* before Rādhā-Mādhava.

I do not want to feel out of place. Social obligations are meaningful too. But right now it is just me and the crickets. Is this my imagination? Do I really hear them asking me a question? Do I really sense them speaking a secret? Do they know what I don't know, the simple facts of life? I turn to the pictures of the *ācāryas* in disciplic succession and to the sophisticated cultural technique of writing symbols on a page.

Soon I will turn to the spiritual vibration. Crickets may "chant" in Māyāpur, but we humans are meant to directly enunciate God's holy names, as Lord Caitanya Himself did in Gauḍa only five hundred years ago.

3

I have been brought here. This is pilgrimage. I have my specific duties. We are all serving our spiritual master in the *dhāma*. My specialization is a detail—the main thing is that whatever I do, there is something rendered as service to the pure devotee. Śrīla Prabhupāda advised us to taste the *rasa* of preaching. He said the quickest way to attract Kṛṣṇa is to bring other people to Kṛṣṇa consciousness. Spread the word, "make" devotees. Whoever does so is the dearest servant of the Lord and there will never be one more dear.

Preaching can be intense. The preacher has to constantly qualify himself. His audience demands the real thing. If he preaches surrender, then the preacher must surrender. If he preaches love of Kṛṣṇa, then he must love and serve and worship Kṛṣṇa. Just as a doctor or professor has to attend so many intensive seminars throughout his career to keep abreast of developments in his field, a preacher has to stay in touch with the *japa* of the holy name and with the pastimes of the Lord. He also has to stay in touch with his own honest self. He has to ask himself, "Am I a devotee? Why am I practicing Kṛṣṇa consciousness? What benefit am I deriving from it?" Greed *(lobha)* is the price of love of God. It is also called *laulyam*, intense desire to serve the Lord.

O Kṛṣṇa, do you need another writer of poems? I know You don't *need* me, but can I develop myself to help one of Your poets? Can I learn to compose poems for You? Or, if it is not to be my service, then what can I do for You eternally?

I think if I serve my spiritual master in this world, that will be sufficient qualification to guarantee me some service in my next life and to gain eternal service. It's best to bet on a sure thing. The stakes—life and death—are too high to take a wild chance on a dark horse. Go with the strong one, the lover, the teacher, the revealer of the *dhāma*.

And if I do not desire to enter Rādhā-Kṛṣṇa's pastimes—because I do not possess the strong greed to do so—at least I can return in my next life to associate with Śrīla Prabhupāda and his movement, to live with Prabhupāda in this world. His movement will increase for the next ten thousand years. There is time enough to return and qualify myself. But what am I waiting for? Bhaktisiddhānta Sarasvatī Ṭhākura prods us, "Finish up your business in this life." We have to give up whatever exploitative mentality we have and live in this spiritual movement, which is meant not for fulfilling someone's personal motive, but to benefit people all over the world.

4

I am a tiny person, a happy person, a village teacher, a street sweeper, a bird in the woods. I am Satsvarūpa dāsa, New York-born and raised, Brooklyn College literary magazine poet. I am the Swami's man. And I want to write to win people for him—like a conqueror. Call it proselytizing or evangelizing if you like. I do it as I can. And for this I will need to go as deeply as possible into Gauḍīya Vaiṣṇava realization of the soul's relationship to Rādhā-Kṛṣṇa. For this we have come to spiritual India.

This is my aspiration, now let me demonstrate sincerely to Kṛṣṇa that I want it. I don't want to merely be a shadow representing a weak or mixed desire. I know I cannot immediately accomplish whatever I desire. There are always obstacles and my mind gets distracted too quickly. But I pray to be fixed in determination. I seek inspiration from those with similar vocations to be Śrīla Prabhupāda's followers. Let us develop good qualities and inspire one another. Why should the *karmīs* or devotees in other *sampradāyas* have attractive qualities and not us? We must love one another. Ah, why do I say, "we"? *I* must

. . . let me be the one to begin. Let me move to love. Let me by myself. Let me accept others as they are—as they aspire to be, as they are at best. Let me help them to become better, but not by attempting to control them or overpower them or gain their worship for myself. Can there be a society of honest, submissive *sādhus* who permit each other space to live, and who can permit the creative urge? Yes, may we flourish.

We want to be learned in Vaiṣṇava *siddhānta*, to be realized with the unique twist of the followers of Bhaktivinoda Ṭhākura, Bhaktisiddhānta Sarasvatī, and Śrīla Prabhupāda. We want the *ācāryas* to be pleased with us. May we not only take what they have given, but develop it fully. We must beg them to reveal to us how to do this. I do not want to accuse or revile those who are not followers of my Guru Mahārāja; instead let me appreciate the God consciousness they are trying to develop. I want to be strong enough to speak boldly when required (as befits a follower of Śrīla Prabhupāda), and I want to do it with my own voice, not as an imitation of Śrīla Prabhupāda. I want to be surrendered to him so that I am serving him with my self. In that way, I will be able to serve him wholeheartedly and develop an understanding of all that he teaches and represents.

5

I went to see where Sāmba works constructing the Māyāpur city. Then I went to the old GBC rooms, then visited the present facility. All that is in the past for me. I looked at the picture of Śrīla Prabhupāda in his thatched cottage and he looked back at me. Śrīla Prabhupāda's face combines a "dressing down" of the foolish disciple as well as an inscrutable, compassionate gaze into his soul. He wants to help us. He is able to help us if we follow him.

This is my last night in Māyāpur. The green *kadamba* leaves move in the breeze. I hear the train horn in the distance. The *gurukula* boys are off on a boat, propelling it with a long pole. They have moved to the center of the flooded plain. One of them dives from the boat and a moment later, the sound of the splash reaches my ears. Then another boy dives. I wish I could be with them instead of watching. Their lives seem simple and sublime, living in a grove of palm trees and clean mud huts.

Now they have brought their boat ashore. The muggy heat and the Rādhāṣṭamī feasting leave me feeling lethargic. I am counting on early morning to revive my mind with pointed and flowing expressions. If I get up enough drive tonight, I will return to reading aloud from Prabhupāda's books. It doesn't look like Bhaktisiddhānta Sarasvatī Road will flood. Our brief stay in the *dhāma* is coming to an end.

Before I leave the *dhāma*, I want to remember that it is an offense to commit violence to any of its residents or "to consider Navadvīpa and Vṛndāvana different." Can I make a list of everything ordinary I can think of here? Give homage to lights across the water as night comes on. Drum sounds coming from different directions. Radio—violins and a cinema singer. The red sandstone railing on the roof. The pinnacle of the Yoga-pīṭha. Madhu's bowing down after each *japa* round while facing in that direction.

An army of ants surrounds a piece of *iddli* on the floor. When I removed the *iddli*, the ants panicked and ran back and forth. Two *gurukula* boys made me two *daṇḍas* and I gave them each a "silver jubilee" ISKCON pen as gifts. I saw the gazelles in the zoo standing on the high ground. I thought they looked happy until I saw the big one with the horns push the smaller ones off the hill into the water.

Tall Rādhā-Mādhava in the temple with Their broad shoulders. I saw the golden back of small Rādhā-Mādhava during the *abhiṣeka*. We poured green liquid, then red, then yellow.

Jananivāsa told me not to use my left hand and my feet felt tired on the cool marble floor. Bengali devotees leave off the "a" when they sing, "*Jaya* Rādhā-Mādhav."

I pray to take these impressions with me. I returned to sit in the old GBC room and allowed twelve years of memories and ghosts to pass by briefly. But then I saw no profit in staying there. The sun is bright now in the land of Gaura-Nitāi. "Peaceful." Someone wrote that in the guest book. Sweets. Clear water, four showers a day. It didn't flood, but we saw it come close.

Bombay

6

Dr. Patel came to Śrīla Prabhupāda's *guru-pūjā* wearing his usual white pants and shirt. He also wore a white glove on one hand. He looks all right for his years. We talked a bit. He complained that "they" (the Bombay devotees) don't treat him right; he doesn't even have copies of *Śrīla Prabhupāda-līlāmṛta*. "Not like I was treated by Prabhupāda when he was here. It has gone down . . . I don't know what it is like in the States . . . " I gesture with my hand that it has gone down, but we are still trying to follow Śrīla Prabhupāda.

Yes, that is how it is, he says. It goes down when the *ācārya* leaves.

"Try to forgive us," I say.

"Forgive! Oh! What am I?" he asks. "I am just a small man." But still, he complains. We all do. In a sense it was truthful to openly admit that it has gone down. Did you think that it could be the same when the great soul was here blazing the way for us, pushing and creating a harmony that no longer seems possible? We must be loyal, and it is loyal to admit that things were special when Prabhupāda was here.

7

ISKCON Bombay—the lights on in the hotel room, the marble floor, our own bathroom . . . the elusive present moment, present day . . . the big old typewriter on the desk, but little time or presence of mind to use it. Always a crunch wherever you are in the world of going to write while hungry and empty and dumb.

I remember going to hear about Kṛṣṇa. Quietly going down to *maṅgala-ārati*, the wealth of the ISKCON Hotel and the Hare Kṛṣṇa Land *mandira*. Quiet, tropical weather, the walk on the beach. Prabhupāda is never far away there. So much to do. Misgivings that I didn't meet with someone who wanted to see me.

The look of happiness on Dr. Patel's face as he encouraged Tamal Krishna Mahārāja and Girirāja Swami to take the Deity *caraṇāmṛta* before him. Then he took it himself, the creamy liquid in his palm. A few moments later I looked back and saw him again. He looked old and sad, distant and lonely, feeling neglected I suppose.

Śrīla Prabhupāda's *vyāsāsana*—a whole gazebo of a *vyāsāsana*—almost a little chapel unto itself. I went and touched his feet under his saffron silk.

Later, we went to Ahmedabad. I remember the crowded airport and the two *sannyāsī* members of Swami Nārāyaṇa's group wearing fez-shaped turbans and red dots on their forehead . . . and I don't remember so many other things. I remember the feeling of time passing and then noticing that it had all passed. I watched the bright marigolds in the garden. My first impression of the temple was that it was a house, with no outer sign to indicate that it was a temple. Gradually I grew to know the place.

M. and I joke about the "double talk" of so many Indians. They never speak straight about what time a program will be held, how long it will take to drive there, and whether we will go or not. Expect anything, even after you think you have made all arrangements. Indian "standard time," Indian evasiveness, Indian gentility, and the honor they give all *sādhus*.

America

8

There is always pain somewhere in the body with only brief respites in between. No pain can be stopped permanently. Time is getting shorter and my death is coming closer. There is no time to waste.

I try to spend my time in these two rooms constantly, enjoyably, studiously, prayerfully, moving from reading to writing. Let there be no duality between my search for Kṛṣṇa consciousness in *japa* and hearing and my expression of that in the written form. Like most ISKCON devotees, I am following Śrīla Prabhupāda's directions to maintain Kṛṣṇa consciousness in places all over the world. "Vṛndāvana is inspiration only. Our real field is worldwide preaching." I am at a stage where I had to leave Vṛndāvana, yet for the first time in my life, I am seriously trying to maintain the Vraja mood.

It is evening and I have nothing to say. After all, this is not Vṛndāvana. There is a soft, white moon in the blue sky. It is mid-January, 5:00 P.M. Isn't this also God's country? But it is not Vṛndāvana. I burn a votive candle and feel the quiet of this cabin. The moon is so white and full through the branches of the leafless trees. The heat creaks through the wall panels and somewhere a dog barks a few times.

In Vṛndāvana I knew I could write whatever I observed and it would be close to Kṛṣṇa. Vraja is special. Where am I now? Is it worthless to record my vision of the full moon because it shines over Pennsylvania?

When I was in India, one of the devotees wrote me several times that I shouldn't allow myself to forget Vraja. That advice occurs to me again. It seems easier to go back to my former forgetfulness and to justify it as the reality of life in the West. How can I imply that Vraja consciousness is unreal for me? The fact is, I will have to learn to accommodate Vraja even at Gītā-nāgarī. The white winter moon is picturesque and within Kṛṣṇa consciousness, but don't forget Vraja.

9

This morning when I was singing before Rādhā-Dāmodara, I thought of Vṛndāvana. O Vraja, I am so far away from you. Please, can I directly address someone? My spiritual master, Śrīla Prabhupāda? Don't say that I cannot address anyone because if I can't, then I am utterly alone. And God doesn't want me to feel that way.

It is cold out. That means a bottle of whiskey for some, or crime—the jagged panes of anger. All are told, "Love God and be kind to others." What can it mean to someone shivering in the cold of illusion? There are millions of cities—all bigger than that little dirt town of Vṛndāvana in Uttar Pradesh, India. Vṛndāvana has poor electrical lines—sometimes they glow and flames shoot out—it has no central heating; it is an insignificant place. But from our viewpoint, Vṛndāvana is the hub of the world. Boston is not the hub, or Chicago, or New York or Los Angeles or London, Paris, Moscow. A small town named Vraja is the hub.

When that earth tremor occurred, all the Vrajavāsīs started shouting, "Rādhe! Rādhe!" and running to the Yamunā. They took it as a divine manifestation of *prema-bhakti* and were ready to die in some *līlā*. The poverty and elegance of New York City are appalling and ignorant compared to Vṛndāvana.

10

"Dear Lord of the *bhaktas*, I don't want to go back to Godhead leaving behind the poor fools." That's what Prahlāda said. But Bhaktisiddhānta Sarasvatī Ṭhākura also said we should ignore the demons, as is befitting a *madhyama* preacher. Mixing with demons only increases their ridicule of the Supreme Lord, "thus further deteriorating their polluted existence." The preacher should avoid imitating the Lord's pastimes of apparently hating the demons because "there is danger that his mind will become bewildered by such association [of powerful atheists]" (*Bhāg.* 11.2.46, purport). So the Vaiṣṇava preacher meditates how to save envious people, but he discriminates in how he gives them mercy.

We follow directions like these. Tricky decisions have to be made constantly along the way. *Mahājano yena gataḥ sa panthāḥ*.

I pray my hesitating pen will find the right course.

But what conviction do I have that today will be any different than yesterday? What hope that I will become that much more advanced? Partly I could tell myself, "Have faith in the process itself." We all have to have that. Then I could tell myself to apply myself more. Reading sacred texts will have a good effect. As for making huge, quantum leaps ahead, why should I expect it to be so easy? Prayer is prayer. When it is sincere, it always seems to bring us back to the beginning stage. We have to admit we are struggling to remember Kṛṣṇa, that we don't really *love* Kṛṣṇa, and we have to beg for tears of remorse. Our goal is to one day assist Kṛṣṇa's intimate associates. We need to practice more and more.

Pray to serve, and serve, and serve. I heard Śrīla Prabhupāda say with conviction—and experience—in his voice, "The preacher is not afraid to go to heaven or hell for Kṛṣṇa. *He will go to hell to preach.*" The devotee-preacher will do whatever Kṛṣṇa wants; he takes the holy names and distributes them to everyone he meets.

For me, this preaching spirit should be nondifferent than my internal cultivation. They are both ultimately part of the same state. They are both part of spontaneous love. Neither preaching nor prayer is external. Bhaktivinoda Ṭhākura prays, "My offenses ceasing, taste for the name increasing, when in my heart will Your mercy shine? . . . When kindness to all beings will be appearing, with free heart forget myself comforting, Bhaktivinoda in all humility prays, 'Now I will set out to preach Your order sublime'" (*Śaraṇāgati*, 9.1.1,8).

Vṛndāvana is the place to become Kṛṣṇa conscious, the best place to relish Kṛṣṇa consciousness. It is what we desire for those to whom we give free meals at our "Food for Life" booths.

11

When Lord Caitanya finished speaking to Śrīla Rūpa Gosvāmī, He had to leave. He left by boat. Rūpa Gosvāmī begged the Lord not to go, or at least to take him with Him. "No," Lord Caitanya said, "I asked you to go to Vṛndāvana and you are not far from there, so go there and write books. I will see you again in Purī." But Rūpa Gosvāmī felt so much separation that he fainted. Then he went to Vṛndāvana. He felt separation from Kṛṣṇa there and followed the empowering order of Śrī Caitanya Mahāprabhu. He was the literary incarnation of Lord Caitanya, writing down all the inner meanings of His mood. He did that service rather than travel with Lord Caitanya.

Ah, me. Please let me have an assignment that brings me close to Prabhupāda and the *ācāryas*. I want to transform this world into Vṛndāvana. This road in the morning, the trees ahead—as brief as it is, as far away as it is from Vṛndāvana, it can promote thoughts of Kṛṣṇa in Vraja. I can still picture walking down that lonely dirt path with a friend, stopping after a mile or so and saying, "There is no place in the world outside of Vṛndāvana where the sand is *cintāmaṇi*." Pointing to the yellow mustard flowers . . . I remember that now, here on a cold, unfriendly road. I walk toward the lopsided moon and relish the cold and the talking to myself. Somehow I am meant to be here and to think alone, but without that contact with my friends, I would be way off the beam.

12

I dreamt of undergoing many hardships while living on a farm. It started out with me searching for my *candana* ball in my *śuci* kit. Then there was no light and no mirror to see if I was applying the *tilaka* neatly to my forehead. The cows were wild and dirty. The man in charge assured me that when this new farm got organized in the future, I would be recognized for my spiritual qualities.

Out of this dream, where to go? Mentally stumbling, I splash my face with cold water. Can I wash those thoughts away with the shock of the cold water hitting my face? I am so far away from Vṛndāvana.

Remember how at the Krishna-Balaram Mandir guesthouse, the floor is made from Indian cement? There was no rug and every time I moved the wooden chair at my desk, it made a loud scratching sound. I kept thinking I must be waking everyone up on that floor. What could I do? I tried writing anyway, and sometimes it worked, although I filled some pages with the sound of pigeons flapping their wings. I was trying to get beyond the externals, although I know I didn't always succeed.

The *śāstras* are vital to my life. They are the key to leaving behind my dreams and the pigeons and to entering the association of the Vaiṣṇavas. I have so many unnecessary demands, but one sincere moment with the *śāstras*, or the sincere offering of *daṇḍavats*, or the sincere recitation of *praṇāma-mantras*, can take me beyond those demands.

I will not be saved simply by returning to Vṛndāvana. I have to prepare myself to meet the same obstacles and probably new ones, and to practice deep, purifying *sādhana*. How can I engage my mind and senses in Kṛṣṇa consciousness and awaken *bhāva*?

13

Improve the quality of prayer. Hardly an inch do I pray. Or maybe I pray and don't credit myself for it. Kṛṣṇa will decide if I am praying.

Then how much can I help myself? I recall a devotee asking Śrīla Prabhupāda, "You say we should surrender to Kṛṣṇa, but then you write, 'God helps those who help themselves.' So?"

Śrīla Prabhupāda replied: "How does one help oneself? By surrendering to Kṛṣṇa." That's the only way we can help ourselves.

This is not Vṛndāvana where I can write with the awareness in my heart and body and being that I am in that special place. The advantage to my rest stop here at Gītā-nāgarī is that I have to become more internal. Is Vṛndāvana within? Yes. Pennsylvania forces me to go within because I cannot just stay focused on how I took my walk on the back road and how I felt when a car passed me. There is junk and distraction in Vṛndāvana too, but it is totally different. If I could have had more presence of mind there, I could have written like a madman, noting down all the details. I would have captured many motes of Vṛndāvana dust on paper. I didn't quite do it. I also have to go within in Vṛndāvana.

Outer Vṛndāvana doesn't seem to tally with what we read in *Kṛṣṇa* book. We need the guidance of a Vaiṣṇava to understand it. It cannot be seen by mundane eyes, cannot be experienced by the mundane senses, cannot be felt by the mundane body. Śrī Vraja Maṇḍala can only be realized by the mercy of a Vaiṣṇava . . . revealed within the heart and mind of a devotee.

Head on in—pray to write truth as best you can.

Dear Śrīla Prabhupāda, I place my head on the floor and pray by reciting your *praṇāma-mantras* first thing. Get me out of the dream-stuff. Please guide a sleepy-eyed person where to go. And now, face and mouth washed, sitting at a desk writing by reflex with a professed good intention, please tell a covered, frightened person what to write.

14

Hurry along, hurry as you do when they rush you through the Indian temples—you can only see the Deity for a moment or two. Life is short and everyone has to pass through these doors, your father and mother, and before them, their father and mother, and before them, their father and mother *ad infinitum*. It is a wonder people don't think they are going to die, as if anyone is an exception. I can preach on this point using myself as an example, then after the lecture, some people will touch my feet. Like other *sādhus* I will then ask, "Where do we honor *prasāda*?" It is the most wonderful, amazing thing in the world.

And who likes the old, the feeble, the dying anyway? Don't they get in the way of our vigorous lives? Don't they disrupt our plans with their measured slowness? Don't they sometimes act in disgusting ways? Śrīla Prabhupāda detected this disparity in his own followers and he commented on it: "They don't like me. They think I am contaminated?" We faithfully went to his bedside and chanted with him, but there was no activity. He wasn't speaking. So we went back to Delhi and caught our flights back to Los Angeles or Germany or London, back to work on Prabhupāda's behalf. Business as usual.

Why these "morose" thoughts on this cold winter morning? My Lord, my guru, I pray that on my deathbed, I will think of you. I want to savor that verse as I savored it during my outdoor walks in Ireland—". . . whoever, at the end of his life, quits his body, remembering Me alone, at once attains My nature. Of this there is no doubt" (Bg. 8.5).

The destination, "My nature," may refer to many different abodes and relationships with the Lord. It does not automatically mean we go to Vraja. Śrīla Prabhupāda writes, "Anyone who quits his body in Kṛṣṇa consciousness is at once transferred to the transcendental nature of the Lord." This statement is like a *sūtra*. If we put it together with all the other statements in Śrīla Prabhupāda's books, we will understand that he is telling us to think of Kṛṣṇa in a particular way—according to the mood of the residents of Vṛndāvana.

Śrīla Prabhupāda first had to convince us of the basics in Kṛṣṇa consciousness. "If one wants to achieve success at the end of his life, the process of remembering Kṛṣṇa is essential. Therefore one should constantly, incessantly chant the *mahā-mantra*—Hare Kṛṣṇa Hare Kṛṣṇa, Kṛṣṇa Kṛṣṇa Hare Hare/ Hare Rāma Hare Rāma, Rāma Rāma Hare Hare" (Bg. 8.5, purport).

At the end of the *Gītā*, Śrīla Prabhupāda makes it clear that by "Kṛṣṇa" and "Hare Kṛṣṇa mantra," he is referring to Kṛṣṇa in Vṛndāvana: " . . . the very form with two hands carrying a flute, the bluish boy with a beautiful face and peacock feathers in His hair. . . . One should fix his mind on this original form of Godhead, Kṛṣṇa. One should not even divert his attention to other forms of the Lord" (Bg. 18.65, purport).

Śrīla Prabhupāda had to first gather us in. He had the responsibility of gathering in the whole Western world. Therefore, when someone asked about Kṛṣṇa, Śrīla Prabhupāda would sometimes respond in a debating spirit, "Why talk of Kṛṣṇa? Kṛṣṇa is far, far away. First understand that you are spirit soul. Do you agree?" Often the guests did not agree that they were eternal spirit soul or that Kṛṣṇa was God. How could Prabhupāda speak of Kṛṣṇa with such persons?

I praise my spiritual master and fall at his feet again and again. I worship his preaching mood and beg from him a drop of that vigor so I can represent him wherever I go. May he bless me to go on learning in the unlimited science of Kṛṣṇa, to become fit for guiding his many followers over the long haul of human life. Let us appreciate the wonderful depth and playfulness and beauty of Kṛṣṇa consciousness in all its varieties. O Prabhupāda, I am a fool. But I desire to join you if there is a place for me, and if I can rid myself of *anarthas*. Fortunately, there is so much work to do in this world preparing ourselves and others, from the lower stages upwards. Seems like we will never get done—so much to do!

15

This morning I decided to take a walk on the streets near the temple. As soon as I hit the street I thought, "This is it. This is the best time of day to walk." It's cold out, but I'm dressed warmly. The sky is beautiful as the sun crowns the horizon and the pale half moon is still visible. There's no one in sight.

As I walked it occurred to me that the different drives should contribute toward one goal. The writing should push the chanting and reading. The writer-self can tell them, "I am being honest with myself and really trying to cry out, so why can't you do the same when chanting *japa*? And why can't you read with reverence even though you've read the books before?" Similarly, the reading and the chanting can help the writing. Otherwise what do I have to write about except my own self-centered ruminations? I can write about the absolutely important subject of chanting the holy name, and reading can supply me with accurate *siddhānta*. Each part of me should fuel and support the others.

This morning's walk felt so good that I decided to take such a walk every day. But when I started back and was about a block from the temple, I entered a scene that ruined everything. The first thing I saw was a man with his dog on a leash. He was standing in the middle of the road, looking in my direction. Then I saw a few kids who I guessed were waiting for the school bus. As I came closer, I saw four different cars parked, motors running, all with parents inside waiting with their children for the school bus.

My first impulse was that this was going to ruin my plans for a daily walk at this time—too many people—but I tried to make the best of it. When I came quite close to the man, I raised my hand and said, "Good morning!" He just stood there staring at me without the slightest acknowledgment. I then looked down at his dog who was straining on the leash toward me, so I tried making a slight comical acknowledgment of the dog. But all I got was stares from the father, and the kids seemed to join in a xenophobic dressing down of the stranger who suddenly walked down "their" block. They probably continued to watch me after I walked past.

16

I am mad enough to come out here in the snow and write. *Śrī-kṛṣṇa-caitanya prabhu nityānanda.* Dead leaves poking through the snow, everything bleached like a black-and-white movie. Where is summer's green? The only constant is truck traffic, as long as America lasts. And Daddy and Mommy and the kids and houses and cars and suburbs, the American way.

Nectar of Instruction, please don't mind that I have put you on the cold desk. I need to look at something to remind me. You are transcendental to the weather, yet I should not expose you to the cold outdoors. Just stay with me a few minutes. Give me your warmth, the voice of my master.

17

Please, Kṛṣṇa, clean our hearts. Let us enthusiastically hear of Your activities. And when we die, we pray to go on serving You eternally—either immediately in Goloka or by hearing of Goloka as we come back to work out our final imprisonment.

Hare Kṛṣṇa Hare Kṛṣṇa, Kṛṣṇa Kṛṣṇa Hare Hare/Hare Rāma Hare Rāma, Rāma Rāma Hare Hare.

Can I still love? Is it too much for me, a fifty-one-year-old man? Am I afraid it will be too scandalous or upsetting to my routine and my placid heart? But I am not fifty or sixty years old, and I am not a male. I am an eternally youthful soul. Don't give us this too-staid-to-fall-in-love routine. You can do more than you think because Kṛṣṇa and His devotees are unlimited. Nothing is impossible. Don't calculate in terms of Dr. Frog's well.

I write to separate out the bogus feelings, to admit them, and then to grasp at the lotus feet of Vaiṣṇavas. Roll in the dust like a madman. The words are weeping. I make a prayer. It is a rather silly display sometimes.

We are all afraid our expressions will be awkward, even though we think we know what we want to say. Kṛṣṇa is bluish, like the sky holding a fresh rain cloud. He has a broad chest. He is not a human, but He sports among humans when He comes to earth. He is a promiscuous lover, but there is no trace of lust. He satisfies the desires of His devotees and also enjoys Himself, but He is not like the abominable debauch who uses women, or anything else we are familiar with in this world.

I cannot understand Him, although I want to. The *ācāryas* say this Vraja Kṛṣṇa is fuller and more radiant and purely spiritual than all the other incarnations. The *śānta-rasa bhaktas* hear Kṛṣṇa's flute and they beat their heads, "Why have we wasted our time in indifferent meditation?" Bilvamaṅgala Ṭhākura said, "I was fixed in meditation on Brahman, but now my mind has been captured by a mischievous boy who wears a peacock feather in His hair."

Vṛndāvana, do you hear me? My clumsy call goes out to you this night. I picture my friends at the Krishna-Balaram Mandir, aware of the sublime atmosphere they live in, doing their duties, walking on the small campus grounds past the big, wooden doors before the altar. I picture them beholding Rādhā-Śyāmasundara and the green-leafed *tamāla* tree, even though it is winter. I picture the dogs and hogs and beggars and our *gurukula* kids in yellow *dhotīs* playing during their free time on the roof. Each of my friends alone with their own altar, chanting *japa* . . .

18

The car engine and heater are running. It's Saturday morning—we're alone without the usual kids waiting for the school bus. Madhu is chanting *japa* softly in the driver's seat. A cold wind is up. Maybe I'll get my snowfall, although the sky looks clear.

Baladeva will rejoin us tomorrow. Maybe we can take a walk together to talk about Prabhupāda. Who really *knows* him? Often we talk of ourselves in relation to Prabhupāda. When you tell an anecdote of Prabhupāda in action, devotees are satisfied. But no one story can capture the total Prabhupāda. The stories are often superficial; we don't always realize the deep import of even Prabhupāda's smallest actions. The *Vedas* state that the pure devotee is unknowable; he appears to move in this world, just as the moon appears to be moving through clouds. I have faith that everything will be resolved with time. We know so little actually. We can only go on serving faithfully, as Prabhupāda wants us to do.

The car clock reads 7:17 A.M. A gray fox suddenly darts out in front of our parked car. He exchanges looks with us and then he runs off, bushy-tailed, over the gray, pebbled road.

This area was designated for a new development, but no one seems to be building houses. The locals use it to come and park on Friday and Saturday nights, drink beer, and smoke. They throw their rubbish out the windows. I inspect it on my morning walk. Thoreau called himself "an inspector of snowstorms." I inspect my heart, but don't seem to get far.

Regarding separation from Vṛndāvana, I am feeling good somehow. I know I plan to go back. I feel a connection. I wait for news. I read. I'm not ready to live in Vṛndāvana full-time yet, but I am prepared to use my time well as long as I live.

The dry leaves are dancing. The plastic fluorescent pink and yellow strips marking the house sites are blowing in the wind. Kṛṣṇa is God and I am cheerfully trying to serve Him. O gurus, you are so kind and lenient toward us, despite our slow ways. May we improve.

19

The day is still young; I can do things. Keep mindful of their *quality*. The days are rushing by. You can't gain immortality in *this* world except by acts which have the eternal quality of pure *bhakti*. They are the currency that can be used in the next life; other currencies all become useless at the time of death, just stacks of meaningless paper.

A strong wind is up. Heavy boards or something are shifting and sometimes slamming against the house. Reminders.

Don't look up at your own reflection in the window. Keep concentrated.

Rūpa Gosvāmī writes, "My dear foolish friend, I think that you have already heard some of the auspicious *Śrīmad-Bhāgavatam*, which decries seeking the results of fruitive activities, economic development and liberation. I think that now it is certain that gradually the verses of the Tenth Canto of *Śrīmad-Bhāgavatam*, describing the pastimes of the Lord, will enter your ears and go into your heart" (*The Nectar of Devotion*, p. 109).

The heaters are rattling. My stomach is asking for something or other. The world demands attention. Link the moments together by different methods of chanting and hearing Govinda's glories and *upadeśa*. I think this is sufficient for me.

The *gopīs* were shocked and bereft that Kṛṣṇa had left them. They were just like she-elephants who have suddenly been abandoned by the male elephant. They addressed the many kinds of trees in Vṛndāvana and asked if they had seen Kṛṣṇa. "O *kadamba*, O *mālati*, O *bakula*, O *bilva*, have you seen the younger brother of Balarāma pass by here? He must have been here only moments ago, because the trees are still bowing down making obeisances, and now the breeze carries the aroma of His garland mixed with *kuṅkuma* from His beloved."

But the trees and plants do not reveal the whereabouts of Kṛṣṇa, nor do the deer. Although the deer seem to say, "Come, follow me and I will show you Kṛṣṇa," they move out of sight.

In the madness of separation, the *gopīs* begin imitating Kṛṣṇa.

You see? Although your voice was dull and frog-like, and your attention ran only along the surface, still, you have reaped the benefit. You heard again of the marks on the soles of Kṛṣṇa's feet and it grabbed your interest. As you mulled over Viśvanātha Cakravartī's explanations—the elephant goad sign on Kṛṣṇa's sole indicates how His devotees may control their minds; the lotus flower under His big toes increases the greed of the bee-like devotees who meditate on His feet; the barley corn indicates all Kṛṣṇa's opulence—as you hear, your mind is washed of extraneous thoughts. Therefore, hear as much as you can.

20

Troubled voices and the faces of my disciples come through the mail. One is now more interested in Christian mysticism than in Kṛṣṇa consciousness. "Yes, I am still (and always was) interested in Kṛṣṇa-GOD-consciousness," she says. So Kṛṣṇa is acceptable to her now in the larger (more nebulous) context of GOD. I myself dallied in Christian ways, so how can I condemn her? Hope she'll return and one day understand Kṛṣṇa is even better and sweeter than GOD.

Others have trouble with following the prohibition against illicit sex. I tell them to look for the higher taste. All things will pass in this world, our quick lives certainly, so maybe the bad habits and deviation of disciples will also pass as they mature with time. But it could also happen that a whole life will rush by without them climbing out of the pit. Why did I initiate them? I took a chance. They were sincere at the time and they promised.

I took a deep breath in the cold air and felt a sense of life flowing by, not in compartmental units which I manage and control like a clerk—but flowing by beyond control. It is an illusion—time seems to pass slowly as I move through my morning, but then it is gone. Then it is *all* gone. Lesson: do as much as you can every day.

21

If your position is so hopeless for gaining *ruci*, *rati*, or *bhāva*, then why do you maintain hope? Śrīla Rūpa Gosvāmī considered this question in a humble way, in *Bhakti-rasāmṛta-sindhu:*

> I have no love for Kṛṣṇa, nor for the causes of developing love of Kṛṣṇa—namely, hearing and chanting. And the process of *bhakti-yoga*, by which one is always thinking of Kṛṣṇa and fixing His lotus feet in the heart, is also lacking in me. As far as philosophical knowledge or pious works are concerned, I don't see any opportunity for me to execute such activities. But above all, I am not even born of a nice family. Therefore I must simply pray to You, Gopījana-vallabha [Kṛṣṇa, maintainer and beloved of the *gopīs*]. I simply wish and hope that some way or other I may be able to approach Your lotus feet, and this hope is giving me pain, because I think myself quite incompetent to approach that transcendental goal of life.
>
> —*NOD*, p. 137

A Godbrother in Germany once asked me after a *Śrīmad-Bhāgavatam* class, "Why does Rūpa Gosvāmī say that his hope is giving him pain?" I could never understand this point to my satisfaction and so I admitted it to my Godbrother. Now reading the commentaries of Jīva Gosvāmī and Mukunda dāsa Gosvāmī, I can give more information. Jīva Gosvāmī says that Rūpa Gosvāmī speaks of "my hopes as another kind of impurity, a hope for attaining Kṛṣṇa with the desire for one's own happiness, and not for the happiness of Kṛṣṇa only. So Rūpa Gosvāmī humbly claims that his own root of self-pleasure is not destroyed completely. Rūpa Gosvāmī laments, but then finds the solution by saying, 'O beloved of the *gopīs*, You meet all the needs of those who are unworthy. I am most unworthy, so please transform my desire for my happiness into Your happiness. That is the real hope I am maintaining, even though present hopes are for my own pleasure.'" Jīva Gosvāmī states that Rūpa Gosvāmī's humility is an example of *rati.*

Commenting on the same verse (*Bhakti-rasāmṛta-sindhu* 1.3.35), Mukunda dāsa Gosvāmī sees Rūpa Gosvāmī's statement of humility in this way: "'Although I have no trace of *prema* at Your feet, yet my inordinate hope itself in You is giving me pain, that is, I am feeling the pain of not attaining You.' Then Kṛṣṇa might reply to this as follows: 'If you say you cannot attain Me because you have no qualification, then why not be happy by giving up all hopes of attaining Me?' To this, Rūpa Gosvāmī would reply, 'O merciful, compassionate one, You are always kind to the most unworthy. Since there is no one more unworthy than I, my hope for attaining You has taken deep root in my heart.'"

In *The Nectar of Devotion*, Śrīla Prabhupāda comments, "The purport is that under this heading of *āśā-bandha*, one should continue to hope against hope that some way or other he will be able to approach the lotus feet of the Supreme Lord" (*NOD*, p. 137). Śrīla Prabhupāda's use of the English idiom "hope against hope" expresses well my own attitude. The dictionary defines "hope against hope" as: "to hope without any basis for expecting fulfillment."

I usually don't even think it out. We go ahead with *vaidhī-bhakti* because Śrīla Prabhupāda told us to. We keep hearing of the brilliant goal of going back to Godhead, but as we read more, we also sense how disqualified we are and how rare it is to attain *bhāva-bhakti*. We also see more our stubborn, remaining *anarthas*. Yet we keep going. We think, "Oh well, if He likes, Kṛṣṇa may be merciful."

My case is rather dull and not thought out. I think I am afraid to face the consequences. For example, Śrīla Prabhupāda says the atheistic hedonists are so afraid to face the consequences of their sinful acts that they summarily dismiss the facts of karma and transmigration of the soul. Similarly, I don't face my own situation. That is my misfortune. That is the lack of contrition, the lack of piteous crying in *japa*. If we admit, even intellectually, that we are not qualified for love of God, and that we seem hopeless for reform—hopeless for attaining that intense, selfless love that drives the *gopīs* out at night, abandoning all pride, shame and morality, *just to please Kṛṣṇa*—then why don't we feel remorse? Why don't we increase our attempts to attain real Kṛṣṇa consciousness before our lives are over?

22

The beauty of a snowy, gray dawn is not to be put into words. No matter what I'm going through, whether my life is sorrowful or I feel I am being tested, I feel uplifted by the natural beauty of a wintry scene. Of course, it's not only the beautiful scenery, but the satisfaction I feel when I am absorbed in a Kṛṣṇa conscious project. The project makes me satisfied and the natural beauty soothes me. I like to walk in the cold of gray dawns and feel the beauty of winter snowscapes.

But where is Vraja in this snow? Not here, that's true. Still, I feel in my bones, in my being, that walking in the snow alone is connected. The snowfall evokes an almost ideal solitude in which to think about Vṛndāvana.

I have letters from devotees in Vṛndāvana—certainly I plan to return—and the work I'm doing now is connected to Vraja. I am reading Prabhupāda's *Caitanya-caritāmṛta*, and wherever he is, that is Vṛndāvana. But somehow I'm here and it's connected.

23

Lord Caitanya continued to describe the unhappy fate of one caught in attachment to a high standard of material enjoyment. Such a person has to remain bound to repeated birth and death. Any temporary life, even a so-called rich and enjoyable one, is actually full of misery. It leads only to more misery due to the laws of karma. Lord Caitanya said that it was Kṛṣṇa who had personally released Raghunātha: "Therefore, the glories of Lord Kṛṣṇa's causeless mercy cannot be expressed." Lord Kṛṣṇa can save any *jīva* who engages himself in pure devotional service. "One cannot express sufficient gratitude to Kṛṣṇa for being freed from the materialistic way of life" (Cc., *Antya* 6.200, purport).

I am writing in gratitude. I am grateful to be able to write and express myself in Kṛṣṇa consciousness. Writing is my service. But the gratitude I should feel is for the total mercy of Kṛṣṇa in my entire life, my being able to get out of materialistic life by Prabhupāda's acceptance of my fallen self. Śrīla Prabhupāda states that there is no way we can fully express the gratitude we owe to Kṛṣṇa for our release from our karma-bound existence. We attempt to "repay" what cannot be paid back by rendering *guru-dakṣiṇā* with body, mind, and words, in service to the spiritual master.

Although we regret we haven't attained full surrender or spontaneous devotional service, that awareness should not overshadow the gratitude we feel for the position we have already attained. As stated by Lord Caitanya to Rūpa Gosvāmī: *brahmāṇḍa brahmite kona bhāgyavān jīva* . . . it is only very fortunate *jīvas* who can become free from the rotation of birth and death in different species of life. This happens by the combined mercy of Lord Kṛṣṇa and the spiritual master (*guru-kṛṣṇa-prasāde pāya bhakti-latā-bīja*).

We need to feel grateful for the great step that has already been taken in our lives, but we shouldn't think we have attained perfection. We are freed from degraded *saṁsāra*, but pure love of Kṛṣṇa has not been attained. O energy of the Lord, O Lord, please engage me in Your service. The gratitude for deliverance from sinful reactions may be kept in mind at the same time we pray and strive for deliverance from the remaining *anarthas* in our hearts. Ajāmila prayed, "I am such a sinful person, but since I have now gotten this opportunity, I must completely control my mind, life and senses and always engage in devotional service so that I may not fall again into the deep darkness and ignorance of material life. . . . Ajāmila fully engaged in devotional service. Thus he detached his mind from the process of sense gratification and became fully absorbed in thinking of the form of the Lord" (*Bhāg.* 6.2.35, 41).

Ajāmila's example is that a devotee, once saved from near-death, should not fall again into sense gratification or complacency. He should remain determined and fervent in his prosecution of worship and practical service. Then he may be so fortunate to remember Kṛṣṇa at the time of death and be transferred to His eternal abode. "The result of perfection in Kṛṣṇa consciousness is that after giving up one's material body, one is immediately transferred to the spiritual world in one's original spiritual body to become an associate of the Supreme Personality of Godhead. Some devotees go to Vaikuṇṭhaloka, and others go to Goloka Vṛndāvana to become associates of Kṛṣṇa" (*Bhāg.* 6.2.43, purport).

24

It's about sixteen degrees this morning, so it's hard to walk. The back road is covered in frozen snow. When I walk on the snow, I fall through at every step. It's about ten inches deep. I tried following tire tracks, but their path is so narrow that I have to walk by putting one foot in front of the other. It's difficult because my ankles keep turning in where frozen clumps of snow hang off the edges of the tracks. Hare Kṛṣṇa Hare Kṛṣṇa, Kṛṣṇa Kṛṣṇa Hare Hare/Hare Rāma Hare Rāma, Rāma Rāma Hare Hare.

Yesterday I said the fir trees looked brownish-green. This morning, they have a silver aura about them in the dawn light. It's beautiful how the white-covered ground slopes up to where the trees are and how the sky above the trees is clear. The sun is rising in the east and the sky has a reddish hue there. It feels unusual to see that color on this cold morning—red usually implies warmth—but it almost looks more like northern lights than the rising sun.

Another problem with walking in this weather is that my glasses fog up from my breath. I can't clean them properly because I have too many pairs of gloves on. I ended up taking them off and putting them in my pocket. All this is like child's play, like pretending you're a survivor on a polar expedition instead of on your way back to a heated cabin. This walk is a chance to think more about service to Kṛṣṇa and to Prabhupāda, because that's what life is for. What more is there to say?

25

It's only nine degrees. I'm not even going to bother wearing my glasses. Another tiny layer of snow was added overnight to the already existing snowfall. Everything is clean again. It's hard to walk, but at least this new covering has given me a little bit of footing on the slippery ice.

I was determined this morning not to complain about my difficulties in walking on the snow. I decided to make the best of it and appreciate the light and that I've been given eyes to see. Everything comes from Kṛṣṇa. Once on a morning walk in San Francisco, I think Upendra dāsa asked Prabhupāda, "How does the pure devotee see Kṛṣṇa everywhere? Does he look at a wall and sees Kṛṣṇa on the wall playing His flute?" Prabhupāda replied that it's more a vision of love. It's like a mother who sees the small shoe of her child and feels love. If we love Kṛṣṇa, then anything we see will remind us of Kṛṣṇa. That was a wonderful reply. We have to remember that Prabhupāda was a devotee of Vṛndāvana, a Vrajavāsī come to America to preach. He had to say things in such a way that we Westerners could understand them. But Prabhupāda always thought of Kṛṣṇa in the Vraja mood. Prabhupāda was not a Vaikuṇṭha *bhakta*, but a Vṛndāvana *bhakta*. He put it nicely for us. The fact is, in whatever we see, we can seek Kṛṣṇa there in the particular form we wish to worship.

Can that be translated into these snowy woods? I think I can do it, but I can't explain it to others. I can feel it within myself, but I can't present a manifesto to prove it. I think I'll stop bothering to attempt it. I just have to go ahead and be Kṛṣṇa conscious. Just be happy that this snow is also Kṛṣṇa and that I'm Kṛṣṇa's devotee.

Walking on a trail following the tire tracks and chanting Hare Kṛṣṇa Hare Kṛṣṇa, Kṛṣṇa Kṛṣṇa Hare Hare/Hare Rāma Hare Rāma, Rāma Rāma Hare Hare . . .

Everything is shining with an inner light. That's not quite the expression I am looking for. I think of iodine, or a cold ocean—the way it looks when you're on a snow-covered beach on Cape Cod. The colors of blue and iodine through the waves.

I think of getting back to where my fingers can thaw out. But I feel a communion with this place, this day. It's hard to keep expressing this, but I am feeling deeply the conviction that I want to become more Kṛṣṇa conscious. This snowy walk may not appear to have anything to do with my prayers, but Kṛṣṇa knows what I want. I don't want wealth. I don't want women or beautiful poetry, although I do want a kind of plain poetry that speaks and reaches Kṛṣṇa. I don't want followers, just a small group of people here and there who want to read what I write. And even that I only want if it's right. But what I really want is to give up everything else and practice devotional service like Prabhupāda is asking us to. That's what I came out here for, although it's hard for others to see the connection. That's what the cold is about.

This is not some impersonal mumbo jumbo. I know what I mean. My body knows what I mean when I come out in nine degree weather to find Kṛṣṇa in this vivid cold . . . the word iodine and now the bright headlights of a car up near the cabin.

26

Nowadays when people write me questions like, "If we chant Hare Kṛṣṇa at the time of death, even though we are sinful, will we go back to Godhead?" I see the naïveté in it. I used to automatically answer that it was possible and not think much about it. Now I know differently. I think that *for myself*, I will obviously have to come back to work toward love of God. And objectively, it doesn't seem possible that so many attached persons are going immediately to Vraja-loka. It should be clear that *I* will have to come back for more service-in-training. But I'm like the person who thinks, "Others have died, but I may be an exception." I don't think it out; I don't know how to face it; I don't realize that the *ācārya*-poets have written with me in mind when they say, "Now I am coming to the end of my life and I see I have not served Rādhā and Kṛṣṇa. Fie on me. Alas!" I looked at it as *poetry*. I *can't* think of it. Although I brag that I have a taste for being alone and reading, I am not introspective. I enjoy the quiet life, the semblance of solitary pursuits, and the atmosphere of "a life of prayer," but I don't enter. *Entering The Life of Prayer* woke me up, but I . . . I can't say . . . I can't say what it is, except I cannot and will not make an estimation of my own spiritual life.

27

Everywhere snow is dripping and occasionally thumping on the roof. The sunshine is here; the evergreens are glistening wet—beads of jewel-like water in rainbow colors. Am I so far away from Vṛndāvana? The blue jays cry their warning. I will take shelter in these transcendental sources—Śrīla Prabhupāda's books, his voice, the *mahā-mantra* which I utter and pray. I will not allow myself to be dragged down the rapids of material anxiety. I belong to a different sphere.

Just now the black dog from next door came right up to the shack and began barking at me. I turned from my writing and looked at him, and he became more convinced than ever that I was an intruder, a madman in my Carhartt overwear. His master shouts his name (I missed it) and, "Get over here!" Yes, they should bring him back. That black scoundrel is disturbing my meditation all day.

I'm used to the squirrels and they are oblivious to me, but if this black dog is going to make a big thing out of his discovery that a man sits out in the shack, then where will it end? His stupid "*woof!*"

The carpet of faded brown leaves is crisp. It covers the forest floor. Under this year's carpet lies last year's, quietly turning to earth.

Don't underestimate the power a place can have on your Kṛṣṇa consciousness. To live in Vṛndāvana-dhāma, to see Rādhā-Kṛṣṇa *arcā-vigraha*, to be able to speak a few words with a Godbrother—all these are favorable. Yearn for service. Live in Vṛndāvana in your heart.

28

We live in this world blindly, Śrīla Prabhupāda said. He said we think that because we are Americans, everything is "settled up." We have our "own skyscrapers," but we don't know that we can't stay here. We have to leave, and therefore all we have gained and enjoyed—he mentioned good food and dress—will be gone. What happens next life?

Prabhupāda chastised the atheists. "They see God in the form of death." Such strong words of transcendental knowledge. We can hear them any time we turn on the tape recorder and give our submissive aural reception. Prabhupāda is forming me by his teachings. I have an aging body like anyone else, although my *sannyāsa* dress looks outlandish to Americans. But more than these outer differences, I am different than them *because of what I hear.*

I want to try this week to take some more stabs at expressing what I'm trying for in life. I am incoherent, silent, perplexed. Attempting to speak may help. If it's *māyā*, I can be corrected by *śāstra*, but I must be free enough to first explain what I am after, what I understand, and what I don't understand. They say, "The body doesn't lie." So I can tell you what hurts. What do I like? What is my fondest dream?

I want to become a *bhajanānandī* who preaches. Someone told me Bhaktisiddhānta Sarasvatī Ṭhākura said, "The best *goṣṭhyānandī* is a *bhajanānandī* who preaches." I want to be fixed in chanting and form a deep attachment to the holy name, and then I want to tell others to try chanting. I want to gain momentum to continue reading Śrīla Prabhupāda's books. I want so many rare things that are not attainable even for great demigods like Brahmā and Śiva. Am I kidding myself? No, I want this. I am praying for it and writing about it.

I want to dissolve my false ego through writing practice and keep on writing, praising, describing, preaching in Kṛṣṇa consciousness for Śrīla Prabhupāda's satisfaction. I want to return to Vṛndāvana. I want to see the *tīrthas*. I want to grow. I want to be honest and go through the required renunciation.

Śrīla Prabhupāda completely accepted the reality of Kṛṣṇa as the Supreme Personality of Godhead. He was born into a family of Kṛṣṇa conscious parents. Does Prabhupāda know the gap we suffer from our ruined childhoods in the West? One brother (who was raised like me in greater New York City) recently remarked, "The first twenty years of my life were a disaster." That's common. The family is dysfunctional, as is the culture we were born into. This nation was (and is) suffering from a mania of epidemic proportions. We were picked up and saved by Prabhupāda. We may have had some past pious activities, but actually, we were picked up the way a mother cat saves her wet kitten from drowning. Now we are hanging on like the baby monkey holds onto its mother.

These days, I am realizing more how much I am hampered by my background. That faithlessness has thrown me into a whirlwind of mercy, so I'm not complaining—I'm happy I survived. Still, I realize more how much I am hampered by the past.

For example, I can pick up *The Nectar of Devotion* and hear about the amazing qualities of Kṛṣṇa's flute. I just picked the book up without any forethought and started reading in that section. Then I caught myself not understanding any of it and a voice (like a wise guy New Yorker in a Hollywood film) inside me saying, "Do you *believe* this? God plays a *flute*? A simple flute and it turns the whole universe upside down? Who are these demigods anyway? Who do you know who has even heard this flute?"

Hmmm. I turn off the New Yorker and pencil in a note in the margin of that page: "It is amazing that a simple flute can do all this. And are we ready to doubt the whole Kṛṣṇa conscious philosophy because of this?"

This is what I have to contend with. Śrīla Prabhupāda is transcendental to this; he is dragging me away from my doubts. Śrīla Prabhupāda has known me since I was a nondevotee. Śrīla Prabhupāda continues to smash me, continues to make me strong enough for something more. I am certainly *nīca jāti, nīca saṅgī, patita adhama.*

29

Rain is like the earth's tears. She feels sorrow at the sinfulness of Kali-yuga. Prabhupāda's movement is meant to offer shelter. The earth cries.

30

I just read a verse praising Śrīla Prabhupāda. It said that he preaches in the most populous cities and doesn't hide in the countryside for his personal benefit. Another verse praised him as the inspiration for preachers, and another said Prabhupāda is the life of those who quietly practice Kṛṣṇa consciousness. He is for all of us; we have to please him.

Just see that sentence, "We have to please him." It becomes a truism. Or it sounds devoid of joy or spontaneity. I don't mean it that way, although I use that phrase often. Writers often expect others to know what they intend by their sometimes repetitive phrases. Unfortunately, whatever dullness I have comes through in my writing. *We have to please him.* I wouldn't want that to be taken like those announcements made after *maṅgala-ārati*, or like the pledge of allegiance to the United States. Am I perpetrating some of the same, Prabhupāda allegiance truisms?

Actually, sometimes I am tired, not in spirit, but somewhere beyond the body. It is the tiredness of a so-called *sādhaka* whose practice slips down into the modes of nature. I once called this "H.D." disease—half-dead disease.

Life is what characterizes the pure devotees' love for Kṛṣṇa—*intense* life. You have to be vulnerable to Kṛṣṇa's hurting you or neglecting you. You have to love Him. Did you ever love anyone? Are you too bound up to love even God?

The Vrajavāsīs are willing to be hurt. They give themselves completely. Rūpa Gosvāmī warns us, "If you are not prepared to lose all taste and standing in material happiness, then do not go to see Govinda at Vaṁśīvāṭa." I state it here, afflicted by H.D., but desiring the cure. This is *not* a material disease. It is much worse.

31

When you write, it doesn't have to be a poem or a big essay with carefully chosen words approved by E. B. White and company. Don't have to show off to yourself either. But send up a flag, a flare, and be true to your upbringing as you were trained by His Divine Grace. Been a while now since he taught you in '66. I don't know anything much.

You don't have to worry so much about performance, repetition (say it as much as you like if it helps you to learn); doesn't matter what size shoes you wear, but don't let them steal your time.

You can't escape the fact that your spiritual master's "only business" was to spread Kṛṣṇa consciousness all over the world. It stands to reason that you better help him do it. He doesn't need you—he has so many able hands in Russia and California—but *you* need to please *him*, so be sure to do it.

My theory is that ISKCON is a preaching movement, and as long as I stay in it, I'm preaching. If my style is "inner life," well, then that's my preaching. Who's to say whose preaching is loudest or most effective and therefore most pleasing to Śrīla Prabhupāda? It all depends.

So, my friends, preach as you know best. Preach in the west and the east and the south and the north, out of your pocket, in your head, with your mouth, for all you're worth. Do your best, and in the north-northeast too.

Ireland

32

I saw the newspapers. The political cartoons show us a planet staggering under burdens it can never relieve itself of. The picture is getting darker. "Children Who Kill—Crime By Kids." Rape and murder. Terrorism. Nuclear proliferation. One nation after another exposed as chaotic, scandal-torn, desperate. No one can help. Everything is complicated and there are no dramatic or easy solutions. Idealogies crash against each other head on.

I read it and think I am ineffectual against it. How can I help the world's problems? If ISKCON is the answer, then what about the fact that ISKCON has its own problems? I can't even accommodate all the different viewpoints in ISKCON. I can't assimilate all their material, can't sympathize with all their projects. It's I who am ineffectual.

For example, the new BTG has an excerpt from a book, *Forbidden Archeology*. I can't assimilate it. An essay from the *Ṣaṭ-sandarbha* about the Supersoul—too much for me. A picture of one devotee distributing food to the mentally ill. I can't take time to read and think about the details of what all these devotees are doing. Then beyond ISKCON, the Balkans. "Vietnam, The New Tiger?" A cartoon: the map of India shaped like a dagger stabbing a man who lies dead. What does it mean? What can I do?

I am speaking honestly of my feelings after a brush with world events. ISKCON devotees don't usually read much about world politics. It's all *māyā*. The world needs Kṛṣṇa consciousness, so we employ ourselves as simple workers to distribute Prabhupāda's books. Some equip themselves to speak more eloquently, but basically, all devotees hold the view that the world is a place of misery and we should engage ourselves and others in devotional service. Our movement is a small force in the world, but we don't feel oppressed by that fact. We are assured that Kṛṣṇa is pleased when we make the effort to serve Him.

In my own preaching, which is directed toward devotees, I repeat the essential teachings: the main limbs of *bhakti*, chanting Hare Kṛṣṇa, hearing about Kṛṣṇa, and remembering Him, should be our main business. I don't really confront the problem in the Balkans, but this is our response to those problems. I am satisfied to speak to the relatively small group of devotees. I don't feel irrelevant or out of touch. Getting involved in material problems on the material level won't solve anything.

33

Oh, I am much better than the flies. I may even be above *kaniṣṭha-adhikārī*. I may be a *madhyama-adhikārī*. I may be in the *nāmābhāsa* stage of *japa*. I do have a bona fide spiritual master and that's much more than the flies have. They know only eating, sleeping, mating, and defending. And yet, as Bhaktivinoda Ṭhākura writes in his commentary to the *tṛṇād api sunīcena* verse, grass and creatures like grass have a modest sense of ego whereas human beings are puffed-up way out of proportion. We tend to think we are the center of existence. Lord Caitanya advises us to be more like a blade of grass. Use human intelligence to become *more* modest and humble than the grass.

Being puffed-up that I have a guru and the fly doesn't is not good. It's like the petty clerk who is abused by his supervisor in the office, so he comes home and kicks his cat. I'm surly because I can't understand so many things. I am out here to write it out. But the flies plague me, so I write against them. We humans have tender skins.

I have a hunch about my shortcomings. It is psychological—I simply can't admit all my shortcomings at once and then take steps to rectify them. I can admit my wrongs, but no one else can tell me about them. I don't want to hear about it from someone else. I'm proud.

Sādhus speak words to cut us from our attachments. They are trying to save us from the pain of repeated birth and death, but they can only save those who submit to them. Their help may sometimes be painful and even appear violent, but their cutting is surgery. It requires expertise. These days, everyone tries to undergo surgery under anesthesia. They don't want to feel anything. Anyway, best to take to prevention before it comes down to the knife.

The *ācāryas* are also encouraging. Śrīla Prabhupāda said that they were eighty percent lenient. They beckon us forward. They offer the milk of Kṛṣṇa's sweetness and then urge us to come and partake. Their medicine is mostly sweet, but sometimes they offer us bitter Āyurvedic potions as well. A little austerity, but not too much. Śrīla Prabhupāda said, "If I told you everything at once [all the rules and practices required for *vaidhī-bhakti*], you would faint."

34

I thought it would be harmless to my contemplation to stop inside the plastic greenhouse and see what Uddhava was doing. There are so many flies beating against the roof that it makes a constant noise. He says this is just a two-week season and then they will go away. He is growing tomatoes and they are coming up well. Last year he didn't know how to do it, and they bushed out but didn't produce any tomatoes. Now he has the ground covered with cloth, and he feeds them in special ways. He says he still doesn't know everything about it. I agreed that it probably takes many years to learn.

Up here in the attic, I imagined the sweet scent of green tomatoes. I like to see a worker contending with natural obstacles and overcoming ignorance in order to do what he wants to do. I too am a tomato-grower, a reader and writer, and I'm not going to allow myself to get too discouraged.

Uddhava said that in a few days, we will see some red tomatoes. I am hoping for the same.

35

There is no door to this room. The entrance connects immediately to a straight-down stairwell, which brings you into the only room on the ground floor (aside from the small kitchen and bathroom). I hear every phone call or conversation below. I asked them to try and be quiet. When I'm trying to read, it doesn't help to hear M. giving the plumber directions on how to reach this cottage.

The calf's name is Yamunā. Last night I helped bring her into the *gośala*. I went up to her and untied her while Madhu stood seventy-five yards away at the door to the *gośala*, holding a bucket of milk. Yamunā tugged when I took too long unhooking her neck chain. Finally it came loose and she ran clumsily toward the *gośala*. Madhu led her into her straw-padded stall and within a few seconds, she voraciously drank all the milk in the bucket. Madhu asked me if I wanted to let her out in the morning, but I could see myself quickly becoming attached to Yamunā. I thought of Mahārāja Bharata whose *bhāva* meditation was stopped when he became too affectionate toward a fawn.

It is raining out now and I see her grazing in her private pasture. Uddhava and Hare Kṛṣṇa dāsī are also here, tending to their gardens. The plumber is trying to fix the pump. Since there is no door to this room, no one should worry 'bout my becoming a hermit.

36

I'm writing in a shed in Ireland. "You've certainly got a different atmosphere in here," said Madhu as he left me. But it is the same thing. You can go to Bengal, but your destiny will go with you.

It's an outbuilding, dark, throwing delicious shadows on the page. A dark, noon sky, rain falling softly. I can still see the line of pines from here and hear Yamunā's dull, jingling bell. Hay is piled up and there are piles of empty plastic bottles, empty flower pots, little beds for seedlings. On the wall, two axes, a pair of grass clippers, a saw . . . Śrīla Prabhupāda would laugh to see me in the midst of this, but he knows me so well that he would probably say, "He's a little crazy, but he's sincere."

The frame of this door leads to the outside world. It's dark because the sun is covered. But at least there are no meat carcasses hanging on hooks in here. No one is cursing. No radio is playing. Only birds calling and trees in the distance. It's dry in here. I have come from reading and hearing and I will go back to that soon. It is the day before Ekādaśī and I will shave my head at noon. Lunch is bliss, even though my fastidious tongue is a bit disappointed by M.'s simple cooking.

Everything is useless (*śrama eva hi kevalam*) unless I serve Govinda. My spiritual master said service must include *saṅkīrtana*—the chanting of the holy names *and* the desire to distribute Kṛṣṇa consciousness to others. Śrīla Prabhupāda was a great figure in Caitanya-*līlā*. Rūpa Gosvāmī broadcast Kṛṣṇa consciousness in Purī and Vṛndāvana; Śrīla Prabhupāda broadcast it all over the world. He is a *rūpānuga*, a direct disciple of Bhaktisiddhānta Sarasvatī, and we are in *that* line. Because we beg to remain in that line, we are chanting Hare Kṛṣṇa and distributing Kṛṣṇa consciousness on Śrīla Prabhupāda's order.

As Śrīla Prabhupāda said of the Bowery bum who did some service, "Just see. His mind is not in order, but he wanted to do some service." (The propensity to serve is eternal in all of us. The pure devotee is so potent that he arouses it. A bum and a writer gone berserk want to offer something, a few rolls of toilet paper for the bathroom, a few books of tribute for fellow devotees. All glories to the eternal spring of *bhakti*, appearing in all hearts by the grace of Kṛṣṇa, the almighty.)

A mourning dove. The rain has become so fine I can hardly see it against the dark pines, and not at all against the light, gray sky.

37

The black cat just walked by from right to left. Earlier, she was sitting on the windowsill, mewing in the window and showing her teeth and tongue. M. said he would feed her. You have to be careful not to spoil her. Lord Caitanya said that even the pet dogs and cats in Śrīvāsa Ācārya's house would attain pure devotional service. Now the door has blown almost completely shut, but there is still enough light to write by.

The rain has potential to soothe my nerves and allow me to feel at peace, but I am resisting it. I am afraid it is too natural, too much part of this world. I am feeling some duality between the world I perceive with my senses and the world I hear of in the *śāstras*. I know I can claim that there is God consciousness in nature—it is Kṛṣṇa's nature—but when we aspire for Rādhā-Kṛṣṇa-*sevā* in Vraja, then the God-in-nature seems too inferior to settle for. It is too much like pantheism, Taoism, nature worship. Where is *kṛṣṇa-smaraṇam* in the sound of the rain? Lord Caitanya said, "I am feeling the world all vacant in Your absence."

Yet we want to feel that simple peacefulness of a man who is at prayer, who is staying in a countryside cottage with no duties other than hearing, reading, and writing. But I am feeling solaced by coming out here to write. Despite myself, the rain is pleasant. Despite my superficially agitated mood, reading *Caitanya-caritāmṛta* touched my soul. My craziness is not so important or all-pervading.

Mādhukara refers to the practice of the bee who takes a little honey from each flower. *Sādhus* who beg a bit of rice from one house and then a bit from another also practice *mādhukara*. I listen a little bit at a time to Prabhupāda, read a little, and in writing, produce only a little honey at a time.

Now the door has blown completely shut, but there is an open space over the door that lets the light in. Rain, rain.

If I can finish this page, it will be the little extra—the extra that makes your heart crack. Disciples and friends tell me some of what they are going through. I reply. Some stop writing because they don't feel enough is coming through from my side to make it worth their while.

Stray straws on the cement floor. Yamunā spends the night here, dumb calf. I sleep on a mattress under a roof, spending my good karma. Where will our souls go in the next life? If one can take birth again and again in Vṛndāvana, and again and again practice any stage of *bhakti-yoga*, that soul is fortunate. Nowadays, life is so hard and spiritual life so elusive that even in Vṛndāvana, some people don't practice devotional service. But we cannot demand more. It requires practice and grace from the Lord.

I heard examples—practicing *sādhana* is like sand in an oyster. But the appearance of the pearl in the oyster is not due to the sand. Practicing *sādhana* is like going to beg money from a patron. He doesn't have to give it to you. There is a hundred rupee note hidden in a book but you don't know it; you leaf through the pages and discover it. Your looking through that particular book was not the cause of the note's appearance. Yet there is *some* relationship between practice of *sādhana* and the independent, causeless descent of the mercy of the Lord and the devotees.

38

The Western version of *bhajana* is liable to be more open to influences from outside of Vedic culture. It's harder to sustain interest in Christian saints while in India. No one sees Maslovian psychologists in Vraja. If you get sick in the West, there are more varieties of medicine to choose from. I am trying to say these things without making a value judgment. It is simply a fact. You can call Vṛndāvana more restrictive or else say it is deeper into Gauḍīya Vaiṣṇavism, but it is different.

In Ireland, I take an early morning walk wearing sweat pants and Wellington boots. I would never do such a thing on *parikrama* in Vṛndāvana. In Ireland, the hills are not connected with Kṛṣṇa's *līlā*, but still we want to see them in a Kṛṣṇa conscious way. It requires an adjustment. You don't bow down and pray to the roots of trees in the West, although you *could*, seeing them as Kṛṣṇa's energy. But it's not the same. Spirit souls in the Vṛndāvana trees are special. When our ferry from Wales arrived in Dublin, we only joked about whether we should get down to touch our heads to "the old sod." In Vṛndāvana, we will actually do it.

It seems that more faith is required in Vraja, but we need a different kind of faith and determination in the West. The *ācāryas* say we should live physically in Vraja, but if we can't, then we should go to Vraja at least in our minds. We are not going to accept Celtic or Catholic spirituality in Ireland, or American Indian or puritan religions in the U.S.A. In Wicklow we read *Bhagavad-gītā*, and in Pennsylvania we get absorbed in *Caitanya-caritāmṛta*. But inevitably, the local genius seeps through. We see God in the Irish mist; we are enchanted by the healing silences of the Tuscarora creek, and our prayers take a certain shape when uttered within a North American forest.

One point I have made repeatedly is that for me, solitude is more available in the West. Therefore, it seems that I can be better situated here than there when I need privacy. But I also want to go to India. The stirrings begin. People start talking about going for Kārttika: "Do we have enough money? Can we get free from other duties? Can we leave our homeland? Who will take care of the house while we are away? Can we go on pilgrimage? Is it really worth it? Remember how the children got sick last time?" A friend of mine even said, "Never again, or at least not for a long time." And travel! Remember the canceled flight and the bomb threat, the long airport waits, especially in India?

Oh, India, how difficult it is to get anything done there. And the culture shock, the cheating, the staring, the heat, the way you get so tired you don't even have enough energy to get up and walk across the room. Just for the increase in energy we might decide, "Let me stay in the West where I can at least read and not fall asleep." Besides, I don't know the language, so how can I preach? And most people in India think, "I know Kṛṣṇa. I know all the gods." Dangerous, dilapidated roads, head-on traffic, drivers constantly beeping their horns . . .

Anyway, I'm going. Or rather, I am praying that Śrīmatī Rādhārāṇī will allow me to come. I am willing to pay the price. I want the real thing. But as long as I am in the West, I will try to mentally live in Vṛndāvana—just as I will continue to accept a few local amenities and influences—and try to help devotees in the West.

39

Rain . . . I cheerfully admit to others my low state. That's part of life. I try to be friendly and good-natured, not giving pain to others, but the laugh is on me and it makes others uncomfortable, the naked admission of distracted prayers and material desires, and mainly, the lack of attraction and devotion to Govinda.

These are serious and relevant topics. Some don't take them seriously. It's like the way various citizens react to social problems. Everyone knows the problems are out of control, but some prefer not to think about them. They know the quality of their lives is affected by the problems of industrial life, but they don't want to get involved. They see it as hopeless. Maybe they had bad experiences with activists before.

Another kind of person, however, wants to do something about social problems, even if only on a community or neighborhood level. He keeps himself informed and does something positive to keep from drowning in a sea of apathy and overwhelming difficulties.

My activism is writing tracts to myself and a few friends: "Let's overcome mechanical prayer. Do you realize how totally we lack spontaneous love for Rādhā-Kṛṣṇa? Listen to how Rūpa Gosvāmī prays. What are we in comparison? Listen to how Ajāmila prays after being saved from the Yamadūtas. He says, 'Oh, what am I? A sinner who has given up brahminical life. And what are You, O merciful holy name!' We should do something, read together, take a *japa* retreat and increase our quota. What do you think?"

I think it's a good idea. Do something today. Feed your attraction.

Rain pattering down on this roof. Breakfast soon. Kṛṣṇa is giving us what we want, we humans who have devised ways to stay out of the rain. No matter how hard it rains, we are dry. We have books to read, and culture and technology and worries with which to preoccupy ourselves. Let it rain, our salt will pour. The grass will grow. The government will take action. "Life's but a walking shadow, a poor player that struts and frets his hour upon the stage and then is heard no more." Save yourself. "Having come to this material world, which is miserable and temporary, O Arjuna, engage yourself in devotional service."

40

I made my presentation to the assembled devotees in the schoolhouse. I tried to keep it simple and positive and to not sound uppity. I told them to add the hearing of Kṛṣṇa's activities to their lives by regularly reading Prabhupāda's books. They don't have to change their way of life or practice special austerities to do this—they just have to read. Husband and wife can read together, or close friends. With a little effort and regular practice, obstacles can be overcome and we can become attracted to Kṛṣṇa's messages. If we avoid regularly hearing about Kṛṣṇa, our work is in danger of becoming *śrama eva hi kevalam*.

No one objected or said it was impossible. Some hinted that perhaps chanting and hearing aren't the only things we need to do to become purified. I agreed and modified my message a bit to suit that point of view. More complications were mentioned such as an honest remark that it seems "dry and artificial and even fanatical when I attempt to discuss Kṛṣṇa after reading." Someone asked, "How do we know when we are over-endeavoring in *sādhana?*"

Later it occurred to me that some devotees in ISKCON give more credence to their own experience than to *śāstra*. They think the personal changes they have gone through and the examples they have seen, both good and bad, are a stronger testimony than some absolute statement in the *śāstra*. The *śāstras* tell of the superiority of *śravaṇaṁ-kīrtanam* over other religious activities, but someone may want to relativize that statement based on what he has learned about his own capabilities, the needs of living in the world, etc. Someone else may be so cautious about getting carried away by any ISKCON authority's "trip" that he may not quite believe the authorities of the *Bhāgavatam* either. I am not saying that anyone voiced that viewpoint today, but it struck me as a way someone might go—

thinking his own experience is a wiser judge of what to do than the words of the Lord or Śukadeva Gosvāmī.

It was nice talking with devotees about how I like to come to Ireland and how I have been able to write here over the years. I told them the special feature of early morning walks in Ireland, where people sleep late and I don't get bothered by barking dogs. We had a *kīrtana* and then I gave out some biscuits. See you next Saturday.

41

A sudden shower, even while the sunshine was out, caught me on the bench and soaked my page. I have run for shelter to the calf's shed. Even one minute in that downpour has drenched my clothes. It's so pleasant. Yamunā watched me as if it were a sport. She probably thought I was foolish to run inside. After all, it was just a quick shower and she is accustomed to standing outside all day long, even in heavy rain. Everything at once—dark clouds, sunshine, and rain! Good for the grass. Always something growing.

This morning, Uddhava asked me something about the relationship of work to favorable meditation on Kṛṣṇa. I was insisting on reading the scriptures. But he has this wonderful field of backyard activities where he can engage his family members in devotional service. All I meant was that while working, in order to think of Kṛṣṇa, we should have fresh subject matters in our minds, and those come from regular hearing.

But I have to be aware of what others are doing before I tell them to do something else. Therefore, all I said was add *śravaṇaṁ-kīrtanam*. Who will not be attracted to the narrations of *uttama-śloka* except one who is a butcher or who is killing his own self? Someone has to remind us to read. That's my job.

42

I can't expect fresh rain squalls in the sunshine quite like this in India. I won't have a friend's backyard to play in where I can trot from the rain into a shed and still be alone. In India, there are always ten people watching. A cowshed like this might be the residence of a big family, or at least a few workers would be sleeping in it, or animals and children would be running in and out. And if I stopped in a shed in India to write, I would immediately draw a crowd. The children would beg something from me—my pen, my watch, rupees. Within minutes, I would have to get up and leave.

Bhajana in the West has its advantages. The wind is fresh and clean. I can relax. I can be safe in my room and leave my door unlocked. There are no radios or cinema songs or loud *āśrama bhajanas*. Just wind and cows and sheep. This is a nice place, although there is no Govardhana here, and no Rādhā-kuṇḍa. I am intimidated by the Indianness of Bhārata-varṣa. I don't feel at home there. I feel pinched by the lack of conveniences. Yet I eagerly await another chance to go there. Just waiting on the visas.

43

Someone entered a church on the Isle of Capri. He is wearing bell-bottomed white trousers and a turtleneck jersey, and he is barefoot. He has been reading *A Thief's Journal* by Genêt. He is drunk on wine. It is not actually a church, just a small road-side chapel with a votive candle burning, a crucifix, and a picture of the Blessed Virgin. He will never get anywhere in religion this way. He is corrupt, he is lost, he is lonely. He will have to go many more miles. He will have to get God's grace in the form of the guru. He will have to come to that.

Then he met Swamijī in New York City in 1966. Now forget all that happened before that, the corrupt pose, the vain seeking, the victimization and the cheating—forget it if you can.

Start again. Hearing lessons in Kṛṣṇa consciousness from a pure devotee of Kṛṣṇa. Never thought it would happen.

Another look—he is entering Naples as a devotee. He sees the city through a porthole on the ferry. Devotees from the local ISKCON temple are waiting for him on the dock. This is a sweeter memory. He lectured on *Śrīmad-Bhāgavatam* under looming Mt. Vesuvio.

A man is sitting outdoors on a cement step in the spring sunlight, reading Prabhupāda's book. Oh, but there are horrible visions too. The torture, the killing in this world. We want to say they are only dreams, but they happen, don't they? Riots in Los Angeles, starving in Ethiopia, a misunderstood child in a house in the Cleveland suburbs, fear at night in Pennsylvania . . . What will happen? Somebody was killed while riding his bicycle. A woman or man had heart stroke, experienced intense pain, and then died. She has been sick so long she can no longer do anything active as she used to . . . They live in a community where no one understands them. Prison ...

It's *māyā*, it's *māyā*. He dreams a tiger is eating him but there is no tiger. Oh, to know it that way!

But you are supposed to be telling about Vṛndāvana *bhajana*. Yes, but I can't just crank it out if it doesn't come that way. These are the layers and complications of reality. I don't really have it all figured out. Why is there suffering? Is it real? Unreal? Are my headaches unreal? Are my memories unreal? Where am I going in my next life?

Matter is insubstantial. Spirit soul is all and God is the Supreme Truth. I don't have much more to say about it. But when I suffer with a headache, it seems that *I* suffer and it affects my ability to serve. That's not real either. Even when I am pinned down, I can still do simple services and become pleasing to Kṛṣṇa. Freedom from pain isn't *more* real, although I can be more active. And then death. We can breathe, "Kṛṣṇa, Rādhā" at the end, if we have spent our time wisely. That is real.

44

Excitement. My heart is beating fast and my shoes are soaking wet. The calf got loose. M. had gone shopping, so I was alone. I ran out and thought I could easily coax her into the stall with some calf nuts and then lock her in. But no, she was more interested in her freedom in the high grass. I put a short rope around her neck and tried pulling her. But even by pulling with all my strength, I couldn't budge her once she dug her hooves into the mud. I was afraid to keep pulling too, because I thought I might choke her.

I ran around excitedly, not thinking calmly. Try the chain that she had slipped out of. No, it's too small to fit over her head. Then I found a small rope, tied it around her, and forced her to a nearby post. She has no leeway now, just two feet of rope, but she's chewing grass there. Not very comfortable. A rough situation for you, Yamunā, but if you won't let me give you a longer rope or put you in the stall, if you won't budge, then you will have to stay there—until I can get some more capable men to figure out the situation.

I spent half an hour like this. Then I phoned a nearby devotee. Only his wife was home. I asked her to call someone else to come and help. Now I am sitting and waiting. I don't mind that Yamunā is tied so tightly, but I am afraid she will get loose again. Once she gets the idea that she can run away, then we will really be in trouble. Hope it won't happen. Hurry up, somebody, come, so I can get back to my calmer, deeper meditations.

Now that I am waiting, I can see better the weak link in my attempts: by my brute force, I failed to move Yamunā. I have her tied up not far from her shed, but I can't force her to cover the short distance to her stall. Basically, I am too squeamish and soft-hearted, and not very good with animals.

I remember Paramānanda telling me of the day he showed a stubborn horse who was boss. He said he was prepared to beat the horse to death. He showed the animal a murderous intent and that horse obeyed forever after. But I am afraid if I get "murderous" with Yamunā, not knowing what I am doing, I might injure her. All the pressure is on her neck. So I am waiting, exposed as an ineffectual pen-pusher. Why is it taking so long for someone to come? Maybe all the men are out on errands.

After about twenty minutes, I started chanting *japa* again. Then Aniruddha dāsa arrived. He instantly showed me the trick. You grab the calf by the tail as well as the neck. He began to move her forward that way, then we did it together, me at her head and he at her tail. In she went where she is now grounded behind two locked doors. Aniruddha said this has happened a number of times. We will try to improve the system with the post and the long rope.

I said, "Let's leave her in the shed until Madhu returns. I don't want to further disrupt my work." So an hour has gone by in cow-chasing.

45

Kṛṣṇa is coming home from pasturing the cows. His *līlā* is eternal. His coming home at dusk is a pastime for all of Vraja's devotees. The *gopīs* watch Him discreetly from the porches and roofs. They embrace Him with their eyes. He is the perfection of handsomeness, the vision of youthful grace and strength. He plays His flute and the cows obey His wishes out of love for Him. They walk homeward, and the cows' hooves raise dust which settles on Kṛṣṇa's body in a delightful way. He appears even more beautiful decorated with that dust.

Nanda Mahārāja and Mother Yaśodā anxiously wait at the house, and when they see the cloud of dust rising in the distance, they search into it for the first sight of their beloved children, Kṛṣṇa and Balarāma.

May this pastime come to me now and at the time of my death. Bhīṣmadeva reviewed many of Kṛṣṇa's pastimes at the time of his passing away. He especially loved to see Kṛṣṇa with the dust and wounds of the battlefield—Kṛṣṇa coming toward him on the chariot, Kṛṣṇa driving the horses of Arjuna's chariot, Kṛṣṇa as Bhīṣma's adversary. And Bhīṣma saw Kṛṣṇa with the *gopīs* in the *rāsa* dance, Kṛṣṇa, the Supersoul in everyone's heart . . .

"May His glittering yellow dress and His lotus face, covered with paintings of sandalwood pulp, be the object of my attraction, and may I not desire fruitive results" (*Bhāg.* 1.9.33).

Astu kṛṣṇe ātmā—"Let my mind thus go unto Śrī Kṛṣṇa" (*Bhāg.* 1.9.34). Let my mind be fixed upon that Kṛṣṇa. May His lotus feet always remain the object of my attraction. At the moment of death, let my ultimate attraction be to Śrī Kṛṣṇa, the Personality of Godhead. Thus Bhīṣma merged himself in the Supersoul, Lord Śrī Kṛṣṇa.

46

Kṛṣṇa drove Arjuna's chariot. Arjuna ordered Him because they were friends. "Okay," Kṛṣṇa said, "whatever you order. I won't fail to carry it out as your driver." But when Kṛṣṇa showed His universal form, Arjuna was afraid. He said, "Forgive me for calling You *sakha* and asking You to drive my chariot and joking with You. You are God, You are not my friend." But Kṛṣṇa wants to be friend, son, lover. The devotees like Yaśodā-mātā and the *gopīs* are always fixed in their intimate *rasa*. Kṛṣṇa likes that best. Arjuna too likes it best when He is the close friend. These are the teachings of Gauḍīya Vaiṣṇavism. I am one of the teachers. Don't laugh, I can do it. Standing in front of a class—I can do it anywhere, at any university. Put me there and I'm not afraid (especially if they are inclined to *some* religion). Put me in front and I can give a lecture. That makes me a teacher.

But the teacher is in the shed saying, *I wish it were all in my heart*. I like Sanātana Gosvāmī's prayer to Lord Caitanya after the Lord finished instructing him. He said, "You have taught me plenty, but how will I, a low person, realize it and speak it to others as You desire? Please put Your feet on my head and bless me with realization." Lord Caitanya complied with Sanātana's request. Sanātana knew he needed it. What good is teaching unrealized precepts of love of God?

The teacher *wants* to go to the shed and shed tears and shed his snake skin and be quiet.

I want to capture a Kṛṣṇa conscious moment and put it on the page. And then I can go to the bathroom, but the sublime moment won't be lost. Is that another vanity? No, not if by "captured on the page" you mean an eternal, small act of offering to Kṛṣṇa. The page may get lost, go unpublished, be destroyed, but not the act. That's our faith.

And when you are writing best, that is what you are doing. You can do it in Texas or in India; you can do it while watching a swallow fly over the greenhouse or when copying out Narottama dāsa Ṭhākura's poem in your own hand. You can do it with candor and no pretension or with a carefully prepared plot and argument. The main essence is devotion.

47

Third day in a row I've developed a headache around this time. Usually I am able to subdue it by the routine of bath-lunch-rest. But it's not fun. At least I am able to appreciate my free time when I have it. I want to fill it with devotional service. Stress brings my headaches on, even the stress of a too-packed schedule.

I don't know exactly when my search for calmness began. I think it began when the headaches were at their worst in 1985–86. At that time, I had to stop everything and live at Gītā-nāgarī as an invalid. I was taking so much medicine that my condition seemed to be worsening. Peace and quiet were the main priorities in my day. I began to cultivate interests and habits that promoted calm and that were at least not stressful, or noisy, or requiring too much personal interaction.

One interest I developed was taking solitary nature walks and communing with the flowers and birds along the Tuscarora Creek. Keeping a diary seemed to fit in with that. Whenever I had time (free from a headache), I wrote down what was happening. I compensated for my inability to do more by seeing value in the small and nearby things. I saw subtle changes in the seasons and recorded them. I also expressed the guilt and uncertainty I felt—was I a malingerer?—in my diary.

That's the history, but even after I recovered a little, I continued my search for a calm environment. Nature-watching became a luxury I could no longer afford. I took up my service again as a traveling *sannyāsī*, but this time I traveled with sympathetic assistants who tried to make my way through the world safe and controlled.

I have found that calmness to some extent by retiring from the GBC and temple management, and by not allowing myself to meet with many people in one day. I still get headaches when the stress levels build, and anyway, I am attracted to the quieter life. It is more conducive to my writing and prayer. And although my external situation is calm, I have found that prayer and writing can be tumultuous. They are full of inner excitement. External simplicity, solitude, and calm are good for prayer life.

At the same time, I keep up a considerable travel pace. When I arrive in the midst of a Kṛṣṇa conscious community, I set up a kind of controlled accessibility. I stay in my van. I don't go somewhere where they demand too much of me. So far this is working. I am gradually meeting new friends wherever I go and taking on more service of guiding and counseling people.

My only fear is that ISKCON's leadership might insist I become more actively involved in their committees, management, etc., but that fear seems unfounded. My Godbrothers seem to accept me as an elderly semi-recluse.

Lord Kṛṣṇa, you have somehow arranged things this way. I am grateful and hope to respond more favorably to Your indications.

(I look out at the plastic greenhouse rippling in the wind. I notice the twinge in my right eye and calculate optimistically that I will be able to subdue it with therapy, just as I have done in recent days. Oh, black cat, you frighten me the way you suddenly arrive at a place, staring under the door with yellow eyes.)

I have grown in a particular direction, just as a tree grows, sometimes straight and sometimes gnarled. Just by looking at the shape of a tree, you can tell what it has had to do to survive. Who can judge the tree's experience? At least it survived.

On the other hand, I shouldn't write my memoir as if it is the last chapter in my life.

Go in and tell M. I've got a headache. He hears it often and we do what we can. He honors and protects my little passage through physical inconvenience. Whoever shares this with me and gives me respect and space to deal with it . . . I am grateful to them. I am trying to reciprocate by showing that a quiet life can yield firm *bhakti* fruits. It is a way of saying thank you to those who have cared.

48

This is a book about clouds. Ireland *bhajana* must reflect the cloudy sky and the blustering chill that produces hardy natures and red cheeks. Now the whole sky is covered except for a few chinks of blue showing through. Rich colored, magnificent gray, Kṛṣṇa's own bodily hue. Prabhupāda says Kṛṣṇa is blackish, but not like the black in this world. No, not the color of black-skinned Africans or dark-skinned Indians, but the color of a fresh rain cloud. That image is good because clouds aren't material in the gross sense. Their darkness is filled with the aura of heavenly light. It's "gray," but it's beautiful, infinite, inconceivable.

Rādhā is said to be "golden," but not exactly like a gold bar or straw or turmeric. A flash of lightning in the gray clouds—this is the metaphor that is used to describe Rādhā and Kṛṣṇa together.

When Kṛṣṇa wants to know Rādhārāṇī's nature from Her point of view, He appears (eternally) as Śrī Caitanya Mahāprabhu. His body is golden and He is immersed in the *bhāva* which is unique to Rādhā—*mahā-bhāva-prema* for Kṛṣṇa, and especially, *madana-mahā-bhāva*, the mad love felt in separation from the beloved.

How far away these emotions are from me, and yet they are also near. If I can shape my life and pay more attention to them, then that will be the best use of my life. Make this the point of your search for a "calm" life.

49

How to carry the Vṛndāvana experience into my Western life? A Gauḍīya Vaiṣṇava wants to serve in Vraja day and night. This is achieved both externally and internally. Externally (physically) he lives in Vraja (in the district of Mathurā, in the state of Uttara Pradesh, in India), or if he is unable to do that, he lives in Vraja mentally *after at least having physically been there for some time*. The physical residence in Vṛndāvana-dhāma enables us to gather sense impressions, which will help our remembrance. Some of my Godbrothers are good at gathering these sense impressions. They recall details of Govardhana *parikrama*, or special moments when they were on Vraja Maṇḍala *parikrama*. One Godbrother is preaching in Germany and recalls how a parrot came and sat on his shoulder in Bhāṇḍīravana. I need to go and collect my own "data" and, I hope, to be transformed by the dust of Vṛndāvana. Then when I come back, I will be able to remember.

We cannot imitate direct service to Rādhā and Kṛṣṇa, but according to our greed, and according to the guidance we receive from our guru, we can pray and hear of Vraja. Hearing this, we may pray to serve there in some future lifetime.

This *bhajana* is best done while living in Vṛndāvana, India. Then we (Prabhupādānuga preachers) will be better able to keep it in our hearts even as we travel. We may also stop here and there in the West and try to recall both the external and internal *bhāvas* of *sevā* in Vṛndāvana.

But—you say—in the West, ordinary things are not sacred in the same way they are in Vṛndāvana. There is no śāstric support, as there is in Vraja, to assure us that the dogs are actually *sādhus* and are about to be liberated, or that the dirt (earth) can give us mercy. Nothing is ordinary in Vṛndāvana, but can that be said of places in the West?

Is it true? Is ordinary life in Ireland doomed to be always ordinary? Or if I am able to see it in a Kṛṣṇa conscious way, is it still not as holy as Vṛndāvana? I guess the answer is that if we become like Śrīla Prabhupāda, then "wherever you are, that is Vṛndāvana." We can "superimpose" impressions of grass in Vṛndāvana on our impressions of Irish grass. It is a matter of meditation.

I like that explanation, but I am looking for more. I want validation that direct experience of Ireland is also a part of the Vraja experience. There is no way to experience Vṛndāvana in Ireland except to be totally immersed in chanting and hearing. It is Kṛṣṇa's pastimes that focus our minds so we can see through the mundane. But neither is meditation on His pastimes a vague form of mysticism. It is Vṛndāvana consciousness.

50

The silent, still pines after a rain. The sky is blue, calm, and bright. I hear a woman and a child singing, or no, it is Madhu singing a children's song from the Murāri band's new collection. "Aghāsura was a most envious demon . . . "

I claim so many distractions and probably if I were free of them, I could go to the center of something. But this is my state. I am semidistracted and trying to serve. Most of my contemporaries are also in this state. We take it for granted that we live in a flux of busy items and noises and intrusions. Some people even like it; it makes them feel "engaged" in devotional service. As long as the phone rings and someone wants to talk to us, it gives us a chance to parry and thrust.

This fresh air and cool weather is the Lord's mercy. Now I am anticipating the monsoon heat. Straw at my feet.

I write out of this center of self while realizing that I am not the center at all. I am a mini-center, an infinitesimal self, a fallen and covered self. I spin in orbit around the Supreme Self. He drives me to come closer, to be warmer, but there is some delay due to my *anarthas*. I am slowly spinning off my unwanted burdens. And just when I feel I am learning sophisticated truths about the science of *bhakti*, I see a tiny, delicately built flying insect on my page and wonder how it fits into the scheme of things. It's a strange world.

Please, language, let me use you. Let me twist you like flowers wound around with string for a bouquet. Let me dig in the earth, using my pen as a spade. Stop and sweat. Say a prayer: "O holy name, I do like to chant, but You don't allow me." Śrīla Prabhupāda said that if we can chant without committing the ten offenses, then we will immediately see Kṛṣṇa.

Days dwindling.

51

Manu dāsa is coming to stay with us at the cottage. He has worked hard in Dublin for quite a few years, mostly alone. He feels sorry that he couldn't establish a solvent temple building and thriving congregation. But he attempted it at a time when other devotees here weren't interested in communal, *āśrama* life. Anyway, Manu has done his best. Now he thinks it would be better if he went to Inis Rath where the temple is more established and where his wife and son can live more peacefully and be fully engaged in devotional service.

So many devotees, each with a story of their own. The men's hair has started to thin. Faces crease with wrinkles. We go on smiling. We ask, "Should we listen to others' opinions? Why is it difficult to understand the depth and gravity of Kṛṣṇa consciousness? When you spoke on the *Śrīmad-Bhāgavatam* verse, *satāṁ prasaṅgān mama vīrya-saṁvido* (*Bhāg*. 3.25.25), I wondered, 'What is real devotion and devotional service,' as mentioned in Prabhupāda's purport. Could you explain it?"

It means the nectar for which we are always anxious. It means that at present, our devotional service is an unripe mango. Real devotion is the ripe mango enjoyed by Kṛṣṇa. We are going through the motions now, and real devotional service means spontaneous love.

"How can we tell if enthusiasm is material or spiritual?" Well, folks, you can tell in this way: if it is selfish, it is material, and if it is for Kṛṣṇa, it is spiritual. Next question?

Of course, anyone can answer these questions, but how many of us can solve the issues in another person's heart?

Someone asks, "How do we keep from getting depressed by a reverse?" They already know they are not this body. They also know everything comes from Kṛṣṇa's mercy. Still, they are brought down when a reverse comes. They need more than the index reference as to what page Prabhupāda discusses this on. Can I reduce someone's depression in a time of reverse? Do *I* get depressed in a time of reverse? If so, what do *I* do?

How about this: "What are the signs by which we can understand that the relationship with the spiritual master is deepening and if it is deepening in the right way?" To answer that, I have to enter the understanding of what a guru is. I was disregarding most of those kind of questions. I was looking for those that seemed suitable, like ones about *gṛhastha* life and another, "How should we meditate during Ratha-yātrā?" But now all questions seem valid.

A question comes whether *gṛhastha* duties are devotional service. And this remark: "I suppose the insecurity is there because living in a temple we were always told to do the needful, so we felt that it was devotional service. As a *gṛhastha*, we may also do the needful, but it appears to be less Kṛṣṇa conscious. Is that a misconception?"

My answer: "What is the needful?" In the temple, all activities are supposed to be dedicated for the good of humanity by spreading Kṛṣṇa consciousness. If a *gṛhastha* sees his wife and children as servants of Kṛṣṇa, then his home becomes a temple and when he does the needful, it is Kṛṣṇa conscious.

52

We tire of hearing mundane stories with mundane heroes, but we never tire of hearing about Kṛṣṇa. "In this way, the reading matter remains forever fresh, despite repeated readings" (Bg. 10.18, purport).

Your inner breast is burning. You are face to face with your lack of surrender. You are impatient and raving. You have found an outlet for this in writing. I may say, "Peace be upon you," but it can't be settled until I learn of my relationship with Kṛṣṇa. I have to give up fascination with everything else, including self-expression, that doesn't touch the spiritual relationship with Kṛṣṇa.

Your Godbrothers are doing what they have to do. Now you do what you can. Don't think you can avoid surrender. Wherever you go, your lack of surrender will face you. Everyone needs Kṛṣṇa and He is waiting for everyone to surrender to Him.

It requires great faith to do as the guru asks us, and faith to do as our institution asks us. They represent Kṛṣṇa. But when someone misrepresents Kṛṣṇa and Śrīla Prabhupāda, then it creates a crack in the foundation of our faith. Once the crack is there, it is hard to mend. We think, "Then all my service and surrender was wasted. I cannot trust anyone in the same way again." This becomes an excuse to engage in sense gratification and to become skeptical.

Some stay in the movement but retain cracked attitudes. Tending to the needs of such devotees is important, but if someone's faith is too cracked, then he can no longer hear. Performing austerity becomes difficult if we have no taste, little realization, and little faith. A humble soul will get down anyway and perform acts of faith and austerity, but other people, nondevotees, will deride the faithful.

Each of us has to examine where we fit into all of this. Are we healers? Are we the strongly faithful ones? Or are we doubters, hypocrites? It requires self-examination and honesty. When a leader in ISKCON falls down, it hurts all of us. Then we see that even one who appeared to be upholding the principles was cheating. It becomes harder to know who is sincere and who is a hypocrite, who we can trust and who we can follow.

Someone says, "Don't worry, you can follow Śrīla Prabhupāda." But we ask him, "Why should we listen to you? You may be motivated." We want to follow Śrīla Prabhupāda, but who among his followers can we trust? And if we can't trust ourselves . . . This is the doubt syndrome; the cracked foundation syndrome.

53

Green grass with reflections of sunlight turning the upside of the blade white and translucent green. The sun is evaporating the beads of dew. In this thick grass sits an uncomfortable, white bench. A washing sound of wind in the pines.

Kṛṣṇa went to Dvārakā. The Vrajavāsīs didn't follow Him there. They meditated on His pastimes with them in Gokula. We may go anywhere to preach the glories of Vraja-nandana.

You look up and think of other devotees in ISKCON. You look down and make marks on the page. In between, you ask your mind what to write. Sometimes you don't even ask . . . faces of devotees . . . bellow of a cow . . . wind rippling the page. I write the "come what may" sentences, not abandoning vows or service, but as a way to get to more sincere expression.

Śrīla Prabhupāda said, "For service, you can step on my head." The sculptor making a Kṛṣṇa *mūrti* puts his foot against the Lord to gain leverage. Govinda stepped over Lord Caitanya's body. You can write in this way—going past crazy thoughts by writing them down.

Grass—because I see it. Breeze—because I feel it. *Kṛṣṇa-kathā* because I remember it. Statements of honesty because honesty is important to me. I am at a stage where the striving for honesty—and the self-criticism it produces—are crucial engagements. Later, I may get past that and be more concerned with *līlā* itself.

But when I start to speak *līlā*, I remain concerned about my sincerity, my level of realization, and my faith. I think about it. When others speak or write *kṛṣṇa-kathā* I also think, "What is their realization? What is this speaker actually like in his life and in the privacy of his mind?" As a kind of service, I tell you. And as an exercise. At least this one person is going to stick to self-scrutiny. It may be obsessive. Anyway, I can see it better for what it is. I don't hate it. It is a part of the *bhakti* process, but it is not entirely spiritual. I mean, it is not letting go and forgetting everything except the service of Śrīmatī Rādhārāṇī and Śrī Kṛṣṇa.

It's asking myself, where am I at truly? Vrajavāsīs don't think like that. They serve and always think what is best for their Lord. So I have to accept myself as I am at present. I am going to Vṛndāvana. It's a good place to get beyond the limited self. I plan to continue writing while there but it may be difficult. That's up to Śrīmatī Rādhārāṇī. I write and She controls it or enters it as She likes. If the *dhāma* enters my writing, then it will be filled with praises of Rādhā and Kṛṣṇa. I will disappear. My contention is that the writing act is my way to invite Them to appear in my writing.

Wind blowing through a fence. At first I thought it was an electric drill. Indigestion. What do you see? What do you want to say? What my body feels. What my emotions tell. What my mind says. What my intelligence deliberates. Prayers of the soul—I attempt them. Idealized cries to God. Gut cries.

54

As I was writing the above, Yamunā the calf came thundering down to where I sat in the far corner of the field. She had broken her rope and wanted me to see. She then romped away. She was being playful, not letting me catch her. She is getting so big (and strong) that it will soon be hard to tether her by the present system of a rope attached to a pole in the ground. I called Madhu to catch her. She was trailing a long cord, so he was able to grab it and put her, for the time being, into the shed.

The black cat usually slinks by at the right time, as if to add her comments on every situation. When Yamunā got her milk last night, noisily nosing the bucket, the black cat appeared high on the top of the hay bales mewing loudly as if to say, "Where's *my* milk?" And when I went to tell Madhu, "We've got a loose calf," the cat walked by silently as if to say, "I told you so. You won't find *me* acting up like that."

55

"Hurry up, please. It's time." The famous T. S. Eliot line. Or the hare in *Alice in Wonderland.* He is running along with a clock in his hand, "I'm late, I'm late, for a very important date." I think that's me, always looking at the clock to time my *sādhana*. Write for an hour; then *japa* for an hour; then half an hour in the bathroom (hurry up, don't be late); then another hour *japa;* then *gāyatrī* and out the door by 5:00 A.M. (5:05 at the latest). If it happens to be 5:07, then I feel like the hare, hurrying along, quickening the pace to make up for the lost time.

I'm late, I'm late for a very important date; I run and then I hop-hop-hop. I wish that I could fly. I'm late, I'm late . . .

Oh, dear, he's late. Where are you going, Mr. Hare? (Alice asks). What a wonderful but frightening, mad world. Oh Alice . . .

Sign on the lectern at the ISKCON Soho Street temple: "Dear respected guest speaker, please finish your lecture by 8:30 A.M." At the Manor, the phrase is added, "Including the question and answer session. And be sure to ask questions of the women."

Poor *karmīs* work hard all their lives and their time is thus wasted. *Śrama eva hi kevalam.* Poor cats and dogs. "Poor frogs," Śrīla Prabhupāda said to the biologist.

Hurry up and serve the people and the earth before it's too late. That's the serious intent—*there is urgency in the Kṛṣṇa conscious message*. That's why devotees are hurrying along through their morning and all-day-long program, because they want to quickly tend to their own needs and then help people. Go out and preach. Don't procrastinate.

But take the time to do it with quality. How fast do you chant a round of *japa*? He said, "Sometimes four minutes, sometimes ten." He is an exception. The average is very fast. I shouldn't talk because fast or slow, I am still "out of it."

The inner life is important. You may appear to be hurrying or slow to you or me, but we can't judge just by the outer movement. Is the hare a fool just because he is hurrying?

Śrīla Prabhupāda didn't rush. He is an excellent example. But he did walk quickly. He didn't spend his whole day chanting *japa*. Writing too was done in the morning. We can't imitate. What he did was surcharged with the urgency of Kṛṣṇa's compassion for all *jīvas*, deep as the *bhakti* ocean, so whether he took five minutes or ten to do something, we can't judge it and we can't imitate it.

Memoir: When Harikeśa mentioned that he was spending two and a half hours cooking Prabhupāda's lunch, Prabhupāda said, "You do not know how to cook. I will show you and do it in one hour."

"One hour?" said Harikeśa, almost in disbelief. "This is amazing."

Later: "Śrīla Prabhupāda looked at his watch. 'One hour,' he said. 'We have cooked nine preparations'" (*Śrīla Prabhupāda-līlāmṛta*, Vol. 6, pp. 121–22).

56

There are so many devotees in Śrīla Prabhupāda's movement. Some of them appear irregular in their character and we are prone to criticize. Just by thinking ill of another devotee or by allowing our minds to criticize someone, we can jeopardize our whole spiritual life. Although we may be inoffensive in our actual dealings, we also have to check our internal offenses. It means we have to become humble in our hearts.

If we can realize, at least somewhat, our own fallen natures, then we may deliberately avoid the cutting, sarcastic words or thoughts we aim at other devotees. According to the narrations we hear in *śāstra*, if we do offend someone, we should approach them directly and beg their forgiveness.

We cannot become offenseless by simply avoiding contact with others, although it's true that thick mixing with many devotees can give rise to offensiveness. But as Lord Caitanya prescribed, we should praise the devotees, both in their presence and in private. We don't want to be superficial, but we should look for the good that exists in each person, and concentrate on that.

I hear children's voices mixing in with the cattle lowing and the sheep *baaaa-ing*. Are the cattle complaining because I am leaving here in a few days? Of course not. But it somehow speaks to my mood in a way that reminds me I have to go. It also reminds us that these creatures are not happy. They are a lower species of life. (Lord Caitanya told the leper that Yamarāja has 84 *lakhs* of hells for offenders.) To err may be human, but too many mistakes and you have to suffer.

57

I am sitting between the cat and the calf. Mādhāi's "nest" is on the other side of the bales of hay, to my left, and Yamunā is outdoors. I can't actually see her, but she is only about twenty feet from where I am sitting. I hope they both stay put so I can write undisturbed.

Prabhupāda dāsa and I had a talk and then read together from *Caitanya-caritāmṛta*. When Prabhupāda dāsa got up, he bumped his head against the low attic ceiling. I am used to it by now, and used to the tight ladder-like stairway. Used to the mattress which is too short (my ankles hang over). Used to the bathroom with hot water. Used to not taking anything to drink or eat after lunch because I can't digest it. Used to taking rest for the night with the sun still up, and to waking up a few times when it is still light out.

I am also used to the low performance of my morning *japa*. But it's nice lighting two votive candles, keeping the room dark, and chanting with earplugs so as not to wake up the others from 2–3. I am used to these things.

Used to yogurt for breakfast (although in a few days, the yogurt fast begins). Used to headaches. Used to having doubts about myself.

Does the phrase, "used to" signify complacency or stuck in a rut? Does it mean "attached to"? Maybe. It also means I tolerate. I am patient. And I think it means I accept these things. I accept my life as it is, though I wish I could improve it by chanting attentively and realizing *kṛṣṇa-kathā*. But what can I do but patiently wait for improvement?

58

The day will come when you will hear the wind washing in the pines and you will think of a Vraja pastime. The grass in Wicklow will suddenly bring you to the grass on Govardhana Hill and the words of the *gopīs:* "This Govardhana Hill is the best of the servants of Hari because it provides fresh grass for His cows."

When your heart is free of material desire (*viṣaya*), then you can see Vṛndāvana. Śrīla Prabhupāda saw Vṛndāvana aboard an Indian tanker on the Red Sea. He saw Rādhā-Dāmodara in Vraja in Manhattan. At such times he yearned to return to

Vṛndāvana, but even more, he desired to carry out the order of his spiritual master to preach Kṛṣṇa consciousness to the Western people. He saw Vṛndāvana where we saw a beat-up Indian bus belching black exhaust smoke on the road to Agra. He brought us to Vṛndāvana and then sent us out to preach again, assuring us "This is best. You have learned to keep Vṛndāvana in your heart."

It's possible to have that romantic concept of Vṛndāvana. That means imagining yourself there amidst the splendid and pleasant trees and ponds and Yamunā . . . imagining yourself merging into the eternal role . . . So visiting Vṛndāvana will smash that and I will gain something better than I imagined.

59

We can't fathom the mind or the activities of Śrī Caitanya Mahāprabhu or His associates. When we judge the behavior of a Vaiṣṇava, we make a great mistake. Their activities may be appreciated and even studied, but never criticized. Neither should their activities be imitated. We have to learn how to follow intelligently.

Kṛṣṇadāsa Kavirāja says that Lord Caitanya tested Sanātana Gosvāmī in the month of May–June. He called for him one day at noon. Sanātana went to Lord Caitanya's residence by walking on the beach where the sand is as hot as fire. He did this to avoid touching the *pūjārīs* who frequent the main road. Lord Caitanya knew this and praised Sanātana Gosvāmī for observing the etiquette. Śrī Caitanya Mahāprabhu then embraced Sanātana Gosvāmī. But this mortified Sanātana because his oozing sores touched the body of the Lord.

The next day Jagadānanda Paṇḍita went to meet Sanātana Gosvāmī. When they sat together and began to discuss *kṛṣṇa-kathā*, Sanātana Gosvāmī submitted to Jagadānanda Paṇḍita the cause of his distress. I like thinking of how the two devotees came together to discuss *kṛṣṇa-kathā*, and yet Sanātana Gosvāmī revealed his personal troubles to his friend. I like to do this when I can, although I find it's rare—to sit and read with a friend and yet feel free to pause in the reading to discuss what's on my mind. Sometimes we can discuss personal topics in love and trust and then return to the scriptural reading. It's not that Sanātana Gosvāmī completely forgot his distress when they spoke about Kṛṣṇa. His distress was, of course, transcendental. It is so elevated that for us to discuss it today is a form of *hari-kathā*.

60

Some thinkers say it is good to forget yourself, to become lost in a larger effort. We want to make the leap to Vraja in our thoughts. Seems we have to develop strong muscles in our minds, like frogs or kangaroos.

See myself admiring the natural scenery and then jump to Kṛṣṇa in Vraja. Like Hanumān in a single bound, land beside your Lord and ask to serve Him. But as you get older, your limbs lose their suppleness. I can't hike, can't climb, can't jump or run except for a little bit if a tiger is chasing me. Can the mind jump or is it only able to make the same, predictable movements?

One devotee wrote in her diary during an especially honest moment, "Oh Guru Mahārāja, I so much want to serve you and love you . . . but even more I want to be alone with time to myself and peaceful in my own house." Oh, leap, leaper. There's a haiku by Issa something like "Go ahead and leap, little cricket, but be careful, that's the ocean." And others encouraging little creative-like crickets or snails to go ahead and climb Mt. Fuji. Comparison of the tiny ones' limits.

Laughter at their herculean efforts. Śrīla Prabhupāda tells the story of the Ganges in flood. Big stalwart horses try to swim across, but they're washed away. A lean and broken-down horse, seeing all this, comes to the river bank and asks, "Is there much current? Shall I cross?" In a different mood: Prabhupāda was criticizing the scientists' attempts (which are often attempts to defy God). A devotee said, "But they see this as bravery." Prabhupāda replied, "Bravely going to hell."

One who can leap shouldn't always crawl. And what about one who can only crawl? We take the pace determined by the snail climbing Mt. Fuji. Śrīla Prabhupāda will take pity on us; you know the story of the sparrow who tried to empty the ocean.

61

We may think that we have already studied all of Śrīla Prabhupāda's books, so now we just need to keep up a refresher reading to keep in touch and to remember details. We don't want to get rusty. This attitude toward reading assumes there's not much new to be discovered. Even new books are examined with a connoisseur's attitude. Is the author presenting new material? Is he using fresh expression to say what we already know?

But another attitude toward study confronts the fact that as yet we are the grossest type of neophytes in devotional service—unrealized, no *bhāva*, still hampered by our *anarthas*. This kind of reading seems more relevant and challenging. We read earnestly, hoping to improve ourselves, because we know our life depends on making sound advancement. We are not concerned with whether we have read the material before; we are looking for deeper and deeper realization.

It's the same with *japa*. We can either chant as if we have been chanting this mantra for long enough to know how it's done, or we can chant for all we're worth. When we chant with heart, we surrender in *japa*. Again and again we pronounce the same mantra despite our failure to be attentive and devoted. We chant it again and again. *This* is our devotion. St. John of the Cross and other practitioners of prayer credit this persistence through arid times as a high order of surrender. As neophytes, we have no other choice but to chant through our lack of taste.

Even a neophyte is not chanting and reading only to taste spiritual sense gratification. He chants because he knows this is his constitutional position. He has to have at least that much realization to continue.

62

We are on our way out of Ireland, driving to the coast. We decided to stop for a day and rest. It's been a busy month.

M. said it is lambing time for the sheep and the herders. That's why the herdsmen are checking more often with the flock. What do I care? M. remarked how beautiful the sea looked. It was filled with windy, white breakers. I didn't say anything because at that moment, M. was driving over the precarious area where there's a sheer cliff and no guard rail. I leaned slightly in the other direction, as if that would help us not get too close to the edge. If your car falls over and plunges into the ravine, what good is a beautiful view of the sea?

63

A date is set, a time, when I will have to leave this body behind. Prepare yourself for that parting. Behave in ways conducive to that fact. Whatever I think of at the end will determine my next destination. For the materialist, death is a reverse. It is a wrenching away, a tragic defeat. Devotees shouldn't die like that. A devotee's anguish is that he or she did not attain *kṛṣṇa-prema*. We will feel that anguish.

At the hour of death, it's too late to develop our chanting, to promise to read more, to serve Śrīla Prabhupāda to our full capacity, to preach and save others. Of course, if we yearn to do these things, Kṛṣṇa will ensure that we can carry them out in our next life.

I'm convinced that at death, we should pray as Narottama dāsa Ṭhākura prayed, for association and service to advanced Vaiṣṇavas. We can't demand to go to Goloka Vṛndāvana if we are not qualified, but we can beg to serve the Vaiṣṇavas no matter what condition of life we attain. Beg to continue hearing and chanting in the line of Śrīla Prabhupāda and Rūpa Gosvāmī.

Death is inevitable. It's not far away. Wind up your material life today. Why do you eat so many sweets? Is it really to keep your body healthy and strong? What acts do you carry out to serve your body but which have no real spiritual benefit? Nothing is more important than self-realization. How gradual does your path have to be, anyway? At my age, the word "gradual" takes on a new meaning. I don't have time for long-term plans. And there are no senior citizen discounts in the spiritual realm.

At this stage of life, sex desire is most ridiculous. Material attachment in any form attacks your integrity. Dhṛtarāṣṭra shamed himself by living in Yudhiṣṭhira's house. Vidura told him to get out at once. It was not the time to find a materially comfortable situation, but to realize the self.

Those old people who dress in sporty clothes and wander around the world as tourists, flashing false teeth smiles, drinking in bars, trying to enjoy sex life at least on the subtle plane—how pathetic and disgusting, how ignoble. They are a disappointment to the human race. Keep this in mind and don't develop your own version of it. Śrīla Prabhupāda was always dignified in his old age—his magnificent seventies and eighties—a regal *ācārya*. He left this world at the age of eighty-two, a saint who gave his body so the world could live in Kṛṣṇa consciousness. We are his disciples. We should follow his example. Keep your honor and keep the goal in mind.

64

I walked across the meadow. Sheep don't use it. I want to communicate. I want to be a devotee happy in life in a temple or community or movement. But life is the way it is. You can feel all right all day and then suddenly, with no apparent cause, in the late afternoon, after a good reading—feel no meaning in anything. So you run out to the cliff, hoping the change of pace and the fresh air and the washing sound of the sea on rocks will bring a favorable change. It's possible that a little physical change can out-trick the doldrums. At least we don't take this down mood as all-in-all. We are steady.

The tide is high, the sky dark and menacing. The air is cool. The ocean surface is smooth as far as I can see; no breakers. Speaking of moods, the sea certainly has its own.

Here comes a red fishing boat, puttering in from left to right. I feel like I am sitting in the first row of an otherwise empty theater. The fishing boat is offstage Atlantic Ocean.

How do I look to the fisherman? He sees a lone figure in a silver coat writing away the afternoon and sitting oddly on a cliff against a low stone wall. Don't I have any work to do? Am I some tourist from America daydreaming while others work?

The boat cuts in closer, although it's not close enough that I can hear its engine or see who is on board. They are doughty boats, well-tuned and with powerful engines. There's room for plenty of fish. Soon he'll pass away.

65

The poor man asks God for money. Śrīla Prabhupāda says, "He is welcome." The *jñānī* wants to serve the Absolute Truth and not *māyā*. He is also welcome. Then there are those who have entered the *bhakti* path a little ways. They are on the shore of the ocean. They don't know how to go further. They need mercy.

They pray on cliffs and beaches. They try to feel that in the washing of the waves and the sea's pounding against the rocks there is some kinship for prayer. Again and again a heart beats. The stone wall is the wall of impediment. They fear the Atlantic's waves, but pray for the waves of the *bhakti* ocean to wash and pound against the wall.

I write this thinking it will help. A chill in my body at seaside is not an ecstatic symptom. A tear welling in my eye from the wind is not a symptom of *sañcāri-bhāva.* These things are on my mind, so I seek the connections. The sea is blue, but there are patches of green and brown and purple. At rock's edge, the spray!

I am a lost child. I am a servant of my spiritual master. If anyone finds me, they should know I belong to Prabhupāda and the Hare Kṛṣṇa movement. Previous identities are all dead, ancient history. I don't feel sorry for myself. I want to see myself on a map. And I want to die to material ambitions. At the time of death, your whole life passes before your eyes and your throat is choked up so you can't chant. King Kulaśekhara prays, "Now let me chant and die." Let me die to all material ambitions.

Italy

66

There are scars on this old, Italian table. We are always moving into places where others have lived and died. I write at their tables. We overturn dresser drawers and use them to eat on. We close their shutters and walk in their yards. I heard this used to be a priest's house and that he was connected with the nearby church. We don't plan to visit there.

Don't stop to figure it out. Remember? You write sentences before you even know what they will be, unafraid that they may start and sometimes end with no obvious Kṛṣṇa conscious content. Millions of sentences, like wriggling worms in the earth. Or big bees that startle you. They have their own world. Don't be afraid.

I don't dare take down the large drawing of Christ's crucifixion which is hanging in this room. Neither do I meditate on it. I allow it to stay and make its statement. It seems to be a kind of background statement. Śrīla Prabhupāda often cited Christ's giving up his life as the best example of the tolerant pure devotee whose "only fault" was that he preached God consciousness. Christ did not even condemn his enemies as they killed him. What a high standard. His influence in the world is no joke. (*Conversations With Śrīla Prabhupāda*, Vol. 30, p. 310)

I like this room because it is airy and light. When I chant *japa* here, I don't have to worry about waking anyone. I don't chant loudly, but I could. I prefer to chant softly, alone. I make a nice indirect lighting effect with one small lamp on the floor behind me in a corner, and two votive candles on the altar. At least the external situation is nice. I stay awake and I give myself ample time to chant.

Chanting is the most auspicious activity. Even uttered imperfectly, the holy name takes away sins and their reactions more than we could commit. The *ācāryas* recommend it as the most direct path to love of God. So put aside other concerns and just hear. Hear your voice sounding the Hare Kṛṣṇa mantra. Think of Kṛṣṇa—anything about Him at all—whatever you have heard from Śrīla Prabhupāda.

Anything at all.

67

"Be yourself. Ask for what you want. Don't let my opinions sway you or pressure you into thinking you should be something *I* want you to be." Someone said that to me yesterday.

What is it I would like to be that's being denied me? I want to be a devotee enriched with *bhakti*. No one is standing in my way except myself and the whole world which is engineered to keep souls in bondage. In prison, if someone asks, "Who's preventing you from being your blissful self?" it comes off as a bad joke.

I want to make a quantum leap. That means letting Kṛṣṇa take over. If I could just stop being concerned with performance, with my bodily inconveniences, with what is being said in the room—I beg to rise to the occasion of a Kṛṣṇa conscious life.

At the time of death, humility and honesty can save us. We have been dedicated to our spiritual master's mission and we may have been modest about that. But then the wave of truth: we have not attained devotion to Kṛṣṇa and guru. We will be fortunate if such a thought should occur to us. Then we can regret our fallen condition and beg for forgiveness and mercy. We can beg to again try to serve the devotees.

Honesty is important because Kṛṣṇa sees through all poses. He knows what we want and He awards us accordingly. We beg Him not to award us on that basis. We beg Him to disregard our desires for sense gratification and liberation. We beg Him to honor what little *bhakti* we have attained. We beg Him to increase that small store of devotion.

Who needs a theme other than impending death? "Again, offering obeisances unto all you *brāhmaṇas*, I pray that if I should again take my birth in the material world I will have complete attachment to the unlimited Lord Kṛṣṇa, association with His devotees and friendly relations with all living beings" (*Bhāg.* 1.19.16).

Śrīla Prabhupāda writes, "Mahārāja Parikṣit was certainly going back to Godhead, but even if he were not to go back, he prayed for a pattern of life which is the most perfect way in the material world. A pure devotee does not desire the company of a personality as great as Brahmā, but he prefers the association of a petty living being, provided he is a devotee of the Lord" (*Bhāg.* 1.19.16, purport).

"You are the spiritual master of great saints and devotees. I am therefore begging you to show the way of perfection for all persons, and especially for one who is about to die" (*Bhāg.* 1.19.37).

Śrīla Prabhupāda: "The question put forward by Mahārāja Parīkṣit is the basic principle for the complete thesis of *Śrīmad-Bhāgavatam.* Now let us see how intelligently the great master replies."

This is my subject, my theme, should I wish to have one. I am frantically writing in the face of death. "Please let me know what a man should hear, chant, remember and worship, and also what he should not do. Please explain all this to me" (*Bhāg.* 1.19. 38).

Later, Śukadeva Gosvāmī will reply *varīyān eṣa te praśnaḥ*, your question is glorious. Ask someone competent to tell you about Kṛṣṇa at the time of your death, now. Let us see how intelligently the spiritual master replies.

As I write this, I see Lord Kṛṣṇa's photo on my desk. He is sitting with His Rādhā on a throne in a Vṛndāvana grove. The message is implicit. Those who can see Kṛṣṇa entering Vṛndāvana forest, playing His flute, with wild flower decorations on His turban, accompanied by His *gopas* and cows, have attained the perfection of sight.

68

I woke this morning and remembered the details of a dream. It wasn't a Kṛṣṇa conscious dream, or rather, it was filled with incomprehensible events in a Kṛṣṇa conscious context. I thought, "Why preserve this?" But the delicate tapestry of it was still hanging in my mind. So I reached out, found the dictaphone, and recorded the dream.

Empty the contents. Fill up again. There is no end to the water in the well. The only limit is my time. Chairs stand without falling over. Windows don't break. Hearts beat smoothly and veins carry the blood supply. No one appears about to die and the world isn't like a plate of peas about to tilt and spill off. The world is not about to break into global nuclear war. The poison in the air, water, and earth is not so bad right now that we will die from it. We can still chuck our garbage somewhere. The businesses are recycling, so we can expect things will go all right. America will slowly recover from her economic recession and Italian businesses will flourish. We can fly comfortably to India via Air France and not expect to get hijacked. But if something happens, I've already said what I could.

69

I played a tape of Prabhupāda speaking to devotees and paused to write what came. Then we had a memorization session. I thought of hard hearts and soft ones, hearts like an ocean, like a city, and like a pond, a cottage. Hearts that don't melt, deep hearts that don't reveal themselves, and hearts that melt like shellac or butter and show themselves quickly. I am stripping away, baring all I can. Is this anti-romantic? Is it necessary? Helpful? I am using whatever tactics I can.

Looking out these barred windows at the green leaves against the back wall reminds me of the yellow room in Baladeva's house in Vṛndāvana. I used to look out that window as I wrote in the evening. Then I would go to sleep, depending on Kṛṣṇa. We got used to living there despite all the austerities—often no lights, so many mice, threat of robbers. We also got used to the routine at the Krishna-Balaram Mandir. I was like an aloof *sannyāsī* who came over to give my lectures once a week and who sat through others' lectures on other days.

It's different here. India is so brown, but Italy in the spring is lovely and bright. The cherry trees are in full bloom and the leaves are all spring green. I can't go outside much because I have hay fever, but the light and the green and the breeze come right through my window. The trees create shadows, so I can see the patches of sunlight and cool dark on the grass.

I could fall in love with all this and pretend it will always be so peaceful. But that is not the nature of this world, no matter how light and how green. Therefore we steel ourselves against misery. Bhaktivinoda Ṭhākura says we should lead a life free of material entanglement, which is born of greed, faultfinding, and material attachment. We should make our lives simple and free from controversy and *ugra-karma.*

"A learned sage should take his satisfaction in the simple maintenance of his existence and should not seek satisfaction through gratifying the material senses. In other words, one should care for the material body in such a way that one's higher knowledge is not destroyed and so that one's speech and mind are not deviated from self-realization" (*Bhāg.*11.7.39).

"One should live in such a way that he can avoid useless activities . . . One should nourish himself in such a way that the tongue and mind do not deviate from *yukta-vairāgya.*"

So we sit here in Italy, reading Prabhupāda's books and watching the spring sunlight on the grass, and I think of praying to Kṛṣṇa in His holy names, of coming into the light of *śuddha-nāma.* Chanting is the only way out of the horrors of Kali-yuga, the only safe place for the melted heart.

70

Sādhana-bhakti gradually replaces lust with love. We can taste selfless love whenever we perform selfless service for our spiritual master. We taste love when we feel attracted to the holy name.

Can we experience spiritual love in this world? Yes, but it is based on pure service and compassion. Therefore we begin in *sādhana-bhakti* to replace lust with love.

Be patient. It is still so easy to revert to material standards when we talk about love. "I love you because you give me pleasure." "I love you because you help me to fulfill my desires." But there is a real love between devotees who care about each other and who are emotionally bound. As devotees, we are not afraid for the ultimate welfare of our loved ones because we know we are not these bodies. We trust Kṛṣṇa to take care of us more than we can take care of each other. Yes, we can love each other and yes, it will hurt when they leave this world before us. But we will adjust our emotions to see it spiritually. We will love each other with Kṛṣṇa and Rādhā in the center and together, we will desire to render Them service.

We can love the world as a *madhyama-adhikārī* loves, by giving it Kṛṣṇa consciousness.

71

The pink roses are beautiful. They grow in tall bushes outside this house. As you come down the dark stairs, there's a small window at the bottom, and you can see the roses blooming outside. "Adopt the pace of Nature. Her secret is patience."

While writing this, I look up and see the tree filled with ripening cherries and above that, a clear sky. The pale half moon has already risen, even though it's only 5:30. Soon the "patronage" star will appear to offer blessings on all those who engage in welfare work.

The moon is as white as a porcelain dish. It influences so many things in this world, and many people spend time foretelling its effects. Pure *bhaktas* simply fix themselves on the moon of Kṛṣṇa's face and pray to see His sidelong glance. They lose all other interests. If the pink roses in Italy don't transport them to Vṛndāvana, then they feel the universe void.

72

Dear Baladeva,

We just spoke on the phone. I'm glad our interests are the same. But it's a fact we are also distant from each other. You are passionately driving your truck, one day in Toronto, two days later in Mississippi, then back up to New York, and I am traveling here and there in Europe.

It's hard for me to write you this letter because two Italian workmen are chatting just outside the house. At least I can't understand what they're saying. They remind me of the workmen in Vṛndāvana. Yes, I imagine myself there.

I spoke to you tonight how I prefer not to own any house or accept any permanent residence in Vṛndāvana. I'm glad you took it gracefully. I liked your wife's remark that Rādhārāṇī tricked you into buying your own house in Vṛndāvana. Let us plan to meet there together. We can talk about writing and Kṛṣṇa and Vraja.

It will be nice to visit Vṛndāvana again. I love it when you get little things for me from the bazaar, things to help with the writing, and when you write me notes with your ballpoint pen on yellow paper. Often you write the same word over and over. It's your way of doodling. I also like your little vignettes describing the so-called ordinary people you meet. You are always encouraging. I want to reciprocate.

Anyway, I just want to tell you that I'm glad we understood each other on the phone today. I am looking forward to seeing you.

73

He says he writes lines impulsively in the morning because the chosen words must survive as they were made—by the reckless impulse of a fallible but hopeful person. "I must be willingly fallible in order to deserve a place in the realm where miracles happen." He concedes that later a poem which came to him as a gift, may be subjected to order and evaluation.

He says poets carry the world for someone. I know what he means. Someone is lost and the poet comes by. He doesn't do anything special. He is just "being a hero, stumbling along." He turns someone's life into a poem, someone's impossibly ordinary experience into something possible.

This is similar to the influence of a devotee. Just by being alive and Kṛṣṇa conscious, he can lift others out of the realm of impossible ordinariness. He revives whomever he meets.

How can we despair if so-and-so dāsa is still going on the altar after all these years? How can we despair if any devotee is still doing their service even though it's hot as hell and people don't always appreciate?

What about the old man at the Krishna-Balaram Mandir who is too old to sew? He gives out the *caraṇāmṛta* with *tulasī* leaves. If he is going on in service, we can too.

Maybe you would like to write a poem?

Poetry

1

Japa

A brown moth goes by.
Eight minutes go by,
sit, sit somewhere else.
I'm on time, mostly.
I think it's going to get better;
it's already subterranean—inside me
and coming out, as a prayer
to Rādhā
and Kṛṣṇa,
to Rādhā and Kṛṣṇa to Rādhā
and Kṛṣṇa.

2

Kṛṣṇa in the heart,
car in the park,
ink in the pen,
when, oh when
will that day be mine?

Holy name at 1 A.M.,
sitting in the dark,
it is never easy before the mind
turns it into—
trains of thought,
snatches of song,
Auld Lang Syne,
saṁsāra dāvā,
remember when?

Holy name, I cheat myself,
but You are ever-kind.
Please grant my wish.
My true *svarūpa* doesn't
want this rambling *aparādha*.
Please enter *once*
and change me forever with
mad hankering for
śuddha-nāma.
Car in freezing cold.
I pray to catch hold
of the humble-courage
of the Vaiṣṇava heart.

O hear me Kāna,
I borrow words,
I do what I have seen the
gurus do; I'm meant for You,
so please pick me up and
place me as an atom
at Your lotus feet.

O Prabhupāda,
I play my part,
an actor on the stage,
in the start of old age,
please touch me again
tell me when.
Let me be your son
as I am, happy serving you
in a way that makes you
smile,
and claim me as a worker
for your cause.

3

Broken Meditations

Two full garlands on Śyāmasundara,
the green *tulasī* and then an orange marigold one.
I was thinking of the interplay
of separation and union between Rādhā-Kṛṣṇa
when someone tugged on my arm.
I couldn't believe it was happening.
But they tugged again.
A brother asked, "Are you going to Kāmyavan?"

I said, "Tomorrow," and turned back
to looking upon Śyāmasundara,
but the mood dispersed.
Eagerly I looked upon Their gold crowns,
white clothing, His red foot,
notice, notice, try to recall,
separation and union
and where you can fit in
to the eternal *līlās*.

4

On the morning walk it's harmless,
green land and blue sky and
no one in sight but cows and rabbits.
That's all behind me now, I sit cross-legged,
this typewriter on top of two suitcases,
and a mourning dove protesting outside.
All these fabulous shapes and sounds
but none of them can satisfy you
deeply and forever.
And you can't live long so
I turn to the books looking for
the key to open them in a *sūtra* like
yasya deve parā bhaktir,
to one who has implicit faith
in Kṛṣṇa and guru
all the meanings of the *śāstra* will be revealed.

5

Winter Walk Poem by A Serious Guy

My new full-suit gear by Carhartt
is "as rugged as the men who wear them."
A 120-pound hulk, I veer down the road,
hoping the school kids won't come out yet
so I can enter the woods alone.
As for my serious purpose,
I have already told: someone has to chart this
new territory. Don't take yourself *too* seriously,
but still, you've got to justify why you're out here
instead of at a temple and why
you don't sit on a committee.
So I told you: I am charting the unknown,
and I'm trying to pick up a poor *japa* standard
and making an open book for a serious purpose.
All this on the order of guru and *śāstra*
just as you too, brother, work under that order.
(Please excuse me if this poem has no music.)

As for play, yes, the deer tracks are fresh,
I raise my arms to the sky. I call it worship
to taste the getting-smaller-moon sliver
and to report back to you.
A grateful prayer for health, though
I know it can't last.
I am not the rugged man,
befitting to wear a Carhartt,
but I am
going my way
for the purpose of serving
in this world and the next.

6

At Hare Krishna Land on a Sunday Night

Men came to clean our room,
empty garbage, replace a light bulb
in the India that has been conquered by Prabhupāda
and those who worked with him
in the tough years.

There is more control in Bombay.
The ISKCON Hotel is formidable.
In Vṛndāvana, I live
in a house away from the temple
with a flimsy front gate.
Wild birds come and perch,
plenty of squirrels in the front yard,
the cows, the field . . .

I don't want to claim
that I feel for Vṛndāvana.
But at least I'm able to recall it.
I look forward to that roof
and to exchanges with disciples.
We are all trying to enter Vraja.

Chant, walk on the beach,
do your business,
but when you are done,
go back to Vṛndāvana.

7

I'll know what to do:
I'll set an example,
and practice to be truthful
so when you panic and
talk like that it
won't be a surprise to your
friends and you needn't
be embarrassed
that you're dying—it
happens to everyone, it
doesn't mean you did something
wrong, but don't pretend
to be a saint.
Cry—I couldn't be a
devotee!
I missed the Lord of Mathurā!
He Nātha!
Ayi Dīna-dayārdra!
O Prabhupāda, take your
boy back and forgive him his
many offenses—
but keep him, next life.

8

Overcome Fear

Afraid to start a poem?
Don't be.
They always come out all right.
But this time?
What do you have to do?
Something about going to the window
to see the thermometer.
Why is it so important?
Something about the pause today,
the hiatus because you were sick.
You think,
"How can I dare start again?"
Fears of death. The red thermometer needle
at unpresuming 40.

You're not prepared. You haven't read today.
That's the fear—I can't reach over
to claim *kṛṣṇa-kathā*. A nagging
by the *vaidhī-bhakta* who is me.
Did you even read? Tell something.

I wrote a book saying I'm sorry but
I can't chant with attention, however
I like to see Kṛṣṇa on morning walks.
Prabhupāda's book, *Caitanya-caritāmṛta*,
is propped open on the bookstand.
It's a new chapter, about the Lord's
separation. It's getting intense.
I'll get some facts from it early tomorrow.
Right now . . .

I decided what to say in New York in a week:
"This place 26 Second Avenue is not decorated
like it used to be. We come here, but actually
we can think of those '66 days anywhere.
This proves spiritual life is in the mind,
by favorable meditation."
That's just a start, then you'll have to remember
the Swami and yourself.
I like the attention, but I know it's dangerous.
That same fear—that if I open my heart
there will be so little,
I'll be embarrassed,
I won't cry,
I'll stutter. You'll grow impatient with me
and when you look away I'll feel sorry I even
tried.

He came here and didn't know the people.
But he was an elderly, sophisticated gentleman of India,
and don't forget, he's a pure devotee. So he dared.
Became a temporary citizen of Manhattan and
joked, "If the whole New York City becomes flooded
with snow you'll be inconvenienced.
And then there is the misery of cold wind."
Mr. Cohen, Mr. Greene . . . Dr. Mishra . . .
If I say, "Mr. Greene, what you have done,
no intelligent man would have done." That means
"Mr. Greene, you are not intelligent."
Kṛṣṇa called Arjuna a fool.
Prabhupāda was gently telling us, what
we were lamenting for,
no learned man laments.

"Mr. Cohen . . . I was telling him,
this is the sacred thread,
of course it is not a very expensive thing,
but it has some significance.
It means this person has a spiritual master.
One who wants to stop the miseries of life,
he requires a spiritual master.
But what sort of spiritual master?
He must be a devotee of Kṛṣṇa."
This is 1965 and Prabhupāda is telling them,
you must find out what is a spiritual master,
so you won't be cheated.
Who in the world could that be, that devotee
of Kṛṣṇa, does anyone know?
How about the Swami himself?
Is that what he's saying, that he is our
spiritual master?

To subdue the pain I heard a tape—
Prabhupāda singing in 1965 at Dr. Mishra's,
a simple, sad tune, he sounds so funky—
plain, alone, simple, very spiritual,
meditative. His Hare Kṛṣṇa *kīrtana* in
a slow way—was peaceful and consoling to me,
I drifted off to half-consciousness,
such a nice *kīrtana* with the Swami and a few.
When I woke my headache was gone.

9

Separate Stanzas

1
Up Early

By Kṛṣṇa's grace,
another early morning of writing.
It feels like me and others
are on the bridge of a ship
sailing in the dark when everyone's asleep.
I learned it from my spiritual master
who for practical reasons chose 1 A.M.
as the best time for his Bhaktivedanta purports.
Get up with him now,
assist in his mission.
Is his dictaphone working?
He's got his books and a mosquito net.
I am with him still
by my own attempts to pray.

II

Thoughts of An Ordinary Man

God save me from a violent death,
he thought, as he walked on the road
coming upon a neighbor's beef cows
broke loose from their pasture.
He had read a lurid report of a man
whom dacoits had cut into pieces.
Please not me, he thought,
but anything could happen.
They say if you are sinful
it will happen to you.
But how does that work? Don't the dacoits
act out of their own maliciousness?
Why do they pick one as a victim?
Is that karma, fate?
He decided he couldn't figure it out
and he didn't want to think of it.
A dirty, white cow turned its face to him—
dumb terror and outrage
in the eyes of the beast.
Disgusting animals.
He imagined how the slaughterers
must loathe the cows
or else how could they kill them?

10

He'd gotten out of the pasture
but didn't know how to get back in
which he wanted to do when he saw me coming.
He was startled in the 5 A.M. dark.
He ruined my perfect meditation.
He was afraid of me and kept
walking ahead, kept
looking for a way to get back into the pasture,
and I kept treading up behind him
because this is where I walk.

He began to jump two feet at a time,
a futile move.
I kept coming and he kept walking ahead.
During this time, I was remembering Prabhupāda
in ways important to me—
it demanded a careful thread of thought,
but I had to stop thinking each time
I got too close to the sheep.
Finally he found an open driveway
to a farmhouse and went in there,
more trouble for him,
this creature who was alien to everything
except the fenced-in meadow
where his fellow sheep cried.

Finally alone, I made up for lost time,
thinking aloud,
promising I will not neglect
my memories of His Divine Grace,
how he came to us in New York City . . .
Approach the tender thoughts
of his actual presence.
Starting today,
a new meditation.

11

This still life facing me
pink, plastic bottle of Rādhā-kuṇḍa water,
a pink piece of paper marked Saṅkeṭ
wrapped around some dust.
The row of four *paramparā gurus*
with daylight shining through them
and on the upraised place, a silver-framed
Rādhā-Kṛṣṇa portrait,
gold and dark,
Śyāma and Rādhā.

12

Where is God?

Little Sarasvatī couldn't find her
Kṛṣṇa *mūrti*. Prabhupāda had it
behind his back,
to tease her, like a grandfather.
She cried, "Where is Kṛṣṇa?"
Her mother said, "Sarasvatī, *think*,
who has Kṛṣṇa?"
She cried, "Where is He?"
Sarasvatī, who has Kṛṣṇa?
Think.

Is He in the trees? Yes.
In the sky? Right.
Is it all right if I see Him that way
and not always in Goloka Vṛndāvana
and Vṛndāvana, India?
Yes, it's all right; He's in your heart,
in your own mind and writing arm.
But *think*,
Where is He? Where does He live?
Who is His best devotee?
How can you reach Him and please Him?

13

A grocer or a butcher can be a devotee—
no wait a minute, not a butcher.
Say a carpenter. As long as they do
their work for Kṛṣṇa as taught to them
by their guru.
So why not a man who
wields a purple pen?
He can do it. All he needs is
a sign from within.

My friend said, "Now I know
the last verse of *Śikṣāṣṭakam*
is spoken by Rādhārāṇī."
Still, I said, it is spoken
by Lord Caitanya.
We sat on the floor and Tulasī-devī,
twin-branched and healthy for an
indoor winter plant,
was above us.

You fold up this poem-sheet
when it's finished, like a
woman wrapping a fish
or a man folding up a blueprint.
It's a careful act, an art,
the folding of the paper.
It's implied, "This is for Kṛṣṇa."
You're an old craftsman
doing his thing. Fortunately it is
not fish or boiled-alive lobsters
or amphetamine that you are
folding.
It is just a little poem with one
stanza on Rādhā, Caitanya Mahāprabhu
and Tulasī-devī
and your friend and you.
Give it as a gift. No charge.

14

The wrinkled gray *cādar*
strewn over Prabhupāda's body
in the Samādhi Mandir.
Two *sannyāsīs* conversing,
their two *daṇḍas*
are also meeting and talking.
I hold back, glad to watch,
sing and move
in a shuffle-dance to keep warm.

Rādhā-Śyāma in white and pink,
pink backdrop.
I can't see so well.
Lack of spiritual love
brings inability to focus the eyes
on the beloved object,
but I linger at Their altar.

15

A misty rain,
cool 5 A.M. in Eire,
do you know what that's like?
While walking I talked
beyond these hedges—
take the easy journey to other planets.
It's not daydreaming but the solid work
of human life. "Take care of your family,"
I preached to the rain,
"but don't neglect chanting the holy name
and hearing of Kṛṣṇa's glorious activities."

16

This has been a monsoon book.
Blue clouds courtesy of Śyāmasundara.
The names have been changed
to protect the innocent.
But mostly they have not
been changed—I just never
knew them—
"The grass, bushes, insects,
and other creatures in Vraja
are all dear to Lord Kṛṣṇa."
They are full of bliss.
I bow down to offer my respects
to all creatures
who reside in Vraja.

17

Imperfect Striving

I

Rau! Rau! Rau!
Dogs in Stroudsburg have no manners.
Pause please and be a devotee before
you go any further.
But how long do you expect me
to wait?
Kṛṣṇa . . . the word, the one word
filters through my impure consciousness,
like . . . It can't be compared.
Kṛṣṇa and Rādhā—pushing aside
other terms and pictures that come.
I "see" Them or I don't?
See Them "through a glass darkly."
Saw Them this morning in the words
of Śrīla Rūpa Gosvāmī, "Please
be kind, please be kind.
This person cries in the forest,
this sinful person begs,
please be kind and give me the
direct service I desire—
Or else how can I live?"

II

The shack is nice, the cold, the calm,
the chance to write from the brain
down to the arm and right-hand fingers.
Not just any words.
I don't deserve.
I like, I do, I serve,
I chant so hard it wears holes
through my gloves in two places.
I avoid gross sins,
I am a member of ISKCON.
What are these claims?
Wait . . . find a better word . . .
Let Kṛṣṇa be glorified.
Let us all take shelter of
the younger son of Nanda Mahārāja
and Balarāma too.
May we always stay in the
shelter of wonderful Kṛṣṇa.

III

I admit all I can do is
copy and paraphrase out of the books.
And record my experience—
once Prabhupāda made me cry over
a mistake I made. Once I walked with
him, and even while he was on the planet,
I served in separation.

IV

I hear him every day; I believe what he says.
Just keep me, don't kick me away.
I'm living for this and
hope to die in good graces, reaching
out to him. I need you, Prabhupāda.
I did not know how much,
and neither did Hayagrīva dāsa.
But at the end we remember.
Better late than never.

May the Lord's mercy descend on
all sincere souls. May their
piety increase—
may we kick off *mukti* and *bhukti*,
achieve a simple obedience and
non-exaggerated
willingness, acceptance of our fallen
ignorance . . . to serve him
with intelligence and creative drive—
like he wanted
from a whole-self.

18

Your Friend Wants You to Be

Now it's starting again—
hardening of the arteries.
You tell yourself, "I'm no poet.
I don't want to go in there and write.
I don't have the music or vision.
All I know is some things
and that's not good enough."

But I told you before,
this is for us.
They look so nice later—
why am I thinking of a sailor hat?
What to do when the pinpoint pain
starts a little behind the eye?
Steer to Kṛṣṇa, you tell yourself.

It means look in that direction—
past the faces of your old critics,
over their heads,
no college marijuana deans,
no petty officer stopping you on the street
to tell you, "Put your hat on or else."
You can go to the Swami in his room—
the people who count don't find it boring.
They long for you to go there.
They don't even insist that they have to go
with you.

They want it for you. They want you
to come out of that room starry-eyed a little
and they'll laugh kindly.
"What did he say?"
You'll say, "It was nice," and
you'll go with your friends to a
quiet place like the empty storefront
used to be in mid-afternoon.
And there you'll tell them
he had his frayed *cādar* on.
The mat he sat on had this design—
you'll gesture with your hand
to show his hand.
He said something no one even remembered
before.
And many things we've heard
are his way—his brick-colored
Bhāgavatam, he sold it to me again,
he called me by my name,
I forgot my pain—
I told him I'm already a vegetarian
and he said, "Then I'll accept you
on Rādhāṣṭamī."

Is this real or imagined?
Is this present more
right now?
It's for remembering in a poem.
With these friends,
they just want you to be,
and not harden,
don't die yet—
or ever. Keep remembering
the Swami and
don't be afraid to go back.

19

Prayer to Write

I love Kṛṣṇa better
than this world.
The truck goes downhill
scraping snow with its plough.
I am hearing the dripping
of the rain on snow.
With inner ear I strain
to hear the world of Kṛṣṇa,
from the mouth of my Gurudeva.
Go on and write, he said,
don't be dull—
with your own words,
like a baby learning to speak—

Kṛṣṇa, You love Your devotees.
I am a devotee of Your devotee.
I want to praise You and repeat
Your pastimes.
Please allow me.

"*Jaya* Rādhā-Mādhava" is
the true picture of God.
He loves the *gopīs* and enjoys
with them.
He is the supreme controller
who gives even the
crab on the beach the *śakti*
to take shelter in the ocean.

And He gives orders to the
ocean, "Don't cross over
this line."
You are the Supreme.
I worship You in the temple and
in writing.
Give me faith to do so.

In "*Jaya* Rādhā-Mādhava"
You tell of Yamunā and the
kuñjas and my spiritual master
sang this song every day.
We join him with *mṛdaṅga*.
Kṛṣṇa is the cowherd boy
who controls the universe,
who plays the flute,
who enjoys with the *gopas* and *gopīs*.
Those who are pure
will hear these *līlās*
with joy, and sincere devotees
will give up their last
vestiges of lust.

I pray to Govinda to let me
write like a child and like
a devotee who knows *siddhānta*—
with no mistakes.
My primitive attempt need not
be rejected . . . if I follow what I've
heard.

20

Take care of yourself

The snow is coming down slowly.
Big flakes and slow.
I'm starting this page with a sigh.
I see the sun, 4:30 P.M., high in the trees.
And the snow.
Some of your letters are unopened,
the rest I have already discharged,
said what came to mind and any
appropriate quote from *śāstra.*
One of the truest things I said—was it
to Dhīrodatta in Miami?—is *you*
have to take care of yourself.
Prabhupāda used to say, "I am
your friend in this sense—that I tell you
Kṛṣṇa is your best friend."
Someone said, "You are lenient" and I
said, "Who can force you?"
But I'm thinking about this alone,
while the precious snow falls.

Sādhana

1

Tomorrow is Ekādaśī. My head is newly shaven, the breeze pleasant. I am living on a transcendental college campus, ISKCON Vṛndāvana. The seminar starts in a few days.

Sometimes I observe all this as if I were an outsider looking in. There is the group of *sannyāsīs*, *daṇḍas* standing straight, waiting before the Deity doors to greet the Deities. I am among them. Three conches blow, the doors slide open, and the Deities give *darśana*. "*Govindam*" plays over the loudspeaker. We all stand, worshipping Gaura-Nitāi.

I observe this, but it doesn't seem right to remain apart from it. I realize now that I have a choice: I can continue my careful, aloof observation, or I can participate fully. This same act has been going on for hundreds and thousands of years—devotees waiting for the Lord to give His *darśana*. What is the real essence? What are we supposed to *do* while we are here? We are meant to make more than an official appearance; life is more than getting through with a decent reputation. One day we will all be gone and the ranks will be filled with another generation. Better to pray to answer the call to your true self, *jīvera 'svarūpa' haya—kṛṣṇera 'nitya-dāsa'*—the self that never dies or takes birth again. Better to pray to eternal Kṛṣṇa that you can know Him in His *līlā*. Better to pray to serve Him by serving your spiritual master forever.

2

"If someone takes advantage of hearing the pastimes of the Lord, the material contamination of dust, accumulated in the heart due to long association with material nature, can be immediately cleansed" (*Kṛṣṇa*, p. 50).

Do you want to leave the world behind? Then plunge as much as possible into Śrīla Prabhupāda's books. Concentrate on *kṛṣṇa-kathā*. Specialize in it. This is why we frown on outside reading—it dissipates the concentration. Enter the world of Kṛṣṇa thought, of Kṛṣṇa's devotees, more and more.

Going on pilgrimage helps, but when we go to the *dhāma*, we inevitably take our destinies there. There will also be other devotees there who still manifest symptoms of material conditioning. We will probably interact with them on that same level. This will continue as long as we have material conditioning. Still, we shouldn't let it become a distraction in the pursuit of inner spiritual life.

If the road to Kṛṣṇa consciousness isn't direct, then leap over present concerns, land in the pond, and start swimming. ". . . Kṛṣṇa was once thinking, 'Today, while I was engaged in tending the cows in the pasturing ground of Vṛndāvana, I went to collect some flowers in a beautiful garden. At that time My friends, the cowherd boys, were unhappy even to tolerate a two-minute separation from Me. And when they found Me, there was competition between us as to who would touch the other first with the flowers we had in hand'" (*NOD*, p. 274). Jump into the pond.

3

Kṛṣṇa is not easy to attain. He gives Himself only to His pure devotee. He is reluctant to give Himself to one who is not really surrendered. So many people pray to Kṛṣṇa because they want something from Him, and Kṛṣṇa quickly fulfills their desires. But if you claim, "I want You. I want loving service in Your intimate company," Kṛṣṇa tests you for a long time, and severely. This is my understanding of *The Nectar of Devotion* statement that *bhakti* is rarely achieved.

You have to serve a pure devotee of Kṛṣṇa. That service may continue over many lifetimes. It is a mystery how the guru returns life after life to assist his disciples and to help them become free of entanglement. Śrīla Prabhupāda said that the guru comes back for slack devotees to rescue them from the house of the prostitute (as in the case of Bilvamaṅgala Ṭhākura and Cintāmaṇi).

To me, much of *bhakti* remains an unrealized mystery. It is theoretical. It is my professed religion. Within this ancient religion and within its modern institution of ISKCON, I act out my own dramas and dilemmas, seeking my personal needs. I have not yet reached pure service.

Purity is a simple thing. Devotional service is easy for the simple and difficult for the crooked. I think of the verses in *Nārada-bhakti-sūtra* where Nārada says that *bhakti* means total surrender; it means loving Kṛṣṇa to the extent that all other desires and work are put aside. Struggling to understand how to enter the topmost relationship with Kṛṣṇa is one thing, and the purity as it exists in any *rasa* is another thing. I think of simple purity as something you may find in a devotee's service to his guru. Such simple purity asks only the question, "How may I serve you?" Then that purity allows the disciple to serve regardless of the work involved. This purity of interest leads to Kṛṣṇa's abode. As the Lord says, "One can understand Me as I am, as the Supreme Personality of Godhead, only by devotional service. When one is in full consciousness of Me by such devotion, he can enter the kingdom of God" (Bg. 18.55).

If we attempt to interest ourselves in *rasa* without overall purity and surrender to the guru—if we fail to give up other ambitions—then we will never enter into Kṛṣṇa's pastimes. Attaining Kṛṣṇa's love is not an easy thing.

I need to work on my chanting. Should I chant more? That is one aspect. But we barely have time to do all the duties required—meeting people, attending the morning program, reading Śrīla Prabhupāda's books, preaching, understanding the science of God in all its subtleties—we just do not have huge amounts of time for extra chanting. Neither did Śrīla Prabhupāda ask us to set aside such blocks of time to improve. So how do I improve?

I don't have all the answers. Life is a struggle. Kṛṣṇa, You accept each of us. This one person who is handicapped with doubts and bad karma calls out to You. Please let me send You a sincere request for pure devotional service while I am here in Vṛndāvana. I seek the benediction of pure devotional service.

Śrīla Prabhupāda writes that devotional service is characterized by joyfulness. Joyfulness is a sure sign of Kṛṣṇa consciousness. Many devotees feel joyful in their services, but how can we know that our satisfaction is produced by right means? Therefore, we seek the benediction of pure devotional service. We pray. Kṛṣṇa doesn't accept rhetoric. He wants to know what is actually in our hearts. If we say, "Please take all the dirty things out of my heart, including my personal ambitions, and give me what is best for me"—then what? Will Kṛṣṇa immediately take us at our word? No, He wants us to prove ourselves. And of course, He helps us.

We struggle for years to find a niche in Kṛṣṇa consciousness. When we do get a service that is both satisfying and helpful to Śrīla Prabhupāda's mission, it would be foolish to abruptly give it up just beause we detect a little *kāma* in our hearts. *Kāma* will be removed in the course of our service. Still, we have to be ready to give up even that service if Kṛṣṇa desires. His will for us manifests as fate or time, as what happens in our lives. The sincere, inner core, the simple essence—this is what Kṛṣṇa is looking for, more than the outer display.

4

Śāstra is filled with directions. To find our way, we have to follow our guru's instructions. Otherwise, how easily we can get lost. Even materially speaking, it's so easy to lose our bearings. Someone tells us how to get to a certain building, but when we start off we think, "Did he say to go left or right at the first stairway? He didn't tell me that part." Soon we are lost.

Follow the guru's directions. If our spiritual master did not tell us what to think of during *japa*, then we should think of him. But he did tell us. He told us to *listen* to the holy names. If we listen, we will eventually remember Kṛṣṇa's pastimes. Listen to Kṛṣṇa's pastimes in the company of devotees and we will remember Him throughout the day. Our guru has already given us many directions.

Carrying out the orders of the spiritual master is nondifferent than thinking of Lord Kṛṣṇa. Thinking how he wanted all people of the world delivered by preaching Kṛṣṇa consciousness is not subject to the external energy. Can you become an instrument to help bring this about? Try to imagine it, contemplate its reality: a person who is suffering, completely identifying with his body as the all-in-all—that person receives one of Śrīla Prabhupāda's books and by the association of devotees, starts to practice *bhakti-yoga*. Even the preliminary practices give him or her great relief. They see the possibility of their life changing. They deepen their commitment. Another soul gets loose from *māyā's* grip.

Taking part in this movement is not a trivial exercise. Make it real. Intensify your participation. To do this, you must first qualify yourself and understand better what it is. This is the purpose of pilgrimage—to become fit to help others. Prepare to give whatever you gain. Please Śrīla Prabhupāda and Lord Kṛṣṇa in that way. If after observing your own copper jubilees or silver jubilees or golden jubilees in Kṛṣṇa consciousness, you still don't have a taste for chanting or preaching, then why are you living?

Kṛṣṇa consciousness is our source of hope. It gives us something to live for. Work to free yourself from the subtle dreams of the material past. Throw yourself loose from petty thoughts of the present. Chant wholeheartedly. You have heard this before. Serve your spiritual master. Do you think you can settle for less? Improve, improve. Do what you must do to improve. Going to the *dhāma*, rendering service there, and praying with your whole heart may help.

5

I lie in bed having stupid dreams; the impure body imposes its material desires. Maybe the Hindus are right when they say the best a Westerner can do is to take a pious human birth in India in his next life. It may be true in my case. All the junk I have done in this life makes it difficult for me to fully enter Gauḍīya Vaiṣṇavism. Yet Prabhupāda assures us that it's difficult, but not impossible.

When I spoke with an abbot of a Carmelite monastery in Belgium, he seemed to think it was incredulous that Westerners were trying to live as Indian monks. I couldn't believe he couldn't see the essence of it. I don't claim to be an Indian or a

Hindu, and neither does Śrīla Prabhupāda make such an artificial imposition on us. The real strain and awkwardness is not to wear the *dhotī* or recite Sanskrit prayers—but the purity required. Any spiritual discipline I attempt, whether in a Western or Eastern tradition, will demand pure faith, spiritual vision, and heartfelt participation. I will have to bump up against my old conditioning until I finally throw it off. When we are free of sex desire and are convinced that the material world is miserable and useless—and when Kṛṣṇa desires—we can enter His *rāsa* dance, His pure, spiritual *līlā*.

That is what I was supposed to be praying for to Gopīśvara Mahādeva last night instead of sitting there stupefied in the alien surrounding, disturbed by the loud ringing of bells and wanting to go home. Why couldn't I have looked on Lord Śiva's face, his hair decorated with garlands, and prayed to him, "Please remove my lust and greed for material life. Help me, inspire me—you are the wisest sage and best Vaiṣṇava, Lord Śiva. Help this creature who sits before you and knows nothing auspicious. Help a Westernized pilgrim. I have come hoping for a dose of mercy to enter Kṛṣṇa's pastimes. When do you think I can? What should I do now?"

6

We walked to a secret grove to chant. At sunrise, some people use the same area to squat and evacuate; we use it to walk back and forth and chant *japa*. I allowed two more men to join us today, "But no talking." They obeyed the rules. We each take a separate space, far enough apart so that we cannot hear each other, but close enough to see each other.

While I was chanting, two young Vrajavāsī boys walked by. They were collecting peacock feathers. It is a way for poor people to make money. The boys stopped and stared at me. I looked down and went on chanting. "Maybe they will help me improve by their presence," I thought. Then one of them signalled to the other and they left me alone by the *tagar* and yellow *kareṇ* flowers.

This spot is nice, I invite you to share it. Don't bring a pillow. Sit on the cold, rock slab. When you feel inattentive and frustrated, slam the point of your walking stick hard into the ground. Twirl it in the air, draw circular designs in the dust. Bow down after each *japa* round, recite the Pañca-tattva mantra and then stand up and brush the dirt off the front of your *dhotī*. The air is cool. You have an hour clear of all other concerns.

At my present level, day after day I fail to use this time as I would like to. At least I stay awake and chant the rounds at a timed clip. But I cannot go deeper. There is no easy answer. So I am here with the cold seat, slamming the poke end of my cane into the earth, getting up and sitting down.

On the way back to the temple, I had the nerve to speak to the others about *japa*. I said devotees are often concerned with whether they are improving in their *japa*. Sometimes they think they are doing better and sometimes worse. We know it is not in our control; it is up to Kṛṣṇa. However, one basic principle is that the more you put into it, the more you get out of it. This may mean saving the best time in your day in which to chant, giving your whole effort, and trying to connect other things in your life to chanting. My friends had some thoughts about *japa* and spoke them too. We will remember this later, this nice spot for chanting . . . and how on Ekādaśī so many people were out walking on *parikrama*. Find that best place to chant. The thing about the grove near Rāmana Retī is that it is nice, but still I cannot chant in love. Kṛṣṇa knows my desire. He will help me as He sees fit.

7

You are all alone in the world, even when you stand amid many supposedly like-minded devotees on the marble floor of the temple room. Maybe I feel especially alone at this time. Do the others feel that way? I think Śrīla Prabhupāda liked to see many of us gathered, chanting the holy names together. He sacrificed everything for Kṛṣṇa, so the Lord brought us together to dance and sing the *mahā-mantra* before Śrīla Prabhupāda on the *vyāsāsana*. We do it every day. I want to be part of the crowd if it pleases him. But he knows it also makes my heart ache. It has become a formality in some ways, especially to do it every single day for hours at a time, going through the same rituals with many persons. It doesn't seem natural anymore. We crave at least significant parts of the morning alone or with a few friends.

Although there are so many "group conclusions," many matters in spiritual life are individual. Each one of us is alone with Kṛṣṇa and the guru. But brothers don't talk about aloneness. We talk about plain affairs or deep philosophy, technical jargon of spirituality or about ourselves, but hardly ever, "I am alone and it is best, but I appreciate your friendship very much." If we could truly face this about one another, perhaps we would feel less need to impose on one another or exert control over one another.

I am not sure what this has to do with the Gauḍīya Vaiṣṇava *siddhānta*, but I am sure it must fit in somewhere. For example, Kṛṣṇa teaches that we will always be eternal individuals. "Yourself, Myself, and all the millions of persons on the battlefield always exist as persons; in the past we were individuals, now we exist, and we will never cease to be living persons." We don't merge with God when we attain *mukti*. We are not destroyed at death or turned into nonpersons by meditation on *nirvāṇa*. We each see the world in our own way and we each see Kṛṣṇa from an individual viewpoint. Each person has an eternal, unique relationship with Him. In this way, Lord Kṛṣṇa enjoys His *līlā* with innumerable pure devotees, numberless boys and calves and *gopīs*. There is room for everyone.

Pure devotees find the time to glorify Kṛṣṇa together and alone.

Enough of this. This may be the concern of a conditioned soul—too much assertion of self and not enough focus on Rādhā and Kṛṣṇa. But it can be purified. It *must* be purified.

8

Any genuine practice helps. Increase by small increments. We are on the move in *bhakti*. O Kṛṣṇa, help this little group to move forward and not to jostle each other roughly. Let us be kind to one another, or where is the question of making personal advancement in love of God?

The dogs are fighting. Another beast moans. Pigeons flap, fighting for all-night roosts on the trees. They are always ready to fly off if danger comes. I don't want to pay their dark kingdom too much attention. Leave them alone, God is taking care of them. Go ahead on the human path to higher consciousness.

In a little while I have to get ready for *maṅgala-ārati*. Although I stand before the large *mūrti* of Śrīla Prabhupāda every morning, it is rare that I can continually meditate on the meaning of the *Gurv-aṣṭakam* as I sing. Flashes of appreciation come though, as day after day I am cleansed in the association of Prabhupāda and his devotees. It is really up to me to make *maṅgala-ārati* more than an empty ritual.

Śrīla Prabhupāda, you want to save the world. I want to help maintain the enthusiasm of those who are already practicing so that they don't go away and become lost again. But first I have to save myself. Please give me the strength to serve you. I pray for your guidance. I want to chant and distribute chanting; I want to read and distribute books; I want to encourage others and be encouraged myself. I want to appreciate *kṛṣṇa-līlā* and then broadcast it in suitable ways. You demand much from your workers—you want us to stay busy in preaching and to stay absorbed in Kṛṣṇa consciousness. The day will come, you say, when the *vaidhī-bhakta* will taste the bliss of loving service. He should not become disappointed. The happiness of preaching and serving guru is immediately available. I don't want to be left out.

9

There are nice pictures in the Vṛndāvana mood which I can assemble on a table while I chant *japa*. I can keep sacred sand, water, and rocks. I can stop to read a verse here and there. But a brother said we shouldn't become too dependent on the pictures and paraphernalia. The offering of *bhajana* comes from the heart. Find the heart and worship from there. "The same advice is in the *Philokalia*," I said. "They stripped their lives of everything and practiced asceticism so they could face the nothingness in themselves. But their concept of God was also not much more than nothingness."

"They could only reach the point of feeling remorse for sins," he said, "but that is only the beginning."

Even that beginning eludes me. Without it, our collection of verses and pictures doesn't bring us to *bhāva-bhakti*. The *ācāryas* encourage us, however, that steadfast performance of *vaidhī* will lead to higher stages. We have to yearn for the transformation: when will the day come? When can a fallen rascal obtain the mellows of the holy name? When will he be able to chant "Rādhā" and "Kṛṣṇa" with a choking voice and beg to be admitted to Their service at least in his mind? When will a small drop of that mercy fall on him by the descending process? When will he at least look toward and meditate upon the cloudbank of sweetness, just as the *cakora* birds turn to the thunder cloud and refuse to drink any water except that which falls from above?

We need to see and hear Kṛṣṇa's pastimes. Keep alive the reality of those pastimes in your own life. They are not something that happened long ago in the distant past, and neither are they mythology. Those pastimes are available now to those who have the ointment of love of God smeared on their eyes. Prabodhānanda Sarasvatī writes that even today, devotees living in Vṛndāvana have seen those pastimes. That is extremely rare. "In beautiful Vṛndāvana, which is filled with jeweled trees and vines bearing wonderfully colorful, blissful flowers, in the shade of a *kadamba* tree risen from the golden ground, a fair and dark couple is now before our eyes" (*Śrī Vṛndāvana-mahimāmṛta, Śataka* 2.38). Śrīla Prabhupāda recommended the attitude of the six Gosvāmīs, who cried out, "*He* Rādhe! Where are You now? Are You just on Govardhana Hill or on the bank of the Yamunā? Where are You?" They never became fulfilled, but remained in anticipation, *vipralambha*, "Where is Kṛṣṇa? Where is Rādhā?"

10

I liked reading a devotee's homework answer. He said, "Vṛndā-devī makes all arrangements for Kṛṣṇa to always be here. So Kṛṣṇa consciousness is actually Vṛndāvana consciousness. I come every year to absorb myself in the Vṛndāvana consciousness. And what makes me appreciate Kṛṣṇa more and inspires me to engage in His loving service is to take this mood of Vraja and keep it firmly in my mind for eleven months.

Śrīla Prabhupāda took Vṛndāvana and Kṛṣṇa all over the world and we should make sure it stays like that. I just pray at the feet of the Vaiṣṇavas that I will be able one day to understand Rādhā and Kṛṣṇa and Śrī Vṛndāvana."

And Śrīla Prabhupāda writes:

> Cultivating Kṛṣṇa consciousness in Vṛndāvana is the best means of being liberated from material bondage, for in Vṛndāvana one can automatically meditate upon Kṛṣṇa. Vṛndāvana has many temples, and in one or more of these temples one may see the form of the Supreme Lord as Rādhā-Kṛṣṇa or Kṛṣṇa-Balarāma and meditate upon this form. . . . Therefore, if one somehow or other gets the opportunity to live in Vṛndāvana, and if one is not a pretender but simply lives in Vṛndāvana and concentrates his mind upon Kṛṣṇa, one is liberated from material bondage. One's mind is not purified, however, even in Vṛndāvana, if one is agitated by lusty desires.
>
> —*Bhāg*. 9.19.19, purport

The pilgrimage is ongoing. Accumulate what you can, go away to assimilate it, and then come back. Don't take it for granted; don't for a moment be ungrateful or unaware of the rare opportunity to advance.

A letter from a disciple:

"I had a little realization just after two weeks of my arrival here in Vrndavana. Since my last visit, two years ago, I prayed, I dreamt, I wished, I wanted so much to come back and live here. But after my arrival I understood that I am not ready at all. It is not easy to live permanently in Vrndavana. I felt my lack of austerity, purity, and many other qualities. I understood that my desire was immature and maybe sentimental. Anyway, I am eager to purify myself, clean up my heart of material desire and be able to really appreciate the simple and deep life of Vrndavana's people and to share it with them.

Although it was painful to see myself so unqualified in a certain sense, I felt happy because the Lord was taking care of me. He had listened to my prayer, but He also made it clear to me that I asked for something which I am not ready for."

Maybe this letter also states my own situation.

11

Chanting *japa* before a table-altar full of pictures, I look up to the open window. The day-after-Ekādaśī thin moon, a reddening dawn—I curse myself that I indulged in so much illicit sex in this lifetime. That small bit of enjoyment now prevents me from entering Vṛndāvana where Rādhā and Kṛṣṇa are *yugala-kiśora*.

Stay awake and pray in *japa*. I look at the pictures of Kṛṣṇa's pastimes, but they don't always "work" for me. I cannot expect to *see* the spiritual world unless there is the ointment of *premāñjana* on my eyes. I try to hear. If that doesn't work, I fall back to the mechanical practice of counting up the quota, getting it done. Only by descending mercy can we improve. May Kṛṣṇa hear my cries and sighs—I require that mercy and will do anything to obtain it.

I write friendly notes of inquiry to brothers here. That way I can expect a note from someone who will give me tangible hope.

A harmonium sound drifts over . . . the *chaukīdār's* whistle, the night of lurking *guṇḍās* and dacoits. The skinny dogs of Vṛndāvana are on the prowl, but some are sleeping on the road in the November cold. I don't know what is going on in the big world of newspapers. All I know is the news the devotee announces after *maṅgala-ārati*. I am also getting news from the spiritual world. Ring the bells, it's time for Kṛṣṇa to wake up and show us His blissful face.

12

I always feel hopeful about the next morning's *japa*. Maybe it's not warranted. I shouldn't analyze it so much; just accept it. See the sitting mat, votive candles in glasses, three shelves of pictures, boxes of memoirs from Vṛndāvana, incense, my beads . . .

O Harināma, please forgive my offenses. When I come to You in the morning, please overlook my mistakes. Please appear in my heart.

This morning I finished eight rounds while sitting in a darkened room. The votive candles illumined the holy pictures, and the moon shone full through the windows. A few times, I tried recalling that I am fallen.

I may not make full progress in this lifetime. It isn't the worst thing that could happen to me, but it seems likely that I will have to take birth again. Will I ever just accept it as a matter of fact, that the higher powers will transfer me to my next life? As Bhaktivinoda Ṭhākura prays, let it be an insignificant life in the family of devotees. At least allow me to take birth where devotees are chanting Kṛṣṇa's name and hearing His pastimes.

As I wait for death, I don't want to waste my time in defeat. Go forward expectant that someone like me can still make significant gains. But I have to admit this: so much about me seems closed and implacable, like a wizened Chinese man. Who knows what goes on in this mind and heart? Is there a warm heart at all? Before I can feel regret, I will have to admit that I am closed to those feelings. Why don't I open to the truth about myself, the real truth, and live in *that*? Why am I living in the back room of my self with only a small light on?

My mornings are long and filled with the heavy training befitting an Olympic athlete. Be alert. Even as I run through my *japa* like a conscientious runner, there may be moments when I find myself on my knees begging to serve. Watch for that moment.

13

I have to become more humble. You say you want to improve chanting? Then the most essential element is *tṛṇād api sunīcena*. For example, guruship is a great responsibility. You cannot goof off and be silly with hundreds of people expecting you to guide them in the most important way. There are many ways to be a silly ass; you have to strive to avoid them.

But humility doesn't mean being focused on yourself as grave, as guru. You have to be able to laugh (or cry) at yourself. Humility includes being a well-loved servant of the devotees. It means not indulging in sensual or mental gratification. It means not living only for yourself.

Think of what it means to be humble. If you have no idea and no practice, then how can you chant the holy name? How can you read in that mood?

14

I am chanting in Pennsylvania. Early this morning in the perfect quiet, I heard the faraway drone of a small-engined airplane. I wondered, "How could such a small plane fly at 3:00 A.M. over an unlit area?" Then I thought of the lonely pilot in the cockpit. Somehow, I too am hovering high above, lost, not focused.

I don't think and feel when I chant. I get up and, restless, turn on the light. The purpose of this written report is not to hit myself on the head. Poor *japa* is punishment in itself. I am thinking of my thoughtful Godbrothers who also work to improve their *japa*, and of younger devotees who look to us for a sign. How can we help each other?

I have no doubt in the process, but for myself, I can't seem to focus. I wander like a little plane in the sky with no worthy mission, it seems.

"Why fly at this hour? You're just an amateur. You have no radar. There is nothing you can do that can't be accomplished better by the big jets. Why don't you come down and stop disturbing our sleep?"

That pilot won't listen. He *must* fly. He's a *vaidhī-bhakta*. He is deeply impelled by something beyond himself.

I ask forgiveness. "Where am I in comparison to the all-auspicious chanting of the holy name of Lord Nārāyaṇa?" (*Bhāg.* 6.2.34). Śrīla Bhaktivinoda Ṭhākura says, "I fall at the Lord's feet, having taken this *mahā-mantra*" (*Aruṇodaya-kīrtana*, Part 2, verse 5).

Not waiting for inspiration, no time left in this life for studying Sanskrit, not much use left for English structures either.

My morning *sādhana* practice is like practicing jump shots in a big empty gymnasium. I used to practice those one-handed jump shots until I got good at it, but I was always too short and too shy to be a "jock" in my high school days. Ah, if only I had known of devotion to Kṛṣṇa then. If only I had known the protection of a guru. What a wasted youth! So now in the swiftly diminishing hours of my life, I burn a candle and wish I could pray. To become a deer living in Vraja, or a peacock messenger, something connected to Vraja service, to *guru-sevā*. Thank you, Gurudeva, for rescuing me. Please allow me, O Lord of the senses, some life duration and concentration on chanting and hearing the most splendid pastimes, beyond all study; allow me to practice my Hare Kṛṣṇa mantras and one day please You in a simple way.

Make a setting for another early rising. It is the way of the Vaiṣṇava saints and I will follow them. A mat is placed before the altar. Matches, incense, candles, pictures, *japa-mālā*, the room itself is solitary, the house quiet. . . . The scene is set with external details, but the *bhāva-sevā*, the inner *arcana*, cannot be substituted by creating an atmosphere. You must have heart, attention, prayers of contrition.

The page and pen await me too. As in *japa*, so in writing, the pen is merely the medium: there must be a person praying to his guru, praying to Prabhupāda. Please accept me, Śrīla Prabhupāda. Give me the taste of my unworthiness. Please give me the holy name. Keep my greed to hear of Kṛṣṇa alive.

15

This is just one point of view: it seems the simpler and steadier the life, the better I can put aside other concerns in the morning when I do *nāma-bhajana*. Should I take a small airplane into Essequibo (Guyana) or the speedboat? What will I say to the troubled person I have to speak to? You can't eliminate these dealings, but you can simplify them.

The light of my votive candle illuminates the feet of the Pañca-tattva picture I worship. I could turn on the light and read a verse, but I need time just for hearing the holy name. How boldly Śrīla Prabhupāda asserted this "impossible" proposal: "*What is the question of controlling the mind? Just hear.*"

Count your rounds. There is no harm in that (*saṅkhyā-pūrvaka-nāma-gāna-natibhiḥ*). But then also, what about *nidrā-hāra*, conquering sleeping and eating? What about becoming "always meek and humble, enchanted by remembering the transcendental qualities of the Lord"? I can't imitate the six Gosvāmīs.

Yes, a simple life, but you have to be working for Prabhupāda to get the mercy. And you have to be scrupulous in avoiding offenses to the Vaiṣṇavas. Because I commit offenses, I cannot relish the holy name.

How simple and trusting we are in our *vaidhī* following of our spiritual master. Because he says chant, we chant. He told us that chanting is most important and we accept that. If anyone hears the holy name in any context, with any attitude, they get spiritual benefit. We believe that. But I say, "I don't chant with any comprehension of the act."

Beg, borrow, or steal to get the nectar of the name. I will be back for more; there is hope. I can simply chant and hear, driving single-mindedly into the place of no return, the place where I will simply hear like a madman. Kṛṣṇa takes pity on the lost fool trying to chant *harināma.*

16

There is a wonderful communication going on between Śrīla Prabhupāda and his avid, serious readers. Śrīla Prabhupāda delivers faith in Kṛṣṇa and the experience of Kṛṣṇa consciousness. His readers receive it wholeheartedly. They can attest to his mercy in their lives, which they in turn dedicate to Śrīla Prabhupāda.

Śrīla Prabhupāda does more than point in Kṛṣṇa's direction. He gives more than academic knowledge. He gives more than spiritual knowledge. Only his readers know what he gives them, and they share it with one another. They also desire to share it with the whole world by taking his books into the streets of the world and distributing them to everyone.

There has been abuse committed by persons citing the authority of Śrīla Prabhupāda's books. There have been quarrels between those who differ as to what Śrīla Prabhupāda actually meant. But Prabhupāda's wonderful gift will persist and be available to future generations. That gift exists in private reading where it creates faith and intimacy with Prabhupāda, and understanding of Prabhupāda's presentation of Kṛṣṇa.

As devotees read more in Gauḍīya Vaiṣṇavism, and as more books become available to us in translation, there is a tendency to compare what Śrīla Prabhupāda wrote to what the commentators said in their original writings. There *is* a science of Kṛṣṇa, and Śrīla Prabhupāda did not invent it. He comes to us as a representative of *paramparā*. Yet when we read him, we come away with *his* understanding. When we explain the science, we have to account for why Śrīla Prabhupāda said things exactly the way he did, why he simplified certain points, why he omitted other points, or why he gave a particular expression with an emphasis that may differ from the previous *ācāryas*.

This should not be a cause for bewilderment. Reading privately, deeply, with submission, opening up to him, making no critical comparisons—Kṛṣṇa becomes revealed to us. He settles deep within us. We become convinced.

Prabhupāda's books carry this gift for each of us. I don't ever want to lose this gift, even in the name of searching for more thorough explanations of Gauḍīya Vaiṣṇavism. I want to regularly read Prabhupāda's books.

17

What is it? It's so subtle. Hold onto the sound of Hare Kṛṣṇa, Hare Kṛṣṇa. Hold it in your mind. It is not like the breeze or the rain, not sensual like that. The mind is more subtle.

The mind eats up plans, ruminating like a great beast. Recent impressions carry it away.

My prayer is feeble. I utter my prayers and my inattentive *japa* at the base of Tulasī's table. She sees me chanting without attention, staring blankly.

I "finished" my rounds for today, a bare sixteen. I also finished breakfast, a walk, lunch, brushed my teeth. Tonight I'll swallow a spoonful of *triphala*. *Japa* is one of those things I do; it's part of my *sādhana*.

What is blocking me? Did I commit a serious offense to a Vaiṣṇava? Did I split an ant with a straw? Am I suffering some past life karma or is it something in this life I have forgotten or that I refuse to face? We say atonement is unnecessary, but where does that leave me?

There is a stone in the throat of my desire to love Kṛṣṇa by serving His holy names. Brothers and sisters, please pray for me to unlock this mystery. I want to be free.

Do you doubt that anyone chants nicely? Do you look to see if they get ecstatic bodily transformations? No, no, I can't know what they do or feel. That's not my business. Bowing at the base of Tulasī's table, I pray to remember Nāma Prabhu and to ask, "Please allow me to chant sincerely, as service. Tell me what I can do to improve and give me the strength to do it."

18

Prabhupāda says that tears are a way of expressing the consummation of Kṛṣṇa consciousness. In another place he says tears are the price we pay for love of God, meaning that we should cry to attain the perfectional stage. One of the primary ways to practice *bhajana* is to chant the Hare Kṛṣṇa mantra. As with other practices, there should be special emphasis on practicing it with heart, not just mechanically. We are supposed to hanker to live in Vṛndāvana, and we are supposed to feel real separation from Vṛndāvana and the Vrajavāsīs.

But before we can feel these things, we have to pray for the mercy of the holy name and cry in the mood of Bhaktivinoda Ṭhākura's "Gopīnātha" about our unworthiness and sinfulness. This is relevant because it deals with just where we are now—stuck in mechanical chanting. We don't know how to feel deeply when we chant the holy name. Of course, crying and spiritual emotion cannot be imitated; spiritual emotion is given to us by Kṛṣṇa's grace.

I realize that it is one thing to study Prabhupāda's books and try to assimilate them, and another thing to get below the surface, below the intellectualized, verbalized discussion and emerge as a new person with deeper convictions in Kṛṣṇa consciousness. We are looking for a very definite focus. It means we have to break through our mechanical attitudes and attachments. It means we have to specifically be trying to make advancement.

Kṛṣṇa consciousness can be grasped intellectually without fully surrendering. I expressed this to one of my Godbrothers in Vṛndāvana one day. We are not just trying to become "hip" to the scriptures without giving our hearts to following them. Surrender means a change of heart. In the material world, just being "in the know" constitutes realization, but devotees want to go beyond the intellectual into the soul.

When I last wrote at this desk, the fir trees looked chilled in the early morning cold. Now the sunshine pours in. Can I drag myself back to the disciplines—to the studies I want to pursue?

My day goes up and down. I have the most exalted books in the world within my reach; at least physically I can take them off the shelf and try to read what's written on their pages.

19

Learn what it means to live within. Did you ever do it before, maybe as a child? Children have their own worlds. Those worlds are real and children sustain them, but they are internal. Now my own inner world revolves in thoughts of Kṛṣṇa, of Vṛndāvana, of chanting and praying.

I have heard of people entering a cave that opened into a world of lakes and skies and trees. They had to enter deep within the cave to find the interior world. They had to crawl through the dark crevices and hear the bats screech overhead before they found their paradise. I am entering the cave of my mind. I sing *bhajanas* to ward off the bats and I hear and remember pastimes to get past the obstacles of my mind. I write my way in. The obstacles try to convince me that the "real" world lies in a realm of the senses. "Step aside," I tell them. "My guru wants me to hear the Hare Kṛṣṇa mantra and the sounds of Kṛṣṇa's eternal realm."

20

Śrīla Prabhupāda writes we should long for the day when tears will come to our eyes by chanting Hare Kṛṣṇa. Imagine trying to squeeze out a few tears—ridiculous. And yet the dry, macho resistance to this is also ridiculous. I don't think of my desire to cry as a hankering for an advanced stage; more, it is an awareness that I am stuck at a very preliminary point—an inability to feel regret. Sometimes I don't feel anything.

Shall I appease myself and say, "This is a nice stage of advancement. This is a time for patience and don't you know, patience is a virtue too?" You think, "Kṛṣṇa doesn't give me a chance to feel anything in His holy names. One day, He may choose to reveal to me the reasons why the nectar of the name isn't mine. He is in the heart and from Him comes remembrance and forgetfulness. Until He does this, I will go on faithfully counting rounds."

The Vaiṣṇava *kavi* prays that he could not attain the nectar of the holy names. He thinks he must be cursed by Yamarāja. What is the sense of living? Bhaktivinoda Ṭhākura states, "With every rising and setting of the sun, a day passes and is lost. Then, why do you remain idle and not serve the Lord of the heart? This temporary life is full of various miseries. Take shelter of the holy name as your only business. . . . Drink the pure nectar of the holy name. There is nothing but the name to be had in the fourteen worlds. It has filled the soul of Śrī Bhaktivinoda Ṭhākura" (*Aruṇodaya-kīrtana*, verses 5–6, 8).

21

Are you afraid to meet God in His holy names? Afraid to meet yourself? Is that why I turn away from full attention? Do you fear Him as Arjuna feared the universal form? It isn't something I have thought much about. Why am I reciting His names day after day if I want to avoid meeting Him? But even great devotees like Dhruva Mahārāja were speechless and afraid when they first got Kṛṣṇa's *darśana*.

According to this theory, as soon as you seriously begin to approach Him by His holy names, you become afraid. Therefore you allow your mind to go off. A whole lifetime could be spent in this way—afraid of what you will become in comparison to Kṛṣṇa when He manifests. So you prefer to keep it all distant, as a ritual, and you candidly confess, "It is very hard to control the mind." You expect your friends will sympathize because they also find it hard. I don't think my fear theory tells the whole story, but I glimpsed it today.

Otherwise, I am left with my overfamiliar, stay-on-the-surface bad habits. There is no way to bypass them, it seems. Neither am I working hard to change them. I humbly accept a low state and count my blessings that I am up earlier than most, I am awake, and there are other services that I can do with more competence than chanting. It's like accepting the fact that you lost your legs in a car accident or that your wife is unfaithful. You live with it: "I'm a poor chanter." Is that the way to go through life?

22

When we are trying to cut ourselves off from matter, dealing with the matter is part of it. For example, we try to see how Kṛṣṇa is working through the material energy, even when we get kicked by it. When Vidura had to suffer at the hands of wicked Duryodhana, Vidura "was not sorry, for he considered the acts of the external energy to be supreme" (*Bhāg.* 3.1.16). That is, he saw that even in material circumstances, the internal energy was helping him and offering him a way to improve his Kṛṣṇa consciousness.

This kind of analysis is favorable, but then we have to directly apply for Kṛṣṇa's mercy. "Please pick me up and place me as one of the atoms at Your lotus feet." Chanting is not a ritual to pacify God; it is a heartfelt calling out to Him for mercy. Chanting is not meant to help us create a favorable, material situation (the eighth offense against the holy name); it is meant to free us from all material situations. But the dullness of body and the tricky nature of the *māyā*-influenced mind often render us incapable of pure chanting. If we can actually achieve *śuddha-nāma*, then we will be freed from the material world. We will then truly understand and act on the realization of *ahaṁ brahmāsmi*. Such an apparently simple act as utterance of *harināma* in devotion can do all this. The *śāstras* compare pure chanting to a lightning bolt making dust out of a mountain peak. The mountain represents our accumulated karma and ignorant thoughts. We should beg for a lightning bolt to strike us, even if we are afraid of the jolt.

What to do with the mind during *japa*? As if I can logically, reasonably, ready the mind to chant. I have tried different approaches. I have tried ignoring the mind. I have tried simplifying my life to the point where my mind's demands have no choice but to simplify. I have given myself lessons in the *śāstra*. I have appealed to my higher nature. Bhaktisiddhānta Sarasvatī Ṭhākura advises, when all else fails, beat the mind with a broom in the morning and a shoe at night.

When we cannot control the mind, when we are dull or paralyzed by illusory conceptions of ourselves, we can still go on with our external utterances of *nāma-japa* with faith. We can also pray that the day will come when we can taste the sweetness of chanting, and when that sweetness will spill over into all our other devotional activities.

Speaking on chanting in a lecture, Śrīla Prabhupāda said, "We should not go to God for material things. We should go to God for begging how one can be engaged in His service. Hare Kṛṣṇa mantra means that. 'Hare' means, 'O energy of God,' and 'Kṛṣṇa' means, 'Lord Kṛṣṇa, please engage me in Your service.' Hare Kṛṣṇa Hare Kṛṣṇa, Kṛṣṇa Kṛṣṇa Hare Hare/Hare Rāma Hare Rāma, Rāma Rāma Hare Hare. *It is simply praying*, 'O my Lord Kṛṣṇa, O Śrīmatī Rādhārāṇī, kindly engage me in Your service.' Finished all business" (Lecture, Hawaii 6/8/73).

This is the desired mood, begging for service. And the immediate service is loving utterances of the beloved names. But there is such a difference between chanting with offenses and chanting with a heart melted in perfect love of God. Chanting is the best and easiest way to attain love of God, but poor chanting is itself the main obstacle.

The Nectar of Devotion lists sixty-four offenses and states that these can be relieved by taking refuge in Kṛṣṇa. If one offends Kṛṣṇa Himself, then one can save himself by chanting. But according to the *Padma Purāṇa*, if one offends the chanting: ". . . one must definitely fall from one's spiritual life should one commit offenses to Lord Hari's name, Who is the best friend of all" (*Bhakti-rasāmṛta-sindhu* 1.2.120).

If someone were to ask me which offense in chanting is my "favorite," I would have to state "*pramāda*, inattention, from which all the other offenses spring." One doesn't care enough—or he is otherwise unable—to pay attention while praying to *harināma*. Often inattention is a result of hearing or speaking *sādhu-nindā*.

23

I am so low it is unspeakable. I mean, so tiny I can't even place myself or estimate my chanting. Unfortunately, I don't *feel* this reality of my position. To be tiny but unaware . . . unconscious.

A Godbrother asked me, "What are you trying to achieve in chanting, to think of Kṛṣṇa at every moment?" He seemed puzzled about why I keep protesting that my *japa* is no good. Does he think staying awake and being attentive to our own voices as we chant is enough? Some think that that is sufficient for now. There is a modesty in this viewpoint that is commendable. I obviously share this viewpoint and yet I also know it is *not* enough.

I am powerless to change. I automatically think of other things as soon as I pick up my beads; thus I treat *harināma* as something unimportant. It is neglect of the holy name. Someone comes to visit and because I have so little desire to associate with that person, my mind continues to flit from this duty to that thought to the clock, so much so that I can hardly hear or concentrate on the exchange I am having with that person. It is offensive.

I know my appreciation for *harināma* leaps up when I am in physical danger. I cling to Him, and utterly believe, and stay as close to Him as possible. Then there is no room for other plans or persons—just my relationship with *harināma*. I know at that time that Kṛṣṇa is nondifferent than His name. This transformation is understandable, and Prabhupāda describes it in *Kṛṣṇa* book on the occasion when Nanda Mahārāja became afraid that Kṛṣṇa might be in danger:

> It is quite natural for a devotee in danger to think of Kṛṣṇa because he has no other shelter. When a child is in danger he takes shelter of his mother or father. Similarly, a devotee is always under the shelter of the Supreme Personality of Godhead, but when he specifically sees some danger, he remembers the Lord very rapidly.
> —*Kṛṣṇa*, vol. 1, p. 43

I write this after having chanted my first six rounds. In a couple of hours I'll go back to chanting. I'll try again and, even if I fail to improve, I will take solace in the fact that *harināma* still visits me and is willing to stay with me throughout my life.

24

In *The Nectar of Devotion:* Rūpa Gosvāmī (and Śrīla Prabhupāda) say that if one has developed spontaneous attraction for chanting the *mahā-mantra*, then he has reached the highest perfectional stage. Śrī Kṛṣṇa told Arjuna in the *Ādi Purāṇa*, "Anyone who is engaged in chanting My transcendental name must be considered to be always associating with Me. And I may tell you frankly that for such a devotee I become easily purchased" (*NOD*, p. 107).

It is conceivable that I could just take a more simple, resolute attitude and begin paying more attention to *japa*. Sometimes you notice that there is no attention at all. You might as well be saying different words, "Hair Mary, Har

Roomy, Krist, Krsipt." But no, attentive or not, I am trying to enunciate carefully. I have got that down. So why not just put your attention into it?

Try it now: Hare Kṛṣṇa Hare Kṛṣṇa, Kṛṣṇa Kṛṣṇa Hare Hare. Is it so hard? Is it better?

You think it's unproductive. Where is the tangible result? If you write a page, you get a page. If you roll a *capāti* and eat it, you get a belly full of *capāti*. Do you think chanting has no result?

O fruitive mentality, go back to simple prayer. Your prayer is the Hare Kṛṣṇa mantra.

One good sign: When I chant *japa*, I am reluctant to let go of the beads when I am finished with my rounds. The reluctance comes from my hand. The hand itself feels like I am tearing away a valuable, lovable object.

> For persons who are not inclined to clear the dust from their hearts and who want to keep things as they are, it is not possible to derive the transcendental result of chanting the Hare Kṛṣṇa mantra.... As soon as one develops his spontaneous service attitude [under the guidance of the spiritual master], he can immediately understand the transcendental nature of the holy names of the *mahā-mantra*.
>
> —*NOD*, pp. 107–8

In the compilation *Nāmāmṛta*, there is a heading: "One Develops a Taste for Chanting By Chanting." The statement from Śrīla Prabhupāda's purports says that chanting is nectarean; the more you chant, the less you tire of it. The more you chant, the more attached you become to chanting. I agree, but I am unhappy that the statement doesn't apply to me yet. A statement more in line with my experience is this one: "Attacked by jaundice, the tongue of a diseased person cannot palatably relish sugar candy. . . . *Avidyā* (ignorance) similarly perverts the ability to relish the transcendentally palatable name . . . " (*Nectar of Instruction*, text 7, purport). Even this "jaundice" statement, with its assurance that "if he chants, he *will* develop a taste for chanting" is something that hasn't happened to me. Another verse: "Unfortunate as I am, I commit offenses and therefore cannot taste the holy names." So I can't complain that the scriptures are too optimistic or lack detail. They pin me down. Another one states that if your chanting is infested with offenses, you can go on chanting for hundreds of births, but you will never attain *kṛṣṇa-prema*. It has all been spelled out.

Since I tend to complain and claim an injustice is being perpetrated on me, I also say, "There is no guide to take me through the required changes. No one has spelled it out, such as who I may have offended (*sādhu-nindā*), or exactly how I can go about controlling my mind against inattention (*pramāda*)."

Response: "Be serious. Do the needful to improve your chanting. And you do have friends and guides, so appeal to them."

I wanted to take advantage of these weeks to improve *japa*, but I may lack the heart or "guts" to do what is required. Besides, it's so subtle. I can't exactly grasp what it is exactly that I need to do. I am up at 1:00 A.M. helplessly rattling the beloved names, but there is no prayer of the heart, not even a prayer of the mind. What to speak of mixing *japa* with Kṛṣṇa's pastimes.

> When chanting the Hare Kṛṣṇa *mahā-mantra*, in the beginning one may commit many offenses, which are called *nāmābhāsa* and *nāma-aparādha*. In this stage there is no possibility of achieving perfect love of Kṛṣṇa by chanting the Hare Kṛṣṇa *mahā-mantra*. Therefore one must chant the Hare Kṛṣṇa *mahā-mantra* according to the principles of the above verse, *tṛṇād api sunīcena taror iva sahiṣṇunā*. . . . Chanting is very simple, but one must practice it seriously. Therefore the author of *Caitanya-caritāmṛta*, Kṛṣṇadāsa Kavirāja Gosvāmī, advises everyone to keep this verse always strung about his neck.
>
> —Cc., *Ādi* 17.32, purport

I pray to the dry leaves and trees. I mean to say, I pray to God, in the presence of the leaves and trees, "Please let us all mentally, verbally, worship *harināma*. Make it a trend for me, an interest—not a fad—but let me understand that it is the gateway to the attainment of pure devotional service. Improving my chanting is one of the most crucial ways to serve Śrīla Prabhupāda, who says that of all the rules and regulations, chanting sixteen rounds is essential. Prabhupāda did not mean mechanical rounds. He meant that we should chant with *prīti*, with love."

25

Situations of dire distress drive us to feel helpless, but we don't realize that we are *always* in distress. We are so unaware. Here I am in a warm house in the middle of winter in the powerful U.S.A. It is quiet here and I have protective hosts. I have a measure of spiritual favor from guru and Kṛṣṇa, and I accept the honor disciples and others offer me. Yet I don't know that my life is slipping away and I still don't fully love Kṛṣṇa. I feel no shame and little regret over this. Is this not a helpless situation?

As for making factual advancement in chanting, I am helpless. I tend to think that my yearning is a yearning just for the cherry on top of the cake, but that I already possess the cake. I am like the materially puffed-up man who occasionally utters Hare Kṛṣṇa.

I *need* the holy name. I *want* to reach out to save myself. I am stuck in a network of material amenities. I am stuck in the role of guru-preacher. I lack faith (or whatever) that the chanting of Hare Kṛṣṇa can fulfill all my spiritual desires and will be the most pleasing service to guru and Kṛṣṇa.

"A pure devotee knows that when he chants the transcendental name Kṛṣṇa, Śrī Kṛṣṇa is present as transcendental sound. He therefore chants with full respect and veneration" (Cc., *Ādi* 2.11, purport).

We each chant alone. We get good advice, philosophy, practical pointers from learned teachers, but then we must go and chant alone. The purports and verses often describe what a pure devotee knows or what an obedient disciple should do, but where are we? We must ask ourselves. No one else can know. We have to do something about our state ourselves. The devotee (whom we aspire to be) *knows* that Kṛṣṇa and His names are identical. But it's a huge step in realization to practice the chanting with that understanding.

Perhaps I realize Kṛṣṇa is His name; I know it to some little degree. Then how can I assume "feeling and veneration"? What else can I say but go on trying? The retreat, the *japa* worship, the daily best time saved for it, the listening to lectures on devotional science to keep me aware how the *aparādhas* will adversely affect me—all these are favorable. I am in the right place and in the right association. I *am* helping myself, and I *am* receiving divine assistance. So keep as humble as possible and hear the sound vibration of my own utterance of Kṛṣṇa's holy name.

Śrīla Prabhupāda emphasized the chanting's simplicity. But we have to persist. Keep at the attentive, concerned forefront. Don't slip back from there. Know that chanting is very important in our life and *always* deserves our full attention. At least that much we should know. Then maybe the regret will come, and the gratitude for His mercy, and the attraction to His pastimes.

26

Waiting an hour before writing in the morning is humbling. I see I cannot chant in deep meditation on Rādhā and Kṛṣṇa—not as Bhaktivinoda Ṭhākura says, "At the time of taking *nāma*, the true meaning of *nāma* should be cultivated with fondness, and prayer should be made to Kṛṣṇa with piteous cry." How can I come to this page and write high-flying *bhāva* if I cannot even pray during *japa*?

And yet I do have a fondness for it. These times are very nice, sitting in the darkened room with a small light focused on the feet of the Pañca-tattva and extending its rays to the six Gosvāmīs. The votive candles flicker in the warmth of the room, while outside, the wind reminds me it is winter. I sit on a blanket on the floor, alone, and chant the holy name. It is the *act* that is successful, not my actual performance of the act. Even the *shadow* of the holy name . . .

Although there is no piteous cry yet—am I afraid to open my heart like that?—and I know this *japa* I am chanting is way below standard, still, my wish to improve is worth something. Improvement is not really in my power, so chanting becomes an act of patience, waiting on the Lord, as is written about the devotee who has developed *bhāva*, "He is always certain that Kṛṣṇa will bestow His mercy upon him." Śrīla Prabhupāda writes, "Because I am trying my best to follow the routine principles of devotional service, I am sure that I will go back to Godhead, back to home."

But when will the day come? Rūpa Gosvāmī says, "I have no love for Kṛṣṇa, nor for the causes of developing love of Kṛṣṇa—namely, hearing and chanting." Śrīla Prabhupāda concludes, " . . . one should continue to hope against hope that some way or other he will be able to approach the lotus feet of the Supreme Lord" (*NOD*, p. 137).

Bhaktivinoda Ṭhākura writes, "If humility becomes very deep and intense, Kṛṣṇa will be merciful. In that case, feelings of *bhāva* will arise in his mind and then these [*anarthas*] will be destroyed in no time. Then favorable and smooth cultivation of *bhajana* will gradually improve" (*Śrī Caitanya-śikṣāmṛta*, p. 218).

27

When I open a book and read of Kṛṣṇa's play in Vraja with His beloved devotees, something good happens. But when I close the book, I leave it far behind. I'm not like a *gopī* whose mind always runs to Kṛṣṇa. Therefore I try and find more time to be with the open book, hearing the pastimes from he who tastes them.

In the West, without an open Kṛṣṇa conscious book, we are bombarded by the most alien, non-Kṛṣṇa modes of living. The reality of Vraja fades. And as the *ācāryas* take pains to explain, that which is the highest and most chaste in the spiritual world (*parakīya-rasa*) is the most sinful contamination in the material world (adulterous, illicit sex). That immoral sex permeates the ether and affects our attempt to worship and taste Kṛṣṇa's loving affairs. Therefore, it is a fight for spiritual survival.

I plan to read the *Bhāgavatam* as a shield against all enemies. And although I complain of inability in *japa*, I know this too is my shelter. When book-words seem too intellectual or distant, I turn to chanting for shelter. Although I plead in *japa*, and although I bounce off the hard resistance of my inattention, I know the holy name is absolute Kṛṣṇa (*pūrṇaḥ śuddho nitya-mukto*).

We have been battling the forces of *māyā* all along, but in a general way, looking for shelter *somewhere* within the realm of Kṛṣṇa consciousness. We pray to Prabhupāda—he has given us specific instructions—but we misunderstand those specifics and take them generally. Prabhupāda says, "Surrender to Kṛṣṇa." He tells us we are "eternal servants of God." We think, "Yes, an eternal servant of God, let me surrender to God." But we have to understand specifically who God is. By Prabhupāda's grace, we now have an internal universe to turn to, a whole world of love to come to understand in Kṛṣṇa's manifestation in Vṛndāvana. Vṛndāvana-Kṛṣṇa is so far from material reality that there can be no more mistake. We protect our interest in Vṛndāvana by continuing the staunch practices of "following the four rules and chanting sixteen rounds," and building on that.

28

How can a mind filled with publishing plans concentrate on the holy names with humble pleas? Śrīla Prabhupāda has written that in the beginning of devotional service, one is first attached to service and later develops actual love for Kṛṣṇa. I can see it that way—love and service can be distinct. You can work hard for Kṛṣṇa and love your work without thinking much about the Lord Himself. It is *your* work and the plethora of things you have to deal with that occupies all your waking moments. You may occasionally have a meaningful *darśana* of the Deity in the temple (and even then your mind is racing elsewhere, "Did the proofreader catch that mistake on page 214? When are they going to the printer? What will I write next?"). It is good, healthy, to work for Kṛṣṇa, but when will the day come when I *love* Him? I wish on a daily basis I could start out with pure entreaty, then I could take up the burdens of service.

My life is quiet compared to others. That's why when I speak to audiences on the importance of chanting, they always respond earnestly, but the first question is, "How can we do it when we have so many duties and things to do and think about?" I don't know, I don't know, but maybe we have to let those duties tail off and save ourselves. Cāṇakya says, "For the sake of a family, a son can be sacrificed; for the sake of a country, a village can be sacrificed; but most important of all, save yourself." We think of Bhaktivinoda Ṭhākura closing the doors at the end of his life and fully entering the pastimes of Kṛṣṇa and Caitanya Mahāprabhu. Śrīla Prabhupāda remained open to us until his last hours.

Save yourself. How to do it? Ideally, while we are inevitably active, we can call out to Kṛṣṇa impelled by the burden of duties, "Kṛṣṇa, please help me to remember You." Kṛṣṇa says without lethargy or false ego, without abandoning your duty, remember Me and fight. Fight also means fight to pay attention as you utter the names.

29

What is good for me spiritually? What combination of diet? As there are doctors of different schools of medicine, so transcendentalists differ. When Mahārāja Parīkṣit sat for his last seven days of life, sages offered various prescriptions: "Mahārāja, try this yoga." But he was only satisfied when young Śukadeva Gosvāmī arrived with the proposal to continuously hear about Kṛṣṇa.

Even among Prabhupāda's followers, we will hear different prescriptions of how to please guru and Kṛṣṇa best. Everyone agrees (theoretically at least) that chanting sixteen rounds of Hare Kṛṣṇa comes first, but do we mean first get the rounds out of the way, *then* we can talk about real service? Anyway, we all agree that the vows we take are the most important. Of course, follow the four rules. Then, "Preaching is the essence, books are the basis," and don't forget *varṇāśrama*—with ox power—*prasādam* distribution, and don't forget the morning program—*maṅgala-ārati*, *tulasī-pūjā*, *guru-pūjā*, *Bhāgavatam* class, *harināma* . . .

What am I getting at? Am I making fun of the plurality of voices in ISKCON and how each one values a particular science? The sun goes down like a burning cinder.

I am trying to say that Kṛṣṇa is waiting for us. Śrīla Prabhupāda told us that all we have to know is Kṛṣṇa. He is the source of everything, He *is* everything. We just have to love Him. I am trying to say that we shouldn't be complacent and think it's all right not to go back to Godhead in this life. We should understand our priorities. We should consult with our spiritual master and find out what *his* priorities are for us. Prabhupāda speaks very strongly on this point, that we shouldn't be complacent about going back to Godhead. I was surprised to hear him emphasize it so strongly because I have been thinking, "Yes, when the devotees humbly say, 'Let me be born next time in the family of devotees,' that seems to be the right estimation." No, Śrīla Prabhupāda says, quoting his Guru Mahārāja, "Finish up your business."

As I enter the holy name's shelter, hearing sporadically, my mind and senses defy me and cannot be fully conquered. But in the future, by guru's grace, my heart will soften, doubts will all fall away, and the vision of Kṛṣṇa, the beloved of Śrīmatī Rādhikā, will appear always in my heart as the handsome lover. I will love Him with nothing else in the way—my ego smashed.

O Lord of light who protects us from death, please do not abandon me.

30

You can attract Kṛṣṇa by service which is pleasing to the spiritual master and by no other way. *Yasya deve parā bhaktir, yathā-deve tathā gurau*. What pleases you the most, Śrīla Prabhupāda? "That you love Kṛṣṇa."

Śrīla Prabhupāda said (I heard it yesterday), "Therefore I don't talk with any rascal. . . . I only talk with my disciples." He meant they are so ignorant and stubbornly atheistic that it is useless to speak with them. Prabhupāda affirmed that, and moreover, it is the śāstric version. Although a preacher kindly mixes with the nondevotees, his actual relationship is with people who will hear him submissively. "Glorification of the Supreme Personality of Godhead is performed in the *paramparā* system; that is, it is conveyed from spiritual master to disciple" (*Bhāg*. 10.1.4). Certainly this is true of the six Gosvāmīs' works. Śrīla Prabhupāda writes, "For *kṛṣṇa-kathā*, topics about Kṛṣṇa consciousness, there must be a speaker and a hearer, both of whom can be interested in Kṛṣṇa consciousness if they are no longer interested in material topics." He also writes, "Since merely talking about Kṛṣṇa is so pleasing, we can simply imagine how pleasing it is to render service to Kṛṣṇa" (*Bhāg*. 10.1.4, purport).

31

"O merciful Lord, how great is my misfortune that I feel no appreciation for Your holy name! In such a lamentable state, how will I be freed from committing the ten offenses to the holy name?" (*Śaraṇāgati*, 7.8.3).

It is right that I enter verses like these into my book. They speak exactly of my condition—except I lack the lamentation.

We say, "The *ācāryas* are liberated, but they write like this for the benefit of the conditioned souls. Plus, in humility, they actually feel like this." Then what is the benefit for us if Bhaktivinoda Ṭhākura or Lord Caitanya Mahāprabhu lament that they cannot appreciate the holy name? Their words are meant to awaken us from our dullness. We have to first regret our inability to chant, and then we have to embrace the shelter of the holy name.

I write the verse down as both student and preacher. Of course, I am first preaching to myself. How great is *my* misfortune. I tend to think, "It's commendable to be concerned about improving *japa*. But if you think realistically, don't you imagine that your chanting is 'pretty good' compared to other ISKCON devotees? I mean, you rise early for *japa*, you aren't sleepy. Who can expect to control the mind? And anyway, when your thoughts go off, you're usually thinking of devotional service. In this age, in the active mission Śrīla Prabhupāda has given us, we can't expect to be *so* attentive to *japa*. We're not living as *bhajanānandīs*. The chanting is not the only form of *bhakti* we are practicing. So the fact that you are enthusiastic and intent for your other Kṛṣṇa conscious duties and can't wait to tend to them—and that makes you rush through your *japa*—it *isn't so bad*."

I lack regret. Now, how to reform?

I can start by noticing the problem. I can start by dragging the mind back to the feet of the holy name. I can start by rejecting any idea that inattentive *japa* is all right because I'm thinking of devotional service. I can hear from the *ācāryas*, the humble, realized *ācāryas* who are intent on saving me by their statements.

I like to record some of these verses so I can look at them often. The verse I just quoted is an unmitigated lament. It offers no solution—that is not its purpose. Bhaktivinoda Ṭhākura has given plenty of recommendations on how to improve, but unless we *want* to improve, unless we admit we need improvement, and unless we feel sorry about poor chanting, then the recommendations will be of no help. Therefore, statements of assurance and the more elevated statements of yearning, as well as descriptions of the intoxicating nature of pure chanting—these all become useful when we are actually trying to improve. Otherwise, they sound like flowery poetry, and our collection of verses on index cards just becomes a hobby.

First comes regret: *hari hari! bifale janama goṅāinu*. Why are we so afraid to feel regret? Of course, we don't want to be artificial about it and beat our breasts with no real feeling. Certainly the nondevotees will deride us. They will compare us to medieval flagellants who beat themselves out of guilt. Body-punishing ascetics, self-accusers, sufferers from low self-esteem —all negative, they say. But we should not concern ourselves with what the nondevotees think.

The real danger for us is not excessive lamentation, but falling into the pit of complacency. At least we can hear the words of the *ācāryas* like Bhaktivinoda Ṭhākura and Narottama dāsa Ṭhākura and take inspiration in our own steps to improve.

"The treasure of divine love in Goloka Vṛndāvana has descended as the congregational chanting of Lord Hari's holy names. Why did my attraction for that chanting never come about?" (*"Iṣṭa-deve Vijñapti,"* Narottama dāsa Ṭhākura, *Songs of the Vaiṣṇava Ācāryas*, p. 63).

" '*This* is humbleness,' Prabhupāda said. ' . . . If you go on thinking, "Oh, I did not perform this duty so nicely, I should have done it this way," then you will improve. Our love for Kṛṣṇa keeps growing as long as we think that we are not doing the most for Kṛṣṇa and that we must do more' " (*Prabhupāda-līlā*, p. 10).

"When one fails to achieve the desired goal of life and repents for all his offenses, there is a state of regret called *viṣāda*" (Cc., *Madhya* 2.35, purport).

" . . . without *tapa* or inner repentance, the soul cannot live as a Vaiṣṇava" (*Pañca-saṁskāra*, by Bhaktivinoda Ṭhākura, printed in *ISKCON Journal*).

Inner repentance. I don't have to show it to anyone, or even prove it to myself. The state called *viṣāda* is a transcendental ecstatic symptom characterized as follows: "One hankers to revive his original condition and inquires how to do so. There are also deep thoughts, heavy breathing, crying, and lamentation as well as changing of bodily color and drying up of the tongue" (Cc., *Madhya* 2.35, purport).

I'm not going to imitate those ecstasies, but keep a flame burning within. It is not right that I chant with offenses. And I *do* chant with offenses or else I would be in ecstasy uttering the holy names. I want to enter the stage of attraction for hearing of Kṛṣṇa in Vṛndāvana, but how can I do it if my foundation in *harināma* is weak? So tend to this. Think how to improve. Take measures. Don't shirk the work or think, "It can't be done by endeavor. If Kṛṣṇa wants to be merciful to me, He can."

Bhaktivinoda Ṭhākura says, "If I sing Your holy name every day, by Your mercy the ten offenses will gradually disappear. A taste for Your holy name will grow within me, and then I will taste the intoxicating spirit of the name" (*Śaraṇāgati*, 7.8.4).

Other things you might do to improve *japa:*

(1) Give time—a week or two—just for that. Don't do any other extensive work. Chant thirty-two rounds.

(2) Keep up the practice you developed in those weeks of chanting *japa* immediately upon rising, for an hour. It gives priority to your weak *bhajana*.

(3) Think of your visits to Vṛndāvana as a way to improve chanting.

(4) Speak about it in classes, in a non-hypocritical way. Write about it sincerely.

(5) Can you pray for it? Before you chant, say prayers. Often we think we don't have time for even ten or twenty minutes of prayer before *japa*. But it could help. Then when we start chanting, we are in a more sanctified state of mind.

(6) There are other little tricks and things like writing *japa* or keeping a *japa* notebook. But these all take time. Ultimately, we have to get down to chanting.

(7) Discuss it with friends who are in a position to help you.

32

Dreams are a lingering, a delaying. You oversleep because of them. They are an attachment to this world. It may be some foolish activity or even horrible detention—but whatever it is, it keeps you asleep. This gives you a glimpse of the fact that due to attachments, you linger in this world of birth and death. They have to be rooted out. Simultaneously, you want to become more absorbed in the activities of Rādhā and Kṛṣṇa. This cannot happen by your own endeavor. Mercy has to descend before the spiritual participation becomes the root of your being, and for the other connections to wither and fall away.

Devotees who preach against all opposition, with faith in the guru's order, gain his blessings. They get lifted out. I think of them, and I hope I am doing something to attract his mercy. Otherwise, I know I can't develop a spiritual mind and body just by reading books and chanting.

O best of mantras, You withhold Yourself from me in Your inner form. I am an outer person when it comes to chanting. I seek the inner form of truth.

By rising early, we may pray and deliberate. Is the body fit today? Can I welcome the opportunities? We ask for grace and protection.

". . . one can neither see, hear, understand nor perceive the Supreme Lord, Kṛṣṇa, by the material senses. But if one is engaged in loving transcendental service to the Lord from the beginning, then one can see the Lord by revelation" (Bg. 11.4, purport).

"Always think of Me, become My devotee, worship Me and offer your homage unto Me. Thus you will come to Me without fail. I promise you this because you are My very dear friend" (Bg. 18.65).

Everyone is dear to Kṛṣṇa. If we follow Arjuna's path, we too can attain perfection. "Don't hesitate, don't worry," Kṛṣṇa says. "Give up all religious activities and surrender to Me."

"Do it today," as the advertisers say. "Don't delay." You chant His holy names, but it takes more than putting a dollar in the mail. Do it today, all day, all night, all day tomorrow. Be prepared to go on chanting and praying for many lifetimes. Pray for the greed; prove your sincerity. Don't think, "I've done enough. Kṛṣṇa should fully reveal Himself to me and take me out of this world to safety in the supreme abode." That thinking is tinged with salvationism. Kṛṣṇa can purify it. We need to show Him we simply want to serve His devotees, either in this world or in the spiritual world.

But if we cling to life here, using delay tactics as in the dreams our minds create, then what? Kṛṣṇa, please break the bonds. I cannot break them on my own. Let my devotion flow to You unobstructed, the way the Gaṅgā flows to the sea.

We don't eat the right things and then we complain of indigestion. Foolish humans. We can love people despite their weaknesses, but our own weaknesses detain us. We say we want devotion to God, but we act in a way to prevent it from happening as fully as possible right now. We act as if it's not urgent, as if it is something that can be tended to later. It's a fact, we say, that we can practice God consciousness later, when we have more time. More time? That last stage is filled with disease and bewilderment and death.

I, Satsvarūpa dāsa Goswami, hereby declare myself in need of Śrī Kṛṣṇa's profound grace. I ask Him to help me. What do I need? I need contrition. I am afraid to become too emotional, and yet . . . Why am I not sorry that I haven't attained Your attention more? Why don't You reveal Yourself to me so that I care for You? Your name, just a drop of its essence, would flood me with awareness of You. I would crave the chanting day and night.

Yes, I'll work on it. I am at my desk filling out the application forms, writing the exam essay. But please don't delay me unnecessarily. I will probably never be qualified.

Dear spiritual master, you are the most merciful representative of Kṛṣṇa. Please give me full devotion. I won't selfishly keep it to myself. I will serve you and your Kṛṣṇa consciousness movement just as you have always asked us to do in your letters, books, and lectures.

It may be wrong to demand attention. I am just one of uncountable *jīvas* who wake up in the morning. How horrible is the grip of *māyā*—the worries, the pains, and the void. . . . People who don't have God and who are cruel to others are headed for worse suffering. Some of us get cushioned by past good karma, then we sit on our cushions, caring neither for others nor to attain real safety in eternal life.

Kṛṣṇa is the Lord of all, but He is especially inclined toward His confidential devotees. How did they earn the right to be in His eternal entourage? By many lives of austerity; by association with Vaiṣṇavas; by favorable meditation on Kṛṣṇa—in some cases for sixty thousand years.

The path of devotional service is direct. In this age, we can't do anything very difficult. Therefore, I am grateful for the holy names. I am afraid of time and *māyā* and the world. I turn to You. But I am sorry I am not a better devotee.

I go on waiting and hoping. "Because I am trying my best to follow the routine principles of devotional service, I am sure that I will go back to Godhead, back to home . . . one should continue to hope against hope that some way or other he will be able to approach the lotus feet of the Supreme Lord" *NOD*, p. 137).

33

In India, I hear truck horns instead of Kṛṣṇa's flute. But I hear *about* His flute, especially early in the morning when I am fresh. I am not indifferent to my material situation. I prefer indoors because there is a fan and no flies.

To make advancement, we have to perform *sevā* for our spiritual master. We have to contribute to the Kṛṣṇa consciousness movement. We have to serve Kṛṣṇa. The whole Vedic system, he told his Lower East Side audience in 1966, is for giving facility in human life so that misery can be relieved. Kṛṣṇa consciousness is for stopping birth and death. People shouldn't live like cats and dogs. I want to always serve the guru who said that, who drove us hard, his voice excited and strong over the barking dogs and car traffic on Second Avenue. That guru has an eternal form that brings Kṛṣṇa pleasure and I will serve him in this life and future ones. Now I am writing. Previously I did other services—I gave him my paycheck, gave lectures, managed things (although I didn't do that well), organized the *gurukula*. In the future I may be cooking or sweeping or grinding sandalwood paste, making garlands—any humble service. The important thing is to be earnest and to do menial service.

34

It has been raining this morning in Vṛndāvana. The table-top is soaked again. I tilt the table and the water rolls off. Then I wipe it as dry as possible and sit to write. We are still without electricity. No loudspeakers! I can hear tremendous choruses of birds—and nothing else. If a bell rings or someone chants, it is only with the power of their own voice. Amplification needs electricity. This is what Vṛndāvana was like hundreds of years ago. But I am here *now*, groggy after my early rising, and aware of my dullness after thirteen mechanically chanted rounds. I did *ask* at several points why this had to be so.

Then I fell asleep for a short while and saw the same old invitations from *māyā* mixed in with current affairs of *Back to Godhead* magazine. It may be that I cannot advance because of what I have done in this lifetime before I met Śrīla Prabhupāda.

"If we ignore Vṛndāvana, which is flooded with the nectar of Rādhā's lotus feet and filled with the bliss of love for Lord Hari's feet, then what are the other things we will talk about?" (*Vṛndāvana-mahimāmṛta, Śataka* 4.85).

Well said, good friend and great *sādhu*, Prabodhānanda Sarasvatī. Why talk of other things? Why ever forget Vṛndāvana? Even these rolling choruses of bird calls and chirping and peacock's "*kee-gaw*" are part of Vṛndāvana. And the trees dripping in the rain. Who can complain about dark morning monsoon clouds in Vṛndāvana? Not me. But the symptoms of inattentive *japa* mean I have a hard heart filled with unredeemed *aparādhas*. I say I live with it. Others are worse than I am, I say. I look for encouragement in that fact and find it. Then I shake that off and turn to the *sādhu:*

"Śrīmatī Rādhikā's forest is the perfect atonement of sins, the ultimate shelter from offenses to great souls, the crest jewel of all principles of religion, and the crest jewel of all goals of life" (*Vṛndāvana-mahimāmṛta, Śataka* 4.88).

Note: it is *Rādhikā's* forest, and that is what makes it so glorious. Just by living here . . . it doesn't mean you can misbehave here, but you can admit, "I am helpless to overcome my bad habits in prayer. I feel no love. Please, I don't like this condition."

I sat in the darkness of my room. There was a little light from a high, barred window, but that light was really more of a lighter shade of darkness. It was similar to my mental conception of a dungeon. From my mat on the floor, I chanted and heard the *japa* of my two devotee friends in the other part of the house.

Later, I paced on the rain-soaked roof in the Vṛndāvana quiet—tenth round, eleventh . . . where was my heart? Where was my feeling for Hare, Kṛṣṇa, and Rāma? I ask why this has to be so.

I can articulate better in writing, so here, on this page, on behalf of my *japa-sādhana*, I ask the Lord of Vṛndāvana to please help me. You make all arrangements in Vṛndāvana. I approach You through Your representatives, Vṛndā-devī (who awards desires), Bhakti-devī, and Yogamāyā. You have already given us so much mercy on this visit—this house to live in, permission to study and write, time to chant in peace. But if we cannot use it to love You, then what use is it? Please give me a clue as to how to find the essence.

"The fortunate bow down before a person who, always seeing the eternal and sweet spiritual forms of Vṛndāvana's grass, bushes, and other living entities, and bowing down before them with great devotion, resides here in Vṛndāvana" (*Vṛndāvana-mahimāmṛta, Śataka* 4.90).

Prabodhānanda Sarasvatī has *niṣṭhā* for Vṛndāvana. I cannot imitate him, although I worship his statements. I hold them up, place them on my head as sacred. He is right! He sees the true Vṛndāvana. I cannot follow him in his advice to always live here—live like a wandering mendicant, bow down everywhere, serve everyone, see even the thieves as saints—but he knows there are persons like me, still in *māyā*, but with a developing affection for Vṛndāvana. He offers us hope as we hear from him and build our own *niṣṭhā* upon his. He will not kick us away as hypocrites just because we are fools. But he will tell us plainly that we are foolish to abandon the dust of Vṛndāvana even for a moment.

35

Kṛṣṇa consciousness is such a nice thing that even when material troubles come, we can turn to Kṛṣṇa for solace. No one should be deprived of it. But out of our minute free will, we may deny our own Kṛṣṇa consciousness. We are all under the grip of the powerful material nature. No one is excused, just as a small child is not excused if he touches fire. Human life is for getting out of the grip of that powerful, punishing material nature.

Kṛṣṇa is our friend and He desires that we come back to Him eternally in bliss and knowledge. This is the outline of our delusion as well as the rescue offered by the Supreme Personality of Godhead. His help comes through His authorized agents, His pure devotees. I am taking shelter of His Divine Grace A.C. Bhaktivedanta Swami Prabhupāda, who is very dear to Kṛṣṇa on this earth. But how far will I be able to give up my material connections and desires in this one lifetime, and how completely will I be able to develop my dormant love of God? If I don't complete this mission in one life, I'll have to come back and be born again, with great risk, to complete my work in future lives. In any case, I am assured I won't fall back into less than human species. I won't lose whatever Kṛṣṇa consciousness I have gained.

Real liberation is to realize these facts and to attain the loving service attitude toward Kṛṣṇa and His devotees. Narottama dāsa Ṭhākura prays, *tādera caraṇa-sebi-bhakta-sane bās, janame janame hoy ei abhilāṣ*, let me be born life after life to lovingly serve the Vaiṣṇavas. Śrīla Prabhupāda teaches that the life of *bhakti* requires compassion for others—by preaching Kṛṣṇa consciousness to the fallen souls. This preaching work will gain us favor with the Lord, who will grant us His association.

36

It would be nice if a day would come when I would be reading and chanting and be qualified to tell people that I am experiencing a taste in hearing and chanting. Too often we speak of things as policy only. "We must preach. We must follow the rules and regulations. We must please our spiritual master." Dreary reminders as if by a government leader. We hear it without joy, without it touching our hearts, without dreaming of its potential.

A day could come when you would spit at the thought of sex. You would chant in connection with the six Gosvāmīs' mood. There would be no controversy or doubt, "Can we do this?" You would be "past" logic and argument.

37

What is the difference between theoretical knowledge and realization? Realization has to descend as a *śakti* on the practitioner. Lord Kṛṣṇa taught Brahmā everything in the *cātuḥ-śloki* of *Śrīmad-Bhāgavatam*, but is that *jñāna* or *vijñāna*? Vyāsa knew that same knowledge, but not until Nārada told him to meditate did the Lord reveal Himself and His energies to Vyāsa in his *samādhi*. Similarly, Rūpa Gosvāmī learned directly from Lord Caitanya, but only when the Lord empowered him did it become realization. Similarly, Sanātana Gosvāmī heard from Śrī Caitanya Mahāprabhu, yet Sanātana begged that the knowledge become realization. Sanātana said, "The conclusions that You have told me are the ocean of the ambrosia of truth. My mind is unable to approach even a drop of that ocean. If You want to make a lame man like me dance, kindly bestow Your transcendental blessings by keeping Your lotus feet on my head" (Cc., *Madhya* 23.121–2).

When you gain realization and attachment (*āsakti*), then you don't notice whether it's cold or not. You don't find satisfaction in long spells of tamasic sleep. You don't notice what clothes you are wearing. You always think of Kṛṣṇa and serve Him and weep.

It's like the difference between thinking about quenching your thirst and actually drinking water. We can therefore conclude we are thirsty and unsatiated. We only repeat what we have heard. But we have faith.

Can we attain realization by keeping company with those who have realization? Yes, to some extent. But we have to practice and one day, in some lifetime, attract Kṛṣṇa's mercy.

On this last day of Kārttika, I want to make this prayer: "O Goddess of the month of Kārttika, I praise You with flattering words and beg the following boon from You: May Kṛṣṇa, knowing me to be Yours, give me more mercy" (*Utkalikā-vallari*, by Śrīla Rūpa Gosvāmī, text 20).

38

The one saving quality in this age is faith in the guru. May we never doubt him even though others may do so. With that one quality of strong faith in the guru, it doesn't matter so much if we lack the other qualities of a Vaiṣṇava. The qualities will eventually come to us. But if we lack faith in the guru, then whatever we have gained will be ruined. This is the conclusion of all Vedic scriptures.

I have always been blessed with undoubting faith, as have many ISKCON devotees, in Śrīla Prabhupāda. I pray to sustain it. I may deepen, mature, reconsider, and that's not unfaithful. But I will never leave the lotus feet of Abhay Caraṇāravinda Bhaktivedanta Swami Śrīla Prabhupāda. As Govinda dāsa says, *bhajahū re mana śrī-nanda-nandana-abhaya-caraṇāravinda re*. Taking shelter of A.C. Bhaktivedanta Swami means taking shelter of the lotus feet of Kṛṣṇa. May he keep us there despite our foolishness. And may we teach this to others.

39

Travel on an empty stomach with empty pen cartridges. Chant Hare Kṛṣṇa in your emptiness, trying to fill the mind with the pure milk of mantra meditation. Empty the cup of dirty liquid, wash it out, and fill it with purity. That was Prabhupāda's advice. Through him comes the whole *paramparā*.

40

Ajāmila's good fortune began when he gave his last son the name Nārāyaṇa. By that "chanting," he was freed of all sinful reactions. Viśvanātha Cakravartī gives the example of a piece of rope which has been burnt. It retains the shape of a rope, but if you touch it, it crumbles to ashes. Similarly, the *nāmābhāsa* chanter may still appear to be a sinner, but the effects of his sins are gone (*api cet su-darācāro . . . kṣipraṁ bhavati dharm-ātmā . . .*). Ordinary persons may see him as a sinner, but devotees know the truth. The Viṣṇudūtas came to rescue Ajāmila because they saw he was freed from sin by his *nāmābhāsa*. The Yamadūtas, however, saw Ajāmila as a sinner.

Ajāmila couldn't gain love of God by *nāmābhāsa*, but he was freed from hell. After being saved by the Viṣṇudūtas, he went to Hardwar, chanted, and attained *bhāva*. That *bhāva* was not for Vraja. According to his qualification, Lord Viṣṇu's four-armed messengers came to him from Vaikuṇṭha. At a temple in Hardwar, Ajāmila attained *bhāva*, then *svarūpa-siddhi* (knowledge of his Vaikuṇṭha destination), then *vastu-siddhi* (his spiritual form). At that time, the spiritual airplane descended and he was taken to Vaikuṇṭha.

In our case (ISKCON devotees who are following strictly), we aren't sinning and neither do we want Vaikuṇṭha. We want Kṛṣṇa in Vṛndāvana. But we can't chant with attention, what to speak of *bhāva*. Can we learn something practical from the Ajāmila story?

One point is that initiation is a great responsibility. Before we joined ISKCON, we didn't know the difference between right and wrong. We were sinners like Ajāmila, like Jagāi and Mādhāi. Ajāmila didn't commit *aparādhas*. He didn't offend Vaiṣṇavas or commit sins on the strength of chanting Hare Kṛṣṇa. Sometimes when devotees hear this they say, "Ajāmila seems more fortunate than we. We commit *aparādhas*." But Ajāmila couldn't attain *kṛṣṇa-prema* by his *nāmābhāsa*. We can attain *kṛṣṇa-prema*, provided we work at overcoming the *aparādhas*. It is responsible work, and not easy.

41

We were discussing how some of us have been chanting for decades but have not attained the higher taste. Even to keep our attention fixed on the holy names is difficult, although attentiveness while reading seems possible. One of the devotees said that Lord Caitanya explained how to chant the Hare Kṛṣṇa mantra in order to attain *prema*. Where did He say it? We searched for a while through *Caitanya-caritāmṛta* and finally found it in the *Śikṣāṣṭakam* chapter of *Antya-līlā:*

ye-rūpe la-ile nāma prema upajaya
tāhāra lakṣaṇa śuna, svarūpa-rāma-rāya

"Śrī Caitanya Mahāprabhu continued, 'O Svarūpa Dāmodara Gosvāmī and Rāmānanda Rāya, hear from Me the symptoms of how one should chant the Hare Kṛṣṇa *mahā-mantra* to awaken very easily one's dormant love for Kṛṣṇa'" (Cc., *Antya* 20.20).

Then Śrī Caitanya Mahāprabhu gave the method for *prema*-producing *japa: tṛṇād api sunīcena* . . . "One who thinks himself lower than the grass, who is more tolerant than a tree, and who does not expect personal honor but is always prepared to give all respects to others, can very easily always chant the holy name of the Lord" (Cc., *Antya* 20.21).

This is our *siddha-praṇālī*, our perfect, eternal form. If I could go somewhere and attain it, if I could give something up or take something on to attain it—but you can't say that to attain it, I will renounce preaching and traveling and live in seclusion. Neither can you claim, "I will attain it by taking on temple management. I will attain it by virtue of my *guru-sevā*." Nothing overnight. It's not such an easy solution for me. But somehow, I have to try in a humble way, staying uninvolved in *kṣatriya* decision-making, and staying in the association of devotees and those innocent people who want to hear about Kṛṣṇa. That will be my balanced program. Balance is the quickest and easiest way to bring about *tṛṇād api sunīcena*; it is the easiest way to find a prayerful situation to petition *harer nāma* and to please guru and Kṛṣṇa.

But still, our sincerity falls short. Our humility seems nonexistent sometimes. We don't know *prema-japa*. How to become humble? Hanumān is humble. He destroyed Laṅkā to please the Lord. He was always chanting Rāma, Rāma, and wherever anyone is sincerely chanting Rāma's name, Hanumān goes there in a leap. He was humble toward Vibhīṣaṇa and all the devotees. Humility doesn't mean lazy or reluctant to serve Vibhīṣaṇa.

Vṛndāvana dāsa Ṭhākura states that if anyone minimizes Lord Nityānanda, he kicks that person on the head. This is also a kind of humility. Baladeva Vidyābhūṣaṇa humbly served all the Vaiṣṇavas and Lord Govinda by defeating the Māyāvādīs' arguments. Anyone who hears insults to Vaiṣṇavas and doesn't reply in defense is an *aparādhi*. So humility means many things and is always a challenge.

The humble devotee never thinks himself to be advanced. He honors everyone, seeing them as the resting place of Kṛṣṇa. The pure chanter of the holy names is also tolerant.

"If one chants the holy name of Lord Kṛṣṇa in this manner, he will certainly awaken his dormant love for Kṛṣṇa's lotus feet" (Cc., *Antya* 20.26).

"Gurudeva! By a drop of your mercy make this servant of yours more humble than a blade of grass. Give me strength to bear all trials and troubles, and free me from all desires for personal honor. Let me be as you are, without desires or aspirations" (*Śaraṇāgati*, 7.11.1).

42

There is nothing nicer than Kṛṣṇa consciousness. Yes, I believe it. Yet I am afraid of so many things. There is fear, then envy. When you have envy, then *anarthas* and *aparādhas* appear. *Aparādhas* are worse. It is impossible to stop being angry, but it can be used in devotional service. But Vaiṣṇava *aparādha* has to be stopped. It is never harmless.

My eyes see someone as funny-looking, as proud and foolish, as stupid, or for no reason at all, I may tend to dislike a devotee. What to speak of nondevotees. Where is the vision that everyone is the residence of Supersoul?

It's my faultfinding nature, but it's not me. I will think instead of Kṛṣṇa consciousness and my desires to serve Śrīla Prabhupāda.

43

I can write to keep warm or to keep my mind off the cold. Similarly, in *japa* time, I can chant quickly and alertly like a man outdoors intent on warming himself by a fire. He *needs* the fire to keep warm; I need Hare Kṛṣṇa Hare Kṛṣṇa, Kṛṣṇa Kṛṣṇa Hare Hare. That is the benefit of the cold—it drives me to take shelter.

I am like a piece of kindling, a straw or small stick that has been drying out for years. It *can* catch fire if I can just hold it close to the fire for long enough. I want to draw close to that mystical source of my deliverance. I want to be aware of how obvious my need is and how easy it is to fulfill it.

Walking back and forth to keep awake, to keep my circulation flowing easily, but I don't go too far. Who would be so crazy as to light a fire on a cold night and then walk away from it? Who would be so foolish as to make a fire and then douse it with water, just when it's doing its best?

This fire bodes no danger. If it were to spread and blaze out of control, what benefit there would be for the world! I chant in the darkness waiting for dawn, waiting for the sun of *śuddha-nāma* to fully rise. When the sun of devotion begins to blaze, then I will see Kṛṣṇa's pastimes, qualities, and forms, and I will sing madly, not caring for what others think. When will that day be mine?

44

I am chanting on a cliff in Ireland, trying to increase my rounds. I don't expect miracles, but I look at the sea and sometimes pray, "Please reveal to me the nature of the holy name." The prayer-application is made and I can also listen closely to any answer Kṛṣṇa gives in my heart. We need to discern if the answer comes from our own intelligence or from the Lord and His pure devotees.

I have also written a note to myself, "Face fears." Yes, the barren seaside is a good place for this. I advise myself, don't panic and then want to break out of here, don't try to prove that you are busy and active in ISKCON; relax and concentrate on the work (and peace) you came here to seek and find.

That means increased *japa* and what can be derived from that. Hear from Śrīla Prabhupāda.

So how are you doing? *Aihiṣṭaṁ yat tat punar-janma-jayāya?* How are you doing in your attempt to overcome inattentive chanting by a quota increase? Is it working? Yes, to some degree. Is it something you'll be able to carry over into your life when you do only sixteen rounds? Could you make a permanent increase?

I don't think I can make a permanent increase in quota, not as long as I continue to chant so slowly, approximately eight minutes per round. I need time to read and write. So sixteen "good" rounds (alert and distinctly uttered, without indulging in distractions) is my present goal.

Sometimes when I face my altar, the pictures "light up" for me. It happens when my mind is receptive. "Everything is there," Śrīla Prabhupāda says. Kṛṣṇa and Rādhā are in Their pictures and in Their names. When we become more receptive, then we realize what has always been true and has always been available for sincere devotees.

Chanting and chanting, nothing seems to happen. But that perception is a lack of faith. It's happening. Try to see it more. Enter the miracle of *kṛṣṇa-nāma*. "Just hear, just hear," my master says. Do you know what that means?

45

I chanted in the hallway, sitting on a high stool, timing the rounds. There's no point in complaining, "I don't think of Krsna's pastimes." I work on staying awake and trying to hear, trying to pray in the most basic way, *Please let me chant with devotion to harer nāma.* It's not an interjected word formula, but a desire manifest in concentrated thought—a call for help.

You have to do it again each time you pick up your beads. In a similar way, I bow down and recite the Pañca-tattva mantra before each round. I have to offer my free will each time I do it. The mind will always say, "You don't have to actually get down on the floor. Just say the mantra. That's just as good." Then I remember Raghunātha dāsa Gosvāmī who bowed down in "scheduled measurement." He became so weak that once he bowed down, he couldn't get up again, but still he bowed down.

When I offer obeisances, I feel something genuine. And then to actually ask the Supreme Persons, Lord Caitanya and Lord Nityānanda and Advaita Ācārya for help in chanting—these are real moments in *japa.*

This hallway is stark. It has an old, cheap carpet in it—a brownish-orange color that somehow makes me think of the word "vomit" to describe it. There are no pictures or furniture. Just our shoes at the front entrance and sunshine through the opaque, colored glass of the front door. It's cold, but it's a good place to chant. It's less charming than outdoors. I am left to face the void in my heart and chant rounds one after another. After lunch, I'll go there again and walk and sit on the high stool and bow down and exert my energy in prayer.

46

Śrīla Prabhupāda said if we don't read, how will we preach? Letter-writing and seminars depend on information and inspiration that is found only in Prabhupāda's books. Lecturing certainly depends on this. I have read Prabhupāda's books enough in this life so that I could get by without reading more, but I know it's not sufficient. It would be cheating to think like that. I would be cheating myself out of new realizations and out of Prabhupāda's constant association. We are practicing Kṛṣṇa consciousness today.

I also listen to Prabhupāda's lecture tapes every day. I want to always continue that. It's part of my life's rhythm. His words enter my bloodstream and circulate throughout my body. They find their way into my consciousness. His words will save me at the time of death.

47

The *śāstras* are conscious. They can confer blessings on us. I especially look for the blessing of becoming attached to them. There are prayers which express this desire. I like the Pracetās' prayer. The Pracetās say that they accept they will be reborn in some material species of life due to their material contamination, but, "we pray that we may associate with those who are engaged in discussing Your pastimes. We pray for this benediction life after life, in different bodily forms and on different planets" (*Bhāg.* 4.30.33).

In his purport, Śrīla Prabhupāda says this aspiration is the goal of life. It is more important than liberation from the cycle of birth and death. "The most important thing for a devotee is getting a chance to hear about the pastimes and glories of the Lord. . . . For a devotee, everything is the spiritual world, for as long as he can hear about the pastimes of the Lord, or wherever he can chant, the Lord is personally present."

Desire to be with devotees who are chanting and hearing. Desire to attain a taste for this (*ruci* and *āsakti*). Ask yourself how your activities contribute to this. Is your life leading to this goal? Don't get caught up in external duties that divert you from this.

48

Sometimes devotees ask, "What does it mean that the relationship with the spiritual master is eternal?" Our existential reply is, "You *make* it eternal. See to it by your prayers and actions that you go to him." That is *gāyatrī*.

Then we pray to Lord Caitanya, "Please nourish our *bhāva*." Someday I may go to Ekacakra and Māyāpur to pray, and even now I pray to the Lord of *audārya:* "Please lead me to spontaneous love, starting with the removal of the many dirty things in my heart. Please, Master, I am Your eternal servant."

49

I read in *Mādhurya-kādambinī* that in the advanced stages of devotional service, one is not calm, is often sleepless, is seen as crazy. I pray for strength to be willing to be upset and anxious for Kṛṣṇa and His service. Śrīla Prabhupāda displayed this by his total, empowered dedication to spreading and maintaining the International Society for Krishna Consciousness. I am his servant and I should also dedicate myself to the Kṛṣṇa consciousness movement. Exactly how I'll do this will unfold. Try to qualify myself and help others to become qualified; that is the order of my spiritual master.

How can we dare to pray for the advanced state when we are on a stage beset by unsteadiness and *anarthas*? Because we feel the need of inspiration—the goal of our regulative practices. Hearing Kṛṣṇa's pastimes, we aspire to become fixed in the goal of Kṛṣṇa consciousness, even though it may take hundreds of births. Kṛṣṇa consciousness is rare. We have to culture it by hearing and chanting in a regulative way.

"These pastimes were wonderful for everyone, even for those proud of their opulence, including the Lord Himself in His form as the Lord of Vaikuṇṭha. Thus His [Śrī Kṛṣṇa's] transcendental body is the ornament of all ornaments" (*Bhāg.* 3.2.12).

Become interested in Kṛṣṇa, and yourself as the servant of His best servants. Desire this—the positive transferal of your identity and energies into spiritual emotion.

"In the states of wakefulness, sleep, and deep sleep, his intelligence becomes firmly fixed . . . The self-conceit, (*ahaṅta*, 'I') of the *sādhaka* seems as if it enters into a *siddha-deha* (spiritual identity) suitable to his desire to serve the Lord and his material body remains almost as if he has left it. His sense of possessiveness (*mamatā*, 'mine') becomes like a bee to relish the nectar of the Lord's lotus feet" (*Mādhurya-kādambinī*, Shower 7).

We are daydreaming that we backward dwarfs can jump and touch the moon, but our aspirations should exceed our grasp, "or what's a heaven for?" We want to hear of a *bhakta's* ultimate states. We want something to ignite the fire of our present condition. If such a great and wonderful stage is our goal, then why are we wasting time in petty pursuits? We must strive to give them up and make realistic advancement from our present condition.

This is the good effect of hearing about what happens in *ruci*, *āsakti*, *bhāva*, and *prema*. They are not easily attained, but to be entranced by hearing of these states, even now, is not harmful. Better this than to be intrigued by the newspaper reports.

Don't forget the compassionate work of helping those who have no idea of Kṛṣṇa consciousness. Devotees who absorb themselves in preaching, who feel satisfied serving the Lord's mission on earth, are fortunate. "For one who explains this supreme secret to the devotees, pure devotional service is guaranteed, and at the end he will come back to Me. There is no servant in this world more dear to Me than he, nor will there ever be one more dear" (Bg. 18.68–69).

50

This morning I read this in Prabhupāda's purport to *Bhagavad-gītā* 18.48:

> Similarly, one should not give up his natural occupation because there are some disturbing elements [smoke]. Rather, one should be determined to serve the Supreme Lord by his occupational duty in Kṛṣṇa consciousness. That is the perfectional point.

There is so much smoke in my writing service—the professionalism I seek, the groping, the criticism I get for writing at all, the passion for creation and publishing and writing insights, the desire for fame and especially acceptance, the admitting that I don't know what I'm doing, the doubts, the pages where I can't write like a liberated soul . . .

"When a particular type of occupation is performed for the satisfaction of the Supreme Lord, all the defects in the particular occupation are purified. When the results of work are purified, when connected to devotional service, one becomes perfect in seeing the self within and that is self-realization."

Prabhupāda's advice sings. He understands what we all go through. He is compassionate. He gives authoritative evidence. We may reject his help, saying, "That's for conditioned souls attached to karma, not for pure *bhaktas*." But doesn't it apply to us? Should we refuse Prabhupāda's help in this way? Can we renounce our imperfect work and go to the level of pure, constant *śravaṇaṁ-kīrtanaṁ-smaraṇam*?

That's not possible, at least right now. Then take heart from Prabhupāda's purport. Don't give up work which is born of your nature, which you actually love, which you are stuck with. It's your service instrument, your livelihood. Do it for Kṛṣṇa. Yes, it's imperfect, but this direction is coming from Prabhupāda and it is meant for us.

51

Śrīla Prabhupāda begins Chapter 19 of *The Nectar of Devotion*, on *prema*, like this:

> When one's desire to love Kṛṣṇa in one's particular relationship becomes intensified, this is known as pure love of Godhead. In the beginning a devotee is engaged in the regulative principles of devotional service by the order of his spiritual master.
>
> —*NOD*, p. 143

Then he gets purified and develops attachment and taste, and in time, this becomes love (*prema*). Later, Śrīla Prabhupāda quotes *Śrīmad-Bhāgavatam:* ". . . if after undergoing all types of austerities, penances and mystic *yoga* practices one does not develop such love for Hari, then all his performances are to be considered a useless waste of time" (p. 145). He adds, "If a devotee is continuously in love with Lord Kṛṣṇa and his mind is always fixed upon Him, that devotional attitude will prove to be the only means of attracting the attention of the Lord."

And so my friends, that's it. It's not enough to just work. It is not enough to be peppy and zesty while we do our favorite things. It is not enough. We have to specifically think of Kṛṣṇa as the person we love. Such a simple instruction, but we miss the point. We even think we are "authorized" in not loving Kṛṣṇa. That's not a fact.

I am mostly telling this to myself. If the books are too scholarly-looking sometimes, then go to the beads. Or write, *but to the point.* "Oh, I could not attain the master of Mathurā! What shall I do now as I die in this state? O Dīna-dayārdra, please have mercy on me." And that prayer I said so much that it entered my bloodstream, "My dear Lord Kṛṣṇa, please have mercy on this sinner." I know better what it means now. This sinner has neglected You even though he has given up sinful acts. So he remains the worst sinner. Please have mercy on him and give him a drop of *kṛṣṇa-bhakti* so he may love You.

52

In my heart is a sick feeling because I don't believe. I am a believer, but some part of me (small only, I hope) does not believe. Or even if part of me no longer actively disbelieves, yet it is not receptive. I read about the Lord and I remain dead. It's like when our van engine wouldn't turn over because of a loose electrical connection. The expensive apparatus is present and apparently in good working order, but something doesn't connect, so it remains dead. A mechanic can fix it.

What is that "dead"? Does it matter whether I know exactly what's wrong?

Oh, it matters. Don't be wholesale depressed. If you can know what's wrong, we can fix it and continue on our journey. Even when we are operating well, however, we will have to accept some limits. The van is slow on the uphill.

I am reading the Third Canto about the kingdom of God. Jaya and Vijaya and the Kumāras are fighting. The Supreme Lord appeared and was pleased with both of them. So why am I displeased? Because I want to see the Lord in His Vṛndāvana feature. Not only that, but I want to see Kṛṣṇa in His Vraja feature even when I read about His pastimes outside Vṛndāvana. I want to be nourished by Prabhupāda's purports. It is he who is providing the current of pure *bhakti* that can bring me back to life.

Actually, I like to hear how the Kumāras smelled the aroma of *tulasī* leaves on the Lord's lotus feet and how that aroma diverted their minds from impersonalism to Vaiṣṇavism. I just admitted that I felt dead, but I want to come alive. If only I could smell those *tulasī* leaves, it could bring me back to life.

"When the breeze carrying the aroma of *tulasī* leaves from the toes of the lotus feet of the Personality of Godhead entered the nostrils of those sages, they experienced a change both in body and mind, even though they were attached to the impersonal Brahman understanding" (*Bhāg.* 3.15.43).

Śrīla Prabhupāda says the impersonalist is "defeated when he sees the beautiful transcendental features of the Lord." I need to see them too in my mind's eye. My mind can be captured by hearing from Śrīla Prabhupāda.

Prabhupāda

1

I want spiritual life. I just read Śrīla Prabhupāda saying that the young people in his first New York City storefront were not offenders to Kṛṣṇa's name and form. They were not from Benares. Lord Caitanya went to Benares with His heavy load of *kṛṣṇa-prema* to sell, but the Māyāvādīs didn't want it. Śrīla Prabhupāda got a better reception when he brought the Hare Kṛṣṇa mantra to New York City. "...the Lord's holy name is so attractive that simply by coming to our storefront in New York, fortunate young people became Kṛṣṇa conscious. . . . The youths who joined this movement were not very advanced as far as purity was concerned, nor were they very well-educated in Vedic knowledge, but because they were not offenders, they could accept the importance of the Hare Kṛṣṇa movement. . . . We therefore conclude that the so-called *mlecchas* and *yavanas* of the Western countries are more purified than offensive Māyāvādīs" (Cc., *Madhya* 17.145, purport).

Reading this, I thought of Śrīla Prabhupāda leading his Western devotees. Wherever he went, we gathered and followed him. He accepted devotees from all races, including Indians. He didn't enter the Jagannātha temple in Purī because his disciples weren't allowed to enter. He almost always spoke English, the language of his worldwide movement.

Is this just a pleasant, sentimental memory? No, it is the true story of Prabhupāda's compassion. He did what no one else dared to do or could do. He went alone with the blessings of his spiritual master. I never want to tire from telling these stories and describing my own participation in those early days.

2

In his room in Māyāpur: Śrīla Prabhupāda, you could always tell me what to do, and I was satisfied to leave this room and carry it out. I am still that way. I felt so solidly assured when you gave me orders.

Here is your old Grundig dictaphone. You played it for me one morning and I heard your purport here in this room.

You are sitting here now. You wear no *kurtā*, just your *sannyāsa* top piece. You are the same Śrīla Prabhupāda we surrendered to so long ago. Now you are in your India in 1974, and we are trying to catch up to you, trying not to be overwhelmed by peer pressure.

Kṛṣṇa book is open before you on your desk. When I entered the room tonight, a boy was pacing back and forth loudly chanting *japa*, oblivious to your presence. True, he had found a good, secluded place for chanting, but *this is your room.* I told him, "Be quiet here and feel Śrīla Prabhupāda's presence."

Here is the kerosene lamp we used to light when the electric lights went out. Jananivāsa will soon be up with frankincense burning in a clay pot. He comes every evening.

Śrīla Prabhupāda, I used to come here many times, relatively speaking, and find you here. I squeezed in with my Godbrothers to hear you speak. You told me to take charge of *BTG* magazine, to take a GBC zone in one part of America, to distribute your books to the colleges. Here I witnessed the tense scene between Tamal Krishna Goswami's bus party and the American *gṛhasthas*. This is your room, and you stayed here during the international festivals for four consecutive years.

But things have changed. Now a boy can walk back and forth in front of your *mūrti*, chanting loudly, and you don't tell him to stop.

You are with us, Śrīla Prabhupāda. I come and sit silently and put my question to you—I don't even form it into words. I am here for you.

A bell and voices are approaching. It is time to do the *pūjā*, "*Oṁ śānti śānti*." I have heard it is to drive out ghosts. Maybe mine will get chased out too and you will see me more clearly through the frankincense smoke.

Was I actually your personal servant in 1974? Was I so fortunate? I stood at the rail outside and Nanda-kumāra advised me to never leave your service.

I didn't even notice, but you are facing the bas relief wooden sculpture of Rādhā and Kṛṣṇa. They are together in the wood. She holds His flute, His arm around Her. A fresh garland of *jui* flowers is carved around Them.

3

I was thinking about separation from Prabhupāda. Unfortunately, we tend not to think so much about it because we are so busy doing our duties. But we *should* think about it; we should do whatever increases our feelings of separation.

But who can feel real separation? Only those who have a sense of strong intimacy and gratefulness to Prabhupāda. If I think of Śrīla Prabhupāda only in fear or only in reverence, the mood of separation will remain beyond my reach. But when I recall his pastimes and his mercy in an intimate way, as my master and friend, then I can cry. If we can cry for Prabhupāda, then we can cry for Kṛṣṇa. Crying is our *dharma*.

4

I heard Śrīla Prabhupāda on a "knockout" morning walk. He blasted the Christians and the scientists. For any of us to talk exactly as he does would be outrageous, but he can do it.

He was saying how they waste semen, which is actually blood. Forty drops of blood in a drop of semen. "Do you like to do something by which you lose so much blood? Can you call that pleasure?"

"No."

Prabhupāda: "And yet you are doing it every night!"

Devotee: "I'm doing it, Prabhupāda?"

Prabhupāda: "Not you . . . "

Just to be near him, we were liable to get thrown into the category of fools and rascals. Oh, how he blasted them for not following the commandment, "Thou shalt not kill." He said he met so many priests and none of them could answer that question, "Why do you kill against Christ's order?" He said that that question, and another, "If you agree God is unlimited, why do you say He has only one son?"—he asked and they could not answer. I used to cringe sometimes hearing these tapes, but I don't anymore.

"As for the scientists, they are not even gentlemen. They say they will do it—create life from matter—in the future . . . "

5

Prabhupāda preached up to his last breath. He urged us to do that also. When he heard that Harikeśa Swami was printing books in thirteen languages, he said, "You are the favorite grandson of Bhaktisiddhānta Sarasvatī Ṭhākura." Other famous statements encouraging preachers: "Go to Bangladesh with the courage of a British soldier and the heart of a Bengali mother." "Your love for me will be tested by how you work together after I am gone." Remember what he said and try to think what it means to you; where it fits into your life.

Recently a devotee asked a *sannyāsī* something like: "How should we consider our own limitations when we attempt to follow the guru's order?" The *sannyāsī* replied, "By the grace of the guru and his order, a lame man can cross mountains and a dumb man can become a great orator." When he was pressed further, the *sannyāsī* was unrelenting: "Change your life to fit the guru's order. Impossible is a word in a fool's dictionary."

I probably would have answered it with more consideration for the earnest yet limited disciple—"Do whatever you can with devotion." But the stern aspect of spiritual life is a reality. I say, "Let us hear what Śrīla Prabhupāda said and think how we can absorb it and surrender to it. Experience has taught us a lot about fallibility and how people make vows but later become weak and unable to follow them. Experience is not everything, however. The order coming down in *paramparā* is in some ways unchangeable. Surrender is surrender: doing that which is favorable to Kṛṣṇa consciousness and avoiding that which is unfavorable."

Be stern, don't compromise, don't give in to your weak side. Don't pamper your body. Don't indulge in whimsy. Stick to the diet Prabhupāda has given, the program he gave.

Do we believe it? How far are we willing to go before we say, "That's all I can take. Let me serve Prabhupāda in an easier way"?

6

Bombay ISKCON is preparing a 1993 calendar and asked me to "write in two or three lines a summary of Prabhupāda's achievements." I could only boil a statement down to four sentences as follows:

"His Divine Grace A.C. Bhaktivedanta Swami Prabhupāda did what no incarnation of Lord Viṣṇu had ever done—spread *sanātana-dharma*, Kṛṣṇa consciousness, all over the modern world. Lord Kṛṣṇa Himself desired the spreading of the Hare Kṛṣṇa mantra and so did Lord Caitanya (who is Kṛṣṇa in the form of His pure devotee). They desired it, because unless people receive *bhakti* unto God, there cannot be peace or happiness in this life or in future lives. That our Śrīla Prabhupāda was alone chosen to go to America, to Europe, then back to India, to Russia, Africa and all over the world—and that he established an international society whose followers continue to practice Kṛṣṇa consciousness seriously—this is the greatest miracle and it is proof that Prabhupāda was empowered by Lord Kṛṣṇa."

Once Śrīla Prabhupāda was asked for information for a short biography. He said a summary of his life should state that he transplanted Vedic culture from East to West. He said, "Just as it is very difficult and requires expertise in transplanting a *tulasī* plant from India to America, so the birth and growth of Kṛṣṇa consciousness required such care."

We may say this is the external achievement of his life. And it is true that the spiritual master has two lives, that of a *sādhaka* and that of a *siddha*. In his *sādhaka* form, he preaches, and that may be considered to exist within Caitanya-*līlā*. (ISKCON is a branch of the Caitanya tree.) In the *siddha* form, the pure devotee spiritual master remembers his eternal identity and eventually joins Kṛṣṇa in Vraja.

Except for occasional glimpses, Śrīla Prabhupāda didn't reveal to us his *siddha* identity. But his role as preacher in this world was so extraordinary that learned persons conclude he was a *śaktyāveśa-avatāra*. If we apply ourselves to serve Śrīla Prabhupāda in his mission to spread and maintain some of its many fields of work—temple life, congregational preaching, book distribution, devotee education, *gurukula*, or any of the other activities that are part of this mission, that is the way to qualify ourselves for further understanding of Śrīla Prabhupāda's identity. That in turn will reveal to us who we are in our own spiritual identities.

The development of our own Kṛṣṇa consciousness is an important service to Śrīla Prabhupāda. That begins with *śravaṇaṁ-kīrtanaṁ viṣṇoḥ-smaraṇam*. Chant Hare Kṛṣṇa, read Śrīla Prabhupāda's books, chant with others—and always remember Kṛṣṇa and devotional service. That will please Śrīla Prabhupāda. Pleasing Śrīla Prabhupāda is the goal of our lives.

7

Yesterday I received two important honors in Vṛndāvana. I was asked to perform the *ārati* to Śrīla Prabhupāda in his Samādhi Mandir at 4:10 A.M., and I was asked to perform the *ārati* at 7:20 P.M. (the time when Śrīla Prabhupāda left this world on November 14, 1977) before his flower-covered bed. Both times there were many devotees gathered, including GBCs and *sannyāsīs*. I was chosen because of seniority—old age—in ISKCON. I'm grateful for this honor and I thoroughly enjoyed performing both *āratis*. I prayed and tried to praise Śrīla Prabhupāda. In the evening, I buried my face in the flowers at the foot of his bed in the spot where his own feet used to rest—and I prayed that all of his followers could come together and serve him in love and cooperation. These are rare moments worth waiting all year for, worth coming to Vṛndāvana for. I wish to be here as long as I live.

When I thanked the *pūjārī* in the Samādhi Mandir, he said I can do this *ārati* every year. He said (in his heavy Dutch accent), "You have written *Vandanam*, so please pray that I may be asked to continue as the *pūjārī* in Prabhupāda's Samādhi."

It's a deal—I'll pray for him and he'll invite me every year on Śrīla Prabhupāda's disappearance day to wave the incense, flame, conch, and handkerchief before His Divine Grace. May Prabhupāda dwell in the innermost core of our hearts as our Gurudeva. May we carry his orders on our head and try our best to execute them. May we know what he wants. May we be satisfied in full communication with him. May Kṛṣṇa be pleased with us.

8

When I think of Śrīla Prabhupāda's disappearance day, two images come to mind: the bell at Krishna-Balaram Mandir, and the curb on Second Avenue.

The temple bell may have different meanings to different devotees. Dhanañjaya Prabhu explained the extraordinary meaning it has for him. He says the heaviest time in his life was when he was temple president here under Śrīla Prabhupāda's direction. Prabhupāda tested him to see if he could follow the spiritual master by putting up the temple bell properly. When Dhanañjaya's efforts failed and the rope broke, Śrīla Prabhupāda said to him, "No brain. Buffalo stool."

For casual visitors, the bell is just a quaint way of keeping time, or possibly an annoyance when it interrupts conversations. For others, it evokes a religious feeling. Some people may not notice the bell at all—it is just one of the many chaotic sights and sounds that form a background to coping with life in India.

For me, the bell means Śrīla Prabhupāda is gone. I was often here in Prabhupāda's last year when he would lie quietly in his bed. We would sit around him holding a soft *kīrtana* with tiny *karatālas*. Through the long afternoon, waiting with Śrīla Prabhupāda, I would hear that bell. When I hear the bell now I think, "He is gone. He is gone. He will never return. We are left without him."

I know the Vaiṣṇava philosophy teaches that we are never without the spiritual master. But there is still the realm of personal feelings. It is not *māyā* to feel the loss when the great soul leaves us. Raghunātha dāsa Gosvāmī grieved bitterly when Lord Caitanya left, and again when Svarūpa Dāmodara left, and again when Rūpa Gosvāmī left. I know that by my mentioning it, my association of the bell with Prabhupāda's departure will not be resolved. It is something that I live with.

The bell also reminds me of John Donne's poem, "Oh, do not ask for whom the bells toll—they toll for thee." As Śrīla Prabhupāda left, I will also leave. I hope I will have time to be here in Vṛndāvana before I leave my body, to hear that bell and then to join Śrīla Prabhupāda.

The other image I have is the curb on Second Avenue. I was sitting on it with my feet in the gutter, looking around one Sunday morning after Śrīla Prabhupāda's lecture. I was wondering what I should do that day. I wasn't initiated and didn't feel the obligation to only serve Prabhupāda. While I was deciding—and my option probably included smoking marijuana—Śrīla Prabhupāda had a boy come out and get me. He had seen me sitting there. I went inside the storefront and Śrīla Prabhupāda asked me, "Do you have to go to work today?"

"No," I said.

"We have a Sunday feast in my apartment. Please come."

Why did Prabhupāda call me? I have been reflecting on this lately. Why did he care to have me and the others as guests at his Sunday feast? He was so compassionately carrying out the order of his spiritual master to save people like me.

9

I'm reading my mail again, dealing with the ads. *U.S. News & World Report* wants to know if I want two free new books. *Christian Science World Monitor* just gave me a free booklet. *Amnesty International* wants to know if I care. Many people want my money, even more people want my time. They all want to know if I am getting the point. We are not worrying about nuclear war now, but something worse—chemical, biological, fuel, and water warfare, and some new methods no one is mentioning. We need a new awareness, a new peace movement. Save the gorillas, those gentle giants. Save yourself.

This field in Vṛndāvana hasn't changed at all in two weeks. That's peaceful. And Prabhupāda has saved me; that hasn't changed either. He brought thousands of us forward to the stage of giving up our sins, our connections with this war-torn world, and he instilled in us the desire to chant the holy name. Where are the mentions of Prabhupāda?

10

I just read a verse where Kṛṣṇadāsa Kavirāja Gosvāmī says Lord Caitanya "instructed Śrīla Rūpa Gosvāmī and empowered him in the philosophy of devotional service" (Cc., *Madhya* 19.114). In his purport, Śrīla Prabhupāda refers to the verse *kṛṣṇa-śakti vinā nahe tāra pravartana* (Cc., *Antya* 7.11). He says that "a devotee who receives this power from the Lord must be considered very fortunate." Śrīla Prabhupāda then says, "The Kṛṣṇa consciousness movement is spreading to enlighten people about their real position.

". . . The Lord also empowers a special devotee to teach people their constitutional position."

It appears that Śrīla Prabhupāda is indirectly referring to himself as the empowered leader of the Kṛṣṇa consciousness movement. There are other purports like this. I raised the question in my seminar and book, *Prabhupāda Appreciation*, why Śrīla Prabhupāda preaches like this. Ordinarily, if a person describes himself as special and empowered, he leaves himself open to charges of pride. I explained that Śrīla Prabhupāda was not proud or filled with false ego. He often demonstrated his humility. For example, while beginning the Eighth Canto of *Śrīmad-Bhāgavatam* he writes, "I am neither a great scholar nor a great devotee; I am simply a humble servant of my spiritual master, and to the best of my ability I am trying to please him by publishing these books, with the cooperation of my disciples in America." In another place Śrīla Prabhupāda states, "The Kṛṣṇa consciousness movement is spreading now all over the world, and sometimes I think that even though I am crippled in many ways, if one of my disciples becomes as strong as Dhruva Mahārāja, then he will be able to carry me with him to Vaikuṇṭhaloka" (*Bhāg.* 4.12.33, purport).

For every statement Śrīla Prabhupāda makes where he alludes to himself as empowered, he also makes disclaimers. Śrīla Prabhupāda saw a need to assert his position in order to protect his followers. People and parties in India challenged Śrīla Prabhupāda and the Hare Kṛṣṇa movement in many ways. Some said foreigners couldn't become *brāhmaṇas* and *sannyāsīs* and that Śrīla Prabhupāda was "ruining the Hindu religion" by awarding initiation to Westerners. Śrīla Prabhupāda defeated those arguments by referring to *śāstra*. Śrīla Bhaktisiddhānta Sarasvatī also defended himself from this charge and Śrīla Prabhupāda was confident of his position. Defending the movement also required defending its leader. People continue to criticize Śrīla Prabhupāda and his movement, and we need the weapons of *śāstra* and logic to defend ourselves. Śrīla Prabhupāda therefore asserted himself as the protective father of his disciples.

In *Caitanya-caritāmṛta*, Kṛṣṇadāsa Kavirāja refers to people "who are not fit to relish this literature, who are envious like hogs and pigs . . ." Śrīla Prabhupāda comments that the Kṛṣṇa consciousness movement is being appreciated around the world but "in India, there are some people who say they belong to this cult but are very envious of the *ācārya*." Śrīla Prabhupāda says they try to "suppress our activities in many ways." He faced the opposition and compared them to envious hogs and pigs. "It appears that even such a great personality as Kṛṣṇadāsa Kavirāja Gosvāmī met with some envious obstacles; what, then, to speak of us, who are only insignificant creatures in this universe" (Note after Cc., *Madhya-līlā*).

The opposition said our spiritual master shouldn't have taken the name Prabhupāda. They didn't help him find land in Māyāpur, but worked against him. They distributed pamphlets against ISKCON in Madras. They made minimizing remarks about Śrīla Prabhupāda to his own disciples, saying he was just a businessman and that's why he was successful in the West. Some said Śrīla Prabhupāda didn't know *mādhurya-rasa*, that if his disciples wanted to understand it, they would have to find a guru outside of ISKCON. It was more important that Śrīla Prabhupāda defeat all those misconceptions rather than remain silent in the name of humility.

A *mahā-bhāgavata* sees no distinction between friends and enemies, but in order to preach, the *mahā-bhāgavata* accepts the vision of a *madhyama-bhakta*. A preacher must distinguish between devotees and demons, and he must instruct his followers in this understanding. Śrīla Prabhupāda certainly had to assert this knowledge. His movement was attacked in so many ways. Even his son tried to usurp the movement, claiming that his father was an ordinary man and therefore his son should inherit ISKCON, the family business.

In so many ways, his followers would have to face these challenges. Śrīla Prabhupāda gave us the ammunition to dispel the doubts and asserted that he was empowered by Lord Caitanya to spread the Kṛṣṇa consciousness movement. The Hare Kṛṣṇa movement is authorized; its founder-*ācārya* is authorized.

These are some of the reasons why he may have alluded to himself when discussing how envious people criticize a special, empowered devotee. It was a source of pain to Śrīla Prabhupāda, but he resisted these envious criticisms and fought back against them on behalf of the worldwide movement. Śrīla Prabhupāda was ultimately defending Lord Kṛṣṇa and the spread of His mission. He was not trying to make himself look good in his purports. At the end of his life, Śrīla Prabhupāda also apologized to his Godbrothers for any offenses or criticisms he made while preaching.

As I read this purport this morning, I thought about the symptoms of empowerment. By examining those symptoms, we can see that Śrīla Prabhupāda is certainly empowered. He brought Kṛṣṇa consciousness out of India single-handedly and transplanted it all over the world. I want to be a worthy, grateful son and assert the empowered position of my spiritual master.

11

Prabhupāda, as he appeared in this world, saved me. Kṛṣṇa sent Prabhupāda in such a perfect form, a form that could attract us. He was an ancient sage. He looked exactly like our idealized conception of guru with his golden complexion, his Indian demeanor, and his simple, ascetic robes. The *tilaka* markings were mystical to us. They spoke to us of esoteric secrets. We had to learn a new vocabulary just to understand him—*bhakti*, the real meaning of yoga, Kṛṣṇa, service, *saṅkīrtana*. He opened for us a world of self-realized souls and incarnations. He was perfect.

I don't know what form Prabhupāda has in Caitanya-*līlā*, but I offer my homage to the one in which he appeared to us on the Lower East Side.

12

Śrīla Prabhupāda, I think I saw your footprints in the sand at Juhu beach. You must have been wearing those canvas shoes this morning when you took your walk. I imagine that you were perspiring. Your strides were long and we must have been struggling to keep up with you. You wore no *kurtā*, so we didn't either. We hoped to overcome any reluctance we might have been feeling in our services. The opportunity to become better disciples is ongoing.

In my mind, I can hear the prayers your disciples made, silently, fervently, as they walked with you this morning. Please allow us to get close to you. Please call us to serve you. Please help us be sincere, serious, dedicated, honest. Please forgive us for praying without enough sincerity. We are trying to improve.

13

Śrīla Prabhupāda, yesterday I wrote a letter to a devotee who is having problems and I quoted something you said. He had a high profile and a brilliant reputation, a *brahmacārī*, and now he is getting married. His stepping down was so abrupt that some call it a falldown. Anyway, the devotees were disappointed and even hurt by his actions, and he was hurt by their attitude toward him. He felt they treated him like he wasn't a devotee at all and should now be shunned.

I wanted to encourage him. I told him how you once wrote me that failure is the pillar of success. I didn't tell him the incident you were responding to when you said that to me, but I remember it. It was around 1971. Some of the GBC members had held a meeting in the Brooklyn temple, but it turned out that our meeting wasn't authorized because we didn't invite all the members and some of the resolutions we passed didn't please you. You even suspended the GBC for the time being. You were showing us your power and teaching us that you were the real head of ISKCON.

Anyway, we were all disturbed that we had been party to such a source of displeasure to you. I remember your sending out an urgent communication that devotees, for the time being, should not listen to the GBC's decisions. You said legal formulas wouldn't help us, that we had to become mad after Kṛṣṇa. I went back to my service at the new *gurukula* in Dallas and to writing for *Back to Godhead* magazine.

You also asked those of us who had attended that ill-fated meeting to explain to you our understanding of what happened. I wrote and expressed myself openly about it, how I was wrong and how I had been influenced by others and what our intentions were. You wrote back without any grudge, telling me not think in such an expansive way. In that context, you encouraged me by saying, "Failure is the pillar of success."

That expression is not a Vedic statement. It is an English adage. But you applied it at a time when I was disappointed with myself and unsure how to proceed. You gave the whole incident such a positive note.

I remember taking that statement and trying to create an image in my mind. A building is knocked down, but it has to be built up again. The builder should learn what went wrong, where to put the pillars and how to make them strong. That very failure would then turn out to be the cause of a stronger building, a stronger spiritual life.

I remembered all this, Śrīla Prabhupāda, and then passed on that one sentence to the devotee in trouble. I knew it would help.

14

What did it feel like to come into Prabhupāda's presence? I remember learning soon after meeting you, Śrīla Prabhupāda, that coming to see you meant surrendering to God and giving up *anarthas*. Probably everyone wants to do these things at heart, but who could imagine a person who can be trusted so much, who is so intimate with God, that by surrendering to him or inquiring from him, we can become pure? Most people think that's impossible. I thought that too until I met you.

In my youth, I wasn't able to surrender to any priest in the Catholic church, at least not the ones I met, and the fact that my family and community tried to force my surrender made it distasteful. I wanted something more.

I remember the different times I offered *daṇḍavats* when I saw you. Those obeisances were never a mechanical act for me; they were my surrender. Why could I suddenly bow down to someone? Prabhupāda, it was your potency. When I bowed down to you, I felt something. I had faith. And the more I did it, the more faith I felt. That was your potency, that you could create faith in someone who did nothing more than offer you obeisances.

I also remember you smiling when we sat up from our obeisances. What were you smiling at? Maybe you were amused at our combination of earnestness and foolishness, at the combination of our purity and gross *anarthas*. But I know you were pleased.

You would ask us what we were doing and we would report to you or ask you a question. I remember one incident in particular when Hṛdayānanda Mahārāja and I went in to see you together. We had been preaching at the colleges. Hṛdayānanda was frank: the students weren't receptive and the college professors were puffed up. You commiserated. You told us it *was* difficult and it *was* disappointing. You gave us the option to continue with our college preaching or to make a new service proposal. Of course, you would make the ultimate decision as to what we should do. You had your own priorities, your overall vision of your worldwide movement, and you might send us anywhere if you thought things weren't working out so well where we were. You sent Harikeśa, who was your secretary, to preach in Germany. You said, "I thought, this is an intelligent boy. Why he should be rotting here typing?" You deployed your men.

But you also listened to what we thought we were doing and how we thought we might continue. Then you would state your priorities. "These standing orders at the colleges are very important." "Work on *Back to Godhead* magazine." "Concentrate on such and such service." You would emphasize to us what was important to you and we would take that order, feeling resolute, knowing what we should do to please you.

We could never convey to others how purified we felt after being in your presence, Śrīla Prabhupāda, or how directed our lives had suddenly become. These things were beyond our expression. We knew we could only act them out through our service.

Remembering these feelings now, I feel bathed by your presence. You recognized us, me, and we felt happy. You made Kṛṣṇa real to us simply by giving us an order to follow. Ten or fifteen minutes of association and we were ready to follow you for life. That is your potency, Śrīla Prabhupāda, to give us service as the most congenial form of intimacy.

15

If I can remember the spirit of living with Śrīla Prabhupāda and serving him, the enthusiasm we felt in his association . . . If I can face my levels of unsurrender and feel regret for them . . .

I yearn for deep memories of Prabhupāda. I mean even the memories of walking with Prabhupāda in particular places—Switzerland or Germany or Māyāpur—and what the trees were like and what he said there—how the park was more like a jungle or how the U.N. program for women exposed their sense gratification propaganda.

Every word Prabhupāda spoke was important, is important. We learned everything from him.

16

Sometimes I think of Prabhupāda's mother and how she must have seen her son. She didn't have any conception of his *aiśvarya*, of how he would become a great preacher and travel throughout the world. Prabhupāda's mother was in a different mood. Her relationship was *mādhurya*, sweet.

Her main desire was that Prabhupāda should survive to adulthood and she did many small, motherly rituals to bring this about. When I think how Prabhupāda didn't come to the West until his seventieth year, I feel indebted to his mother. She was her son's well-wisher, and in that way, we have reaped her blessings.

17

Śrīla Prabhupāda, your spiritual master told you that you were qualified because you heard nicely. He didn't recognize you because you gave donations to the Gaudiya Math or because you got involved in management. He recognized you for your attention to chanting and hearing. In this way, your spiritual master has forever emphasized the importance of these basic, Kṛṣṇa conscious practices for us. And you yourself told us that because you were good at *śravaṇam*, now you were good at *kīrtanam*, preaching.

Another point similar to this one is that you took your spiritual master's instructions so seriously that later they became the basis of your life's work. For example, he only mentioned that you should become a Western preacher twice—once when he first met you and again in a letter he wrote you at the end of his life. He also told you during Kārttika, 1935, at Rādhā-kuṇḍa, "If you ever get money, print books." You allowed his instructions to impress you deeply.

We cannot imitate your dedication to his words, but it teaches us that following the spiritual master to the utmost depends on the disciple's capacity to take seriously and absorb what his guru is saying.

Also, we have to try and follow our guru's instructions creatively. The guru may give us a seed instruction, a *sūtra*-sized mention that gives us an indication of his desire. Then the disciple has to think carefully how to carry it out to the fullest extent.

Śrīla Prabhupāda, you had to think about so many things in order to carry out your guru's instructions, and yet you always did it in faith. Your faith was in the spirit of the instruction and was not always dependent on the "letter of the law."

Neither did you wait for him to spell out the details of *how* you could carry out his order. You used your creative intelligence and you were successful.

You have left us with much more detailed instructions, but even within those details, there is room for creativity. Times have changed and we may have to learn how to adjust our approach in preaching. When you were here, the airports were open and big book distribution was going on full force. Now it is illegal to distribute books in many airports, so we have to think of another way. If we are following the spirit of your instructions, we will be creative in our following.

18

Śrīla Prabhupāda told us the story of how he first started writing the *Śrīmad-Bhāgavatam*. He explained to us that a librarian (and later an army captain) suggested he should write books rather than only put out *Back to Godhead* because books are more permanent. This was the external reason, but he took it as an instruction from his spiritual master.

Prabhupāda then decided to produce the *Śrīmad-Bhāgavatam*. I made a list from Prabhupāda's books themselves of why I thought he chose the *Bhāgavatam*.

1. The *Bhāgavatam* states that after Kṛṣṇa's disappearance, He appears in the form of *Śrīmad-Bhāgavatam*.

2. There is the statement by Vyāsadeva that in the age of Kali, *anarthopaśamaṁ sākṣād, bhakti-yogam adhokṣaje/lokasyājānato vidvāṁś, cakre sātvata-saṁhitām:* "The material miseries of the living entity, which are superfluous to him, can be directly mitigated by the linking process of devotional service. But the mass of people do not know this, and therefore the learned Vyāsadeva compiled this Vedic literature, which is in relation to the Supreme Truth" (*Bhāg.* 1.7.6). Therefore, the

Bhāgavatam is such an essential literature in the age of Kali to relieve people of their suffering and give them Kṛṣṇa consciousness.

There are other reasons too, but they are related to these two. Taking on this work, which would become lifelong, was a great challenge. Prabhupāda began it in his sixty-fourth year.

As soon as he decided to translate the *Śrīmad-Bhāgavatam*, a room became available at Rādhā-Dāmodara Mandir in Vṛndāvana. I like to think Rūpa and Jīva Gosvāmīs were inviting and inspiring Prabhupāda to live in the *dhāma* and carry out this tremendous task. Prabhupāda was not worried about his mistakes in the English presentation. He knew that those who were thoroughly honest would accept it. The *Bhāgavatam* itself states that fact.

Of course, he had to do everything himself—write, collect money for printing, shop and buy paper, deal with the printer, proofread. Finally he had to sell it. Printing these books was part of his mission on behalf of his spiritual master—he had to print books and take them to the West to preach.

After finishing the first volume, he went back to Vṛndāvana and completed the second. He wrote quickly. He was in *samādhi* working on this project, and that *samādhi* is possible for any of us if we sincerely and intently follow the orders of our spiritual master.

Back to Delhi. There he lived at the Chippiwada temple. It was noisy there and he had to walk down crowded streets to get to the printer. Again proofreading the galleys and returning the corrected proofs. In the second volume, he wrote a preface. People might ask, "What kind of a *sannyāsī* goes to New Delhi and deals in the paper trade, printing and selling his book? This is business in the name of *sannyāsa*." But Prabhupāda defended himself by explaining that his only motive was to serve Kṛṣṇa and that made it pure *bhakti*. And then he told his readership that by engaging in *bhakti-yoga*, they were sure to get over all the material obstacles and go to the kingdom of God to associate with Kṛṣṇa face to face.

Śrīla Prabhupāda, every period of your life is wonderful, but I particularly like this one. Thank you for leading such an exemplary life and letting us discuss your pastimes. May we continue to do it forever.

19

I remember the shock I felt when I heard Prabhupāda was going to San Francisco for the first time. We never thought Kṛṣṇa consciousness would go beyond the Lower East Side. Of course, that wasn't meant to be.

I still think fondly of Prabhupāda's days with us in New York City. I felt like we were living in a small family. We wanted to preach for him, but we had no vision beyond New York.

In those days I had my job at the welfare department and I also had my own apartment a few blocks from the storefront. My apartment soon became an annex to the storefront. We did everything under his direction—Sundays in Tompkins Square Park, making a record, Sunday Love Feasts—at least a few devotees had joined. He began to teach us *Caitanya-caritāmṛta* in the morning, because "now you are a little mature." We were disappointed to hear that he was going to San Francisco.

I was among those who thought it wasn't a good idea. I remember discussing it with Rāya Rāma. How could we let our Swamijī go to San Francisco just because someone had arranged for a "mantra rock dance"? Our Swamijī shouldn't be treated like that—it's not respectful. And anyway, *Back to Godhead* magazine is in New York.

I dared suggest to Prabhupāda that he shouldn't go, but I could tell immediately that he wasn't even open to hearing my suggestion. He was determined to preach and to spread Kṛṣṇa consciousness. But he didn't abandon us. He left us with something special: his instructions and the mood of service in separation.

He wrote us a letter from San Francisco explaining that serving the guru's order was more important than serving his physical presence. I remember feeling excited to carry on in Kṛṣṇa consciousness, even though his room was empty and I felt such an ache of emptiness. We knew we had something even the San Francisco devotees didn't have: service in separation.

20

Śrīla Prabhupāda, when you first went to Sydney, Australia, in 1971, a reporter greeted you at the airport. He asked you why you had come. You said you were like a salesman. Just as a traveling salesman goes everywhere to find customers, you were trying to find people intelligent enough to accept the holy name.

When I first saw this remark by you I didn't think there was anything further I could say about it in the class I was going to give on your life. Someone could even take it as a mundane statement. But when I consider it closer, this comparison of yourself to a salesman is transcendental and revealing. It reminds us that Lord Caitanya also called himself a seller of wares.

"I have come here to sell My emotional ecstatic sentiments in the city of Kāśī, but I cannot find any customers. If they are not sold, I must take them back home. I have brought a heavy load to sell in the city. To take it back again is a very difficult job; therefore if I get but a fraction of the price, I shall sell it here in the city of Kāśī" (Cc., *Madhya* 17.144–5).

In your purport to this verse, Śrīla Prabhupāda, you compare yourself to Lord Caitanya, at least in terms of selling the *mahā-mantra*. You said that you invited people to the storefront in 1966, but really never expected that the *mahā-mantra* would be accepted. ". . . fortunately, young people became Kṛṣṇa conscious. Although this mission was started with insignificant capital, it is now going nicely." Your conclusion was that the uneducated young people of America were more purified than the offensive Māyāvādīs or ascetic impersonalists of Kāśī.

Bhaktivinoda Ṭhākura also uses the metaphor of being a salesman in his "Marketplace of the Holy Name." He carefully describes how he and his associates want to serve Lord Nityānanda by distributing Kṛṣṇa consciousness like salespersons.

Many of the devotees waiting for you in Sydney had never been trained by your senior disciples. They had been given a few instructions and told to go preach. They read your *Bhagavad-gītā As It Is*, although they didn't even really know how to lecture. Their daily classes consisted of reading aloud from your book. But they were faithful, sincere disciples, and they proved their sincerity by going out on your order to chant Hare Kṛṣṇa in the streets despite repeated arrests.

The example of the Sydney devotees and their relationship with you is described in the *Bhagavad-gītā:* ". . . there are those who, although not conversant in spiritual knowledge, begin to worship the Supreme Person upon hearing about Him from others. Because of their tendency to hear from authorities, they also transcend the path of birth and death" (Bg. 13.26).

In my class, I won't have time to read all the memoirs those devotees gave, incidents which now seem amusing as they describe their ignorance and your leniency. One of the most remarkable things of that visit is that you brought Rādhā-Kṛṣṇa Deities and installed Them, even though the devotees were unprepared. You did this for a reason—you wanted to expand the movement and Deity worship was part of that expansion—but still, your motives and tactics and timings were inconceivable. No one knows the mind of the *ācārya*.

In Sydney you initiated persons who you knew were not qualified and then left them with Rādhā-Kṛṣṇa. Later you told us that you prayed confidentially to Rādhā-Gopīnātha: "Now I am leaving You in the hands of the *mlecchas*. I cannot take the responsibility. You please guide these boys and girls and give them the intelligence to worship You nicely."

21

I am writing this letter to you, Śrīla Prabhupāda, after the Rādhāṣṭamī celebrations. Rādhāṣṭamī is special for the devotees and Vṛndāvana is the most special place to observe it. I have a personal attachment to Rādhāṣṭamī because it was the day you awarded me *harināma* initiation in September, 1966. Thank you, Prabhupāda.

I'm in a different place now, moving toward the end of my life in this body. I was a young, foolish boy at my initiation, not at all prepared for the grave responsibility of lifetime vows. You gave me your mercy anyway and allowed me to chant your *praṇāma-mantra*. You chanted it first and I repeated it line by line: *nama oṁ viṣṇu-pādāya kṛṣṇa-preṣṭhāya bhū-tale* . . . You also gave me my red beads after you had chanted on them in your room at 26 Second Avenue.

That night I was your simple disciple. I admitted that I knew nothing and was solely dependent on you. Now I pray to always stay in that mood. Śrīla Prabhupāda, I don't know anything and I am still solely dependent on you. You are my eternal spiritual master.

22

Śrīla Prabhupāda tells us we cannot be God. We can create a playful sputnik and throw it into outer space, but only God can create countless huge planets and spin them in their orbits. Man cannot become God but he can attain seventy-eight percent of His qualities in part. Nārada advised Vyāsa to expand on this idea in *Śrīmad-Bhāgavatam*. Mankind needs to accept the supremacy of the Lord.

This kind of preaching on Lord Kṛṣṇa's behalf was Śrīla Prabhupāda's forte. He broadcast an army of topics on behalf of Lord Kṛṣṇa and his spiritual master. Kṛṣṇa asks that we surrender to Him and Śrīla Prabhupāda argues that we should surrender and thus solve the world's problems.

Śrīla Prabhupāda's approach does not appeal to those who will never surrender to Kṛṣṇa. Śrīla Prabhupāda did not pander to his audience. He wasn't trying to satisfy impersonalists or nondevotees. His preaching was meant to reach the innocent, and from that audience, he won many disciples. His call was answered by thousands.

23

When Steve Kowit, my atheist college buddy, read my introduction to *Nimāi dāsa and the Mouse*, he said, "I see you are trying something that is very difficult, to be true to yourself and at the same time true to the teachings of Kṛṣṇa consciousness." He seemed to think it was impossible. I also recall Rāya Rāma dāsa saying how he and Hayagrīva had "intellectual honesty." Therefore they were willing to defy Vedic truths if they didn't mesh with their own intellects. Today I heard Prajāpati dāsa say to Prabhupāda on tape, "For the last 150 years, theologians have had a great problem in reconciling faith with reason . . . They want to believe, but can't reach God by reason." Prabhupāda proceeded to give examples how God is a reasonable truth. He said we have a relationship with everything, for example, with the road we walk on. Since we have a relationship with everything in the world, why not with God who created it? The devotees on the walk persisted in giving agnostic challenges. Karandhara said, "They want God to be proved to the senses. Otherwise they think the devotees are fantasizing." At first Śrīla Prabhupāda replied by saying that devotional service is verified by the senses, because we walk to the temple, smell incense, see the Deity form, eat *prasādam*, but Karandhara said when a devotee offers food to Kṛṣṇa, he believes on faith that Kṛṣṇa takes the food. We don't see Kṛṣṇa doing it. Śrīla Prabhupāda replied, "*You* do not see, but *I* see. You are blind, and I am not so foolish. So you have to come to me in order to see. You have a cataract on your eyes and I shall remove it."

It was a wonderful thing to hear. I was on this particular walk on Venice Beach twenty years ago. I remember when Śrīla Prabhupāda said that: "*You can't see, but I can see.*" I remember how I felt subdued and convinced by his words. The so-called gap between faith and reason was closed by his assertion of his own seeing Kṛṣṇa. The atheist can't follow. Leave them behind. We want to follow.

I want to always keep these feelings with me. I don't want to forget that my spiritual master convinced me again and again. If I allow the feeling to slip away, how will I follow only dogma or ISKCON policy? My following is based on remembering the pure devotee, Śrīla Prabhupāda. It's also based on my cultivating my relationship with him not only in my memory, but now, in the present.

24

"If you did not mount your victorious jeweled chariot, whose mere presence threatens culprits, if you did not produce fierce sounds by the twanging of your bow . . . then all the moral laws . . . would be broken by the rogues and rascals" (*Bhāg.* 3.21.52, 54).

I remember editing this around 1968. I was always satisfied to do that for Prabhupāda, to type and edit. I took on tasks even though we weren't professionally trained. That's the way we did things in ISKCON. Śrīla Prabhupāda encouraged us to learn on the job. Learn to paint by painting. Learn to manage by managing. The main thing was to persist and not leave, even when teenage thugs broke our windows in Allston and challenged us to come out and fight. We persisted in fear, in anxiety, under threat, but we persisted. We saw it as our duty to Prabhupāda.

I am grateful for my youth spent so fully and actively in carrying out Prabhupāda's order. Were my activities external? You could say so. I worked hard, but did not rid myself of important *anarthas*. I didn't know much. But we knew of Kṛṣṇa consciousness, we asserted, we preached, we stuck to it no matter what the nondevotees said or thought. A youth well spent.

All glories to Śrīla Prabhupāda! He was so close to us in those days through his letters, room conversations, and travels, and we loved and worshipped him. It doesn't seem so simple now that he is gone, but I am still persisting and trying to go deeper. I am spending my middle age well and look forward to an old age full of promise. These are Śrīla Prabhupāda's gifts.

Prayer

1

When I came into the house, Prabhupāda dāsa asked me if I still liked to hear things Prabhupāda said about prayer.

"Sure," I said, "I'm interested in prayer." So he gave me this quote from *Conversations with Śrīla Prabhupāda*, Volume One, pp. 85–6:

> Life is short and it is so much disturbed. So how is it possible to practice? Therefore, this one practice—chanting Hare Kṛṣṇa, and hearing—that is very nice. And praying to Kṛṣṇa, "Please give me strength." Hare, "O Energy of Kṛṣṇa, O Kṛṣṇa, I am fallen, I have no strength. Please accept me." That's all. "I have no qualification. I am frail. I am trying, but I am failing." All these appeals should be made. And Kṛṣṇa is all-powerful, He can do anything. Even we, we do not perform, trying our best, if we fail, Kṛṣṇa will help us.

2

Śrīla Prabhupāda, please somehow keep me honest. I cannot live forever in this body. How can I expect to go back to Godhead at the end? You once lectured, "Deathlessness begins at initiation." You say going back to Godhead at the end of this life can be done. You speak of "devotees" and seem to include all your sincere followers. You say Yamarāja cannot touch them. When death comes, you say, it is "merely official," just a quick transfer, a waking up and discovering we are in Goloka-dhāma. You said we would experience this because we love and serve Kṛṣṇa. I believe what you say—I know it is not an exaggeration—but you yourself know it applies to some and not to all.

You warn us, "Don't leave this Kṛṣṇa consciousness." You want us to constantly preach *hari-kathāmṛta*. You expect complete surrender.

When I think of prayer I think, "You would pray if your life were threatened. You are too comfortable for that now." But I don't want the tension of a physically dangerous or oppressive situation. At least I don't want to pray for that. I think it is valid to want to pray in a peaceful place.

Prayer should be impelled not only by danger, but by meditation on Kṛṣṇa's qualities, *līlā*, and paraphernalia. We shouldn't just cry out because the crocodile has his teeth clamped on our leg when we're trying to enjoy. Those moments will come, but in this rarely attained human life, we have to take the opportunity to pray when our body, mind, and words are composed. There's not much time. And if we can learn to pray when we are relatively peaceful, we will be better equipped to remember Kṛṣṇa during a crisis.

Prayer is not only for ourselves, but for helping others. Use a brief respite from ills and oppressions to help others. That is inner life.

3

Kṛṣṇa, I am far away from Vraja because I want to be. That sounds terrible and foolish. But what other reason is there? Perhaps we can say I am far away from Vraja because in the past, I greatly misused my free will and started a chain of sinful reactions. I lost all memory of Your sweet association. Recently, Your Śrīla Prabhupāda has rescued me and I am gradually reviving my interest in serving and residing in Vraja.

When I leave Vraja, it's not because I want to embrace *māyā*. I have service outside the *dhāma*. I pray to tell others of Vṛndāvana's glories and then to be allowed back into the *dhāma* myself.

O father, spiritual guide, best friend Śrī Kṛṣṇa, my life is blessed by even a slight touch of Your mercy. Thank You.

4

Don't keep saying Kṛṣṇa is far away or that you have no attraction for Him. It sounds too negative and offensive. Why write, "I don't love You"? It's too painful.

But I have to tell the truth. Maybe it's better to beg for mercy: "Kṛṣṇa, please help me become attached to Your lotus feet." I want to go on hearing of Your pastimes with Your devotees and how You are like a maddened bumblebee. I want to hear how You lifted Govardhana Hill and how today, Your dear devotees go to Govardhana, circumambulate the hill, and worship the rocks. I want to reside again in Vṛndāvana, if Your Śrīmatī Rādhārāṇī will allow me.

Kṛṣṇa, there is no need for me to be so negative and declare, "I don't love You." I *do* love You.

5

Is that a cliché only, "Praise Kṛṣṇa"? How do you do it? Is it just a matter of saying "*Haribol*"? No, praise is a quality of appreciating God's greatness—either His majesty, His *karuṇa* (mercy), or His beauty—whatever quality that attracts you. Praise must be sincere.

So often all we can do is ask for help, "God, please fix my life." Praise starts *after* that point, although it should come in the beginning, middle, and end of remembrance. In all the *Vedas*, *Upaniṣads*, *Purāṇas* and their supplements, either directly or indirectly, Lord Hari is praised by devotees who know the purpose of life.

I pray that He who is life, who grants intelligence, memory, and sincerity, will allow me to praise Him. Lord Kṛṣṇa, You are the greatest. You are giving me the rare opportunity to hear of Your pastimes. You are giving me a chance to serve Lord Caitanya's *saṅkīrtana* movement in ISKCON. You are allowing me to praise You. Please allow me to do it sincerely.

O Lord who chastises the demons, O Lord who is the perfect judge of time and circumstance, O Lord who plays and enjoys music with the *gopīs* in the forest of Vṛndāvana, I long to become strong and free to praise You and serve You.

6

O Vaiṣṇava Ṭhākura, please be merciful to me. Let me serve you. By your grace I may control my senses. From you I will learn *divya-jñāna*. Kṛṣṇa is yours. I am simply running after you crying, "Kṛṣṇa! Kṛṣṇa!"

Uttarā prayed: O Lord of Lords, O Lord of the universe, O soul of the universe, please protect me in this world of death.

Prahlāda Mahārāja prayed: O Supreme Lord and master, You have asked me to take a boon in return for my devotional service, but please don't speak like that. I am born in an asuric family and we tend to be materialistic; don't incite me to take a reward. I serve You out of love, as this is my constitutional position. You are my master and I am Your eternal servant. If I take a reward from You, I will become like a *baniya*, a businessman.

Śrīla Prabhupāda prayed: O my spiritual master, evangelic angel, you hold the mace. You have the right. If you had not come to teach Lord Caitanya's message, the world would remain in darkness with no trace of hope. You gave us a fresh life. I worship your feet, your Divine Grace.

The Vaiṣṇavas' prayers keep us alive in spiritual life. By following their teachings, we will be able to remain aloof from the modes of nature. Māyā-devī will not capture us. We will remain servants of Kṛṣṇa and His devotees.

Let us protect our devotional plants and keep them growing. Let us fence in our creepers to protect them from Vaiṣṇava *aparādha*. And let us water them with chanting and hearing.

7

Kṛṣṇa comes home at twilight, leading the cows through the pastures, then through the forest, and into the village. His body is covered by the powdered dust raised by their hooves. He is beautiful.

O spiritual master, please allow me to serve you. Grant me the vision of Kṛṣṇa's pastimes. Please engage me in your mission and allow my service to be acceptable to you. Please teach me how to improve.

O Lord who loves *tulasī* plants, O Lord of the demigods, grant me the vision to know You as the residents of Vraja do, as their son, friend, and lover. You are the God of gods, and yet Nanda sees You only as his son. O Lord, dearest friend of Balarāma, O Lord whose mother hides Him indoors when she sees Śiva coming on his bull-carrier, O Lord who smiles in His sleep, O sweet Lord whose mother sees His newly formed teeth and rejoices, O ancient, self-sufficient philosopher who is awarding everyone's desires, O regulator of karma and Yamarāja and all planets, O subject matter of the *Bhagavad-gītā*, O holy name, O source of incarnations—everything from beginning to end is Kṛṣṇa Himself, and yet You say, "I am not there." You are hankering for the autumn nights when You will arrange for the *rāsa* dance through Yogamāyā. You do not much care for Lord Brahmā's prayers, but You like the *gopīs'* insults. Please be the only aim and object of my life.

8

This is my prayer-application. Śrīla Prabhupāda used this word to describe how 16,000 princesses got Kṛṣṇa as their husband. They were captured by the demon Bhaumāsura, but they made their "prayer-application" to Kṛṣṇa, requesting Him to save them and marry them.

I have filled out applications for jobs, licenses, and visas, and now I am applying for love of Kṛṣṇa. I hope He will have time to read my application and consider me favorably. When Śrīla Prabhupāda left India in 1965, he made an application to the Bank of India to get their permission to leave. At first their agent said no, because Swamiji didn't have an institutional patron in America. But Śrīla Prabhupāda insisted that his file be passed to a superior for reconsideration. The superior came and told Prabhupāda, "Don't worry, Swamiji. I have passed your case."

We wait. We are not qualified. But the saints are kind. Even if someone "up there" wants to turn me down, my spiritual master will not reject me. Maybe he will decide favorably, but postpone the fulfillment of the application. I sit here and chant and wait.

Kṛṣṇa consciousness means intimate love of God. We can practice to attain this intimate love by hearing. Hear about those eternal souls who serve Kṛṣṇa in Vraja. Focus on service to Rādhā-Kṛṣṇa. Lord Caitanya said, "There is no worship of

Kṛṣṇa better than that of the *gopīs* of Vraja." Follow them. And He also said, "As Kṛṣṇa is worshipable, so His Vṛndāvana is worshipable."

Please, therefore, give up fear and the search for sense gratification. Take shelter of the lotus feet of Nanda-nandana. Dear mind and self, please take shelter of Kṛṣṇa and His devotees and cooperate with your whole self. All this is included in my prayer-application.

Sometimes application forms state, "Give further information on the back page. If more space is required, attach additional pages." I am attaching hundreds of pages, making my case. But sometimes what I write can be held against me. Still, it is my testimony. What I write is evidence that I am not properly engaged in this material world in a material body. I want to go back. I love Kṛṣṇa. I am afraid to live in His material energy any longer without Him. I have been writing my experiences and I present it all for His consideration, or for the review of His secretaries who read such things. Please consider my case.

And not just me, but I write for others too. I am applying for all of us. My spiritual master made me an agent on behalf of so many other *jīvas*. Please consider all aspiring *bhaktas* who want to attain the lotus feet of Kṛṣṇa.

9

One of the markings on the sole of Kṛṣṇa's right foot is "an elephant goad, which brings the elephants of His devotees' minds under control" (*Bhāg.* 10.30.25, purport). We often hear how powerful the mind is, how god-like and fierce it is in going its own way and dragging the soul with it. Similarly, an elephant is more powerful than a human, but the iron goad used to control elephants can inflict pain. It presses into the soft skin on the elephant's head and is pressed right against his brain. It will be painful to submit to Kṛṣṇa's goad, but we need His control. Often, just the sight of the goad is enough for us. We know Kṛṣṇa is our controller.

Let's meditate on His lotus feet: "At the bottom of the middle right toe, Lord Acyuta has a lotus flower, which increases the greed for Him in the minds of the bee-like devotees who meditate on His feet. At the base of His small toe is a thunderbolt, which smashes the mountains of His devotees' reactions to past sins."

Let's pray to Kṛṣṇa's lotus feet: "Please increase my attraction to You. Please smash all reactions, even mental ones, to the mountains of sins I have committed. And if I do not submit, but prefer to go my own way, then Lord, please apply your elephant goad to my mind as You see fit. Just show it to me and I will submit."

10

Śrīla Prabhupāda, when I say I want to know the truth and yet I am fearful, what does this mean? I know I don't like to admit weakness, but I have to. It will help me to remember how dependent I am on you. It's not that you helped me only in the beginning, but you are always with me. I had bad karma, not "pretty good" karma as I recently wrote. I was misspending my good karma in illicit acts and heading for hell. I believe it.

I am asking for a miraculous vision of all that I was and all that I am. I am asking you to let me be honest, to write truthfully, and to love you. Let people see that a Kali-yuga victim can become a devotee.

Kṛṣṇa, You know everything and You possess everything. They say, "Ask and ye shall receive. Knock and it shall be opened to you." So I ask You for *nāma-rasa* for *śraddhā*, for whatever I need. I am afraid of severe trials, but I will accept them if they are what I need to attain You. I don't want to live in safety just to keep my good reputation intact. I want to get rid of *anarthas* and attain Your lotus feet. This is my service to my spiritual master.

Please do with me as You see best. Give me the strength to endure trials. Śrīla Prabhupāda wrote on my letter to him (in Bombay 1974), "You are pure. May Kṛṣṇa protect you from calamities." He cared for me and wished me well. He also knew there would be spiritual and material calamities. He has blessed me to be protected by You.

11

O Lord who manifests Himself through the people of many cultures in many worlds, O Lord whose material energy is infinitely varied and yet is only a spark of Your splendor, O Lord Bhagavān, in Your childhood pastimes, You act as if You cannot even turn on Your side unless Mother Yaśodā helps You. O Lord, Mother Yaśodā prays to Lord Nārāyaṇa for Your protection from evil spirits. She decorates You with black armlets and *kajjala* to protect You. Please protect us and our *bhakti* creeper.

O Lord who appears in Kali-yuga making it the most merciful age, O transcendental Lord who appears in the *arcā-vigrahas* of sincere worshippers and in the hearts and words of bona fide preachers, please accept my attempts to serve You.

12

O Lord who is King and most handsome, O God of gods; O father, O mother, O son of Nanda, O seed of all *jīvas*, O seed-bearing spring (Your favorite)—please reveal Yourself to me and change me. O God of devotees, O Kṛṣṇa in threefold bending form—let me sleep well tonight. Then let me rise early and write better. O God, I don't want to pray for material things. O God, I want to see You with clear eyes and vision and no complaints and take on more to help others.

O God of Lords, O handsome youth of Vraja, You are the lover of the *gopīs* and I bow before You. Please excuse my stupid bowing down.

13

O Lord who is beyond my petty broadcasting, O Lord who is accessible to the pure at heart, You dance and play with Your best devotees. We who don't love You enough, who are absorbed in our illusions and attachments, have to rot in this world of *saṁsāra* and be satisfied with our own attempts for supremacy. Your pure devotees are kind to come and fish us out.

O Lord of supreme bliss, we pray to be roped into the circle of those who hear *kṛṣṇa-kathā*. O handsome, polite, soft Kṛṣṇa, only in Vraja do You serve Your own devotees.

O Lord as time, as fate, as death, as nature, You appear as mountains and sky and sea and planets. The impersonalists contemplate these as part of Your universal body and that's the first step in God realization. But I want to hear of You and see You as Govinda. Please protect me.

14

O tender as a rose Lord who was as hard as Indra's thunderbolt when You killed the Keśī demon; O Lord who may laugh at us; O Lord of English and French and Hindi—why this babble of confused tongues? O Lord who is not to blame but who is sorry when the *jīvas* torture each other. O Lord who comes to tell us, "Come back to God and quit this place," O Lord, how hard is it to get back to You?

O Lord above all and in our hearts, I pray to transcend mechanical prayer. Why am I so afraid to be open with You? Please free me.

O Lord with the peacock feather in Your hair, You like Your devotees who have unalloyed love for You. The tainted ones are like merchants praying for profit and liberation.

O Lord who likes nonenvious devotees, we pray for the day when we can become free of envy. May we be confident of Your love and our place at Your lotus feet.

15

O Lord Caitanya whose body is compared to many full moons, O Lord whose moon in this universe is whole, and half tonight, and sparkling on the ocean waves; O Lord of the universe, kindly be visible to me.

O Lord who appeared in Purī five hundred years ago, Your pastimes are now kept in the hearts of Your pure devotees—I get to serve them and hear from them. O Lord who empowered Kṛṣṇadāsa Kavirāja Gosvāmī to tell of Your *līlā* as Lord Caitanya in Purī, I hope to be a worthy servitor of my spiritual master and to cooperate with his disciples.

O Lord, I write to praise You; I want to serve You with patience and devotion.

O Lord who, as Lord Caitanya, felt the same separation Śrīmatī Rādhārāṇī felt when Kṛṣṇa left Vṛndāvana, I pray to be able to pray to my spiritual master. O Lord of gurus, I wish to know my Prabhupāda and whether I am pleasing him.

16

O Lord, O energy of the Lord, You kindly appear in Your holy names. Please grant me the mercy to chant and hear. Grant me the power to control my mind and fix it on the sounds and meanings of Your names. Please see me endeavoring and find some good in my effort. I cannot go forward without Your grace. I have heard that the heart must be cleansed before You will manifest there. That cleaning begins with *śravaṇaṁ-kīrtanam*. I want to clean my own heart and to help other devotees to do the same. Let us share the bliss of *kṛṣṇa-kathā* and preaching Your glories.

17

O Supreme Lord, You are praised in choice verses which are relished by the best devotees; You know me and all living beings. I desire to be lifted out of the ocean of birth and death. I know You rescue Your pure devotees. You are the swift deliverer. But I am slow to completely turn to You and make it clear that I don't want to enjoy this material world. I beg You'll see some grain of sincerity in me and that You will increase it.

O Supreme Lord, You dance in Goloka. To You and Your pure devotees, the spiritual world is home; this material world, as the center of degradation, is not Your transcendental abode. Still, You come here and enact Your pastimes. You tell us Yourself and through Your teachers that this world and the material body are not places of happiness, peace, or permanence. I wish to absorb this message and with a convinced and humble heart, preach it wherever I go.

18

Deep, basic faith is required at every step. I am not above needing to pray for protection of my creeper in the most elementary ways—freedom from sex desire, from *nāma-aparādha*, from Vaiṣṇava and *guru-aparādha*, from desire for fame, protection from contamination of atheism, from excessive fear of injury to this body, from laziness and sleep—you name it, I need release from all dangers of *anarthas* and *aparādhas*. From top to bottom, I pray to Gurudeva. Please accept my activities, such as these writing sessions, as service to you. Please employ my energy in your service.

One has to go on one's own path within *bhakti*, within ISKCON. Each pilot in his own airplane. That's good, and all flying to Kṛṣṇa under the guru's direction.

19

O Supreme Lord who appeared as Lord Caitanya and blessed the town of Jagannātha Purī for eighteen years, flooding it with the waves of His private and public ecstasies; O Lord whose performance at Ratha-yātrā, dancing in seven forms in seven groups of devotees, astounds the worlds; O Lord who left a record of His life and teachings by empowering authors like

Kṛṣṇadāsa Kavirāja Gosvāmī and Rūpa Gosvāmī; O carefree Lord, best of *sannyāsīs*, we pray to You. Only by Your mercy can we enter Kṛṣṇa's pastimes in Vṛndāvana. O transcendental Lord, please reveal Yourself to me through my Śrīla Prabhupāda.

20

O Kṛṣṇa who lives in Vṛndāvana and never leaves; O Kṛṣṇa who expands Himself to perform *līlās* outside of Vṛndāvana; O Kṛṣṇa who took the form of a pure devotee, Śrī Caitanya Mahāprabhu, please let me be eligible to receive *kṛṣṇa-kathā*. To become eligible, I must understand that I am not the master of anything. You are my master and I am Your servant. I can realize that by serving Śrīla Prabhupāda.

21

I feel joy. It makes me want to write a poem-prayer. I want the word "Kṛṣṇa" to be like the pebbles and the clear creek water. I want to find solitude in which to chant the *gāyatrī-mantras*. *Aiṁ gurudevāya vidmahe*—I know my Gurudeva. I want to meditate on him. Please let me go to where he is and serve him there.

Śrīla Prabhupāda, please take this boy whom you found in New York, who went to Boston for you, and keep training him. Be kind, please be kind. I beg you for that chance. Give me the taste of your menial service.

May that Kṛṣṇa who charms the residents of Vṛndāvana be kind to me and give me the right to eternally serve my Gurudeva.

22

Vṛndā-devī, I don't know how best to pray to you. I expect things to turn out as I want them to and then I consider that I am blessed. But please don't cheat me by awarding my inferior desires. Whatever I have to go through—whatever austerity, poverty, humility, or pain—take me through it to loving service to Rādhā and Kṛṣṇa. I can only attain this goal by Śrīla Prabhupāda's intimate direction. Vṛndā-devī, you know my heart. Please grant me only those desires that are best for the growth of my *bhakti* creeper.

Dear Vṛndā-devī, your Rādhā-Śyāmasundara are beautiful. I am not qualified to be here, but I am allowed to come to Vṛndāvana by your grace and by the grace of my spiritual master. Although I am here, I cannot perceive the spiritual reality. Still, I honor it. I have placed my prayers, requests for self-improvement, and prayers for others at your lotus feet. May you destroy my false ego and the false attachments that prevent me from serving you, even if those attachments are dear to me. Please do the same for other devotees I know and live with. We call it purification. Please take away the *anarthas*.

WRITING

1

I found it difficult to sleep last night. Sleep is such a subtle thing to obtain. You have to lie still, but you can't force it. You think, "All right, even this light rest is doing me good." Maybe writing is like that, at least the "unconscious" quality you seek of deep-place (like sleep for the sleeper)—and you desire at least the dream state which will signify that you are not awake. You cannot force it in writing, so you write on and console yourself, "Even this is doing me some good." And sometimes, without knowing it, I may fall asleep; sometimes I may drift into the deep-place in writing. It's all a gift.

2

In the introduction to his diary, *The Sign of Jonas,* Thomas Merton apologizes to fellow Catholics that the book isn't written in the technical, theological language of Catholic dogma. He asserts himself, "I may be pardoned for using my own words to talk about my own soul."

3

Something came today in these note pads. I'm sorry it wasn't better. I'm really stuck at this particular moment. The windblown door is pushing me from behind and this cinder block I am sitting on is a terrible seat. Crouch down, get on your knees, and pray. Kṛṣṇa, God, dear Lord of my heart, dear soul in my heart, dear spiritual master who has not left but who is with me, you see me. You hear my prayer. Please reveal yourself to me.

I'm not incoherent. When the devotees give me their questions, I line up śāstric quotes to support my conclusions and then I try to answer in a gentle, compassionate way. Here, I deliberately drop that performance as the man with all the answers. Instead, I stare at my emptiness in the mirror of this solitude. I don't do it as an indulgence. I'm serious. I hope out of desperation to write what aches and to drive myself to call out, to finally surrender and cry on the page, like the rain cries on the earth. That doesn't happen, but that's the idea.

4

I worry whether my attempt to write honestly about my life is good enough. I worry what people will say. But when I get past the superficialities and the doubts, then I don't worry so much. *Prema-bhakti-candrikā* is too advanced for me because it is the science of *rāgātmikā*. *Mahābhārata* doesn't move me to write. But my own life does interest me. *Interest* me? It is the biggest challenge. I cannot avoid it. I have to surmount its deficiencies or I will die spiritually.

I say "my" life, but it's life itself as a person faces it. It's not a tale told by an idiot, "full of sound and fury, signifying nothing." No, it's the *bhakti-mārga*. It's riding in a taxi on Bhaktivedanta Swami Mārg under the Bhaktivedanta Swami Arch. It's what is in your heart at that time. Why do you quake when you enter Vṛndāvana? Why do you have cold feet when you meet with your Godbrothers and then feel unworthy and sorry for that? *That* topic is the most challenging, and to tackle it again and again is your own life. And yes, telling it can be inspiring to others who have felt similar emotions in similar situations. They are dear friends.

For example, yesterday I was struck by these lines that I wrote honestly in Māyāpur last year:

> Sometimes I feel tired in spirit. No, not in spirit exactly, because spirit is ever-fresh. I can't touch spirit, and perhaps that's why I feel sad. I can't describe it. It's not an *ennui*. There is a nothing happening, dead-pan expression to the face, a kind of gravity where *nothing seems wondrous*. You go through the motions of *kīrtana* and circumambulate the Deities with Śrīla Prabhupāda's *mūrti* without fully taking part. It seems there is nothing that can drag you into it. You are here only because you are supposed to be, and you hang back unenlivened.

It struck me that this is an accurate analysis of someone performing *vaidhī-bhakti* who is dissatisfied with it and hankering to go beyond. I began to understand that there is more to Kṛṣṇa consciousness and that my feeling dead was the burden of doing only what I was supposed to do *because I was supposed to do it*. It produces boredom and is followed by falldown, or if not falldown, then a kind of half-petrification even while you live and breathe and go through the motions of being a devotee.

How can one *not* be interested in his or her own life adventure? I stumble over a rock and write that down. I sit to hear a *Bhāgavatam* class and write that down. Forgive me, friends, for choosing this topic.

5

Pick up again where you left off in your practice. As a doctor practices, so you practice writing *bhajana*. Don't make distinctions between practice and performance. Don't keep avoiding the point. Writing is living, walking, talking to Kṛṣṇa and the devotees—working things out.

6

I hope that what I wrote between 11 and 12 today may be a breakthrough—admitting how your actual Kṛṣṇa consciousness goes untouched by the pen which is many times removed from life. By the time you start to describe it in words, it's gone. I thought, "That was interesting. Where will it lead? Can writing uncover Kṛṣṇa consciousness and lead to a better way to live?" I felt an impetus to write more and freer in the attempt to uncover more.

Still, I would have to face anxiety when I saw how little my present Kṛṣṇa consciousness amounts to, like peeling layers of an onion and finding nothing at the center.

Such writing wouldn't presume to be Kṛṣṇa conscious, and it wouldn't rest on the assumption that Kṛṣṇa conscious writing means saying what you are supposed to say. It would report findings, yearnings.

Anyway, you asked what I was thinking, so *that*. And I am hopeful that following the day-long schedule so diligently will result in a fixed meditation on Kṛṣṇa consciousness.

7

I don't want to artificially create themes in writing—arrival themes, mid-book themes, in-transit themes, good-bye themes. I want to be honest and try to write what is actually close to me in my attempt to serve Kṛṣṇa. If I feel far away, then say that. Then *try to come closer*.

If in India I get a streak of thinking of America, then go with it and try to come closer to guru and Kṛṣṇa. No forced themes of beginning, middle, and end. Otherwise, you will be in danger of making your literary expression more important than your actual life experience. That limits the potential of what can happen; inhibits your ability to see what actually *is* happening.

8

I opened the door to the shed and was startled to see Yamunā, the calf, here. I started to write, but she stuck her head out and breathed audibly through her nose. Now she is snuffling around at the gate. She was lying down when I surprised her. I had better leave.

Try the greenhouse where the green tomato plants are supported by poles. A few are starting to show spots of red.

Is the calf a distraction or am I the distraction? She's mooing because I disturbed her, and the sheep and cows in the neighboring fields are answering her. The heaviest rain has stopped for the time being. This pen is running out of ink (I have another). The tomatoes are doing their occupational duty, turning red. Uddhava wants to know how all this is devotional service. He can offer it to Kṛṣṇa. What is it I seek in my writing? To offer it to Kṛṣṇa.

Soon I will go to India. In India, there are usually two factors that hinder my writing: (1) health (meaning I have so little energy); and (2) I feel too ashamed and insignificant. I don't dare presume I can write in my Western genres. But when I leave India, I want to write again in the Western way. I reason that it would be better to keep writing there, even though I feel unqualified. That's what I will be trying for this year.

9

In a letter I said yes, when I come to Guyana again, I would like to stay at your house. I don't think your talks were "mundane, personal troubles." You didn't waste my time; I didn't think you were speaking as if you were better than the other devotees, but rather, I accepted you as impartial. But if you think these were your shortcomings, we can all improve. But please don't think I didn't like you. I liked the stay at your house and the breeze blowing the curtains and the utter simplicity of it and the fact that the overhead is so low you don't have to worry about money. Therefore, I said you have an ideal situation to increase your *sādhana*. Your desire to take part more in ISKCON is good, and I know your involvement will increase in a natural way.

I am repeating this just to show myself that I can preach and assure someone and mean it. Just give me a subject, especially a submissive devotee with a desire to improve, and I can go at it. But left to myself, I feel the emptiness beneath the counseling words that I give to others. The emptiness that moves in as soon as I don't read *śāstra* for half a day. And this so-called emptiness is just a pause before *māyā* moves in.

I think it's good to face the emptiness, at least for certain periods, and that's what this writing is. Teresa of Avila said she wished she had two hands to write her overflowing realizations, but she also lamented, when she wrote, her lack of love for the all-deserving, all-attractive Supreme Godhead. She was full of instructions and ecstasies in her life.

So I come here with a sense of abundance, but also a need, a desire to face the emptiness and go past it.

10

Bending the will to think of Him. A laborer bends his back to cut grass in the field. He can't be lazy. He's motivated to eat. I bend my will. To eat? No, but I have to do honest work in return for my food. A *sādhu* has to do service in return for the donations and service he receives from followers, so he gives them spiritual instructions.

These are reasons to write—to please guru, to serve my followers. And I can do it because I want to, because I love to. It's my calling and I must.

One of my main topics in writing is why we write—why I write. That was my topic even when I first began to write stories so many years ago. Where does the creative urge come from? What is the source? It fascinated me then and the answer seemed to be nothing less than the mystery of life.

Now I know that Śrī Kṛṣṇa is the source of all and thus the source of the creative urge. I also know this urge in artists can be tainted by the mode of passion. An artist may want to be a controller, a creator, like Brahmā, the lord of the universe. An artist can write or draw or create music for power. Creativity fills you with power. It can be dangerous.

But the urge to create can be purified. This process is my main preoccupation. Some people call it an obsession. I call it my attempt to serve Śrīla Prabhupāda. It is my *bhajana*.

11

A Godbrother writes me on a greeting card, "Vṛndāvana is a touchstone of extremes: extremely hot summers, extremely cold winters; extremely rude people, extremely loving friends.

Extreme blessings and advancement for a simple, sincere effort, extremely severe punishments for offenses."

The simple weather, the simple bell-ringing—live here as innocently as possible. Don't assume you understand anything. Be open to what you can perceive at any hour. Saintly persons can smell the delicate fragrance of *tulasīs* at dawn when they release their aroma.

I want to be confident (and reckless, extreme)—I want to say that what happens even to me in Vṛndāvana is worth telling about. It may be homely now, but later it can become a jewel. I write as if my tiny words from my tiny point of view have value. I write for no reason at all. I write because I am in Kṛṣṇa's land and as I chanted *japa*, I heard a conch blowing somewhere. I imagined myself standing at the rail of the Krishna-Balaram Mandir, imagined myself watching the *ārati*. But then I turned to this page.

I am not writing exercises for self-discovery. I am trying to *do* something with the self, not kill him or stomp him into the earth. I don't want to chase him down a hole like a startled rabbit. I am looking for that small, simple person with the tiny world view who talks in a Kṛṣṇa conscious way. (Why does he talk in a Kṛṣṇa conscious way? How did he manage to learn that? Is it from realization? I can't say.)

12

I woke up at 10:30 last night wondering what I want to do. Couldn't sleep well. Wanted to think things out. Kṛṣṇa, mercy will descend from You. There is no other way to achieve it. If I say one thing honestly, then another honest thing may come. But even if I am released from all obstruction, my own deepest, clearest thoughts can't reach far. I'm like the astronomer looking through his telescope. The human eye is limited, the brain defective. Spiritual truth descends. So I write, hoping to catch the rain, waiting (and singing) like a *cakora* bird waiting for a moonbeam.

13

Kṛṣṇa isn't much pleased by the behavior of the human species. Even the religionists approach Him with their selfish motives and impossible desires to rectify the material world as a place "safe for democracy," a place "peaceful" for sense gratification. Kṛṣṇa may reciprocate and give them what they want, but He is not pleased by their worship. Even the faithful, loving service of the pure devotees in Vaikuṇṭha doesn't appeal to Kṛṣṇa in His original Vṛndāvana form. It doesn't even reach Him. But He is captured by the songs and gestures of the *gopīs*, and by the loving attitudes of His parents and friends.

Devotional service is tricky. The spiritual master wants us to work in the world and we have to be aware of so many things. We have to talk with lawyers, communication experts, accountants, marketing people, and with troubled devotees. Neither are their troubles all on the spiritual plane. Often they are based on, "I need to get married," or, "I can't follow the regulative principles. What should I do?" or, "How can I get along with the other devotees?" It drags me down as much as the whirlwind of my own mind and senses. The spiritual master wants us to practice pure *nāma-bhajana*. We have to recognize that we alone supply our own distractions. Śrīla Prabhupāda gave us work in ISKCON. It is not detrimental to internal life. But somehow or other, we have to remember Kṛṣṇa.

In his *Śrīmad-Bhāgavatam* lecture, a devotee said that self-realization is attained by hearing about Kṛṣṇa and serving

Kṛṣṇa. When we do that, then automatically we discover our own self. I wanted to question him, but didn't dare in front of a hundred people. I didn't want to sound like a doubtful Westerner who goes to psychologists in search of self-realization. I wanted to ask a question I didn't even know how to form—something like, "Don't you have to keep striving to know yourself and understand yourself in order to best pursue the practice of hearing?"

I was thinking of all the junk in ourselves that others see clearly, but which we are either blind to or are unable to change. Do we have to *do* something to improve? Or is everything—even the intermediate stages of self-realization—attained by attending the *Bhāgavatam* class?

For me, self-realization takes place largely by allowing myself to write. Writing is a way for me to analyze myself and to offer prayers for improvement. It is a way I can come to a clear understanding of my motives and directions.

Yesterday, I visited a brother and heard of his *bhajana.* He does fifteen or twenty minutes of prayers, thinking of the members of the *paramparā* and the residents of eternal Navadvīpa and Vṛndāvana. He mentioned that this year, he had been planning to write a book. He decided instead to spend those three hours a day on internal improvement. I was swayed at first, thinking I should also follow his example, but then I asked myself, "*How can I practice* bhajana *in writing?*"

14

My brother said, "Maybe you *can* write what you are thinking. Maybe you will have to learn how to be artful in a literary sense. Maybe you will have to learn the art of how to present Kṛṣṇa consciousness to readers."

We think of a devotee as first and foremost a devotee of Kṛṣṇa. His writing is a by-product of being a devotee. He writes poems when his emotions overflow with love for Kṛṣṇa, or he writes when his compassionate desire to preach becomes strong.

But to be an artist means he has to discover his own voice and language. The Kṛṣṇa conscious artist can be distinguished from the nondevotee artist by his desire to serve only Kṛṣṇa. Can he be an artist and at the same time a pure devotee? Or, if he *is* an artist, can he purify his art in Kṛṣṇa consciousness? The answer is yes.

Then what does he have to do? He has to accomplish two things: he has to discover his own art forms, and he has to glorify Kṛṣṇa. If he succeeds, you get a harmonious, readable, Kṛṣṇa conscious book. The successful Kṛṣṇa conscious artist attains *kṛṣṇa-prema* sooner or later, not by renouncing his work, but by discovering how to eliminate the material energy from it. Perhaps he will finally drop all art as pretense. Perhaps he will find a way to speak that suits him and that is natural to him, and he will proceed to speak like that. Perhaps others will think he is eccentric.

I found this statement by a favorite author from my childhood, Thomas Wolfe. It is from *The Story of a Novel*, pp. 47–8.

> I know the door is not yet open. I know the tongue, the speech, the language that I seek is not yet found, but I believe with all my heart that I have found the way, have made a channel, am started on my first beginning. And I believe with all my heart, also, that each man for himself in his own way, each man who ever hopes to make a living thing out of the power and substance of his one life, must find that way, that speech, that tongue, that language, and that door—must find it for himself as I have tried to do.

15

Some Godbrothers have implied that insistence on writing is like *karma-yoga* in which you give the fruits of your work to guru and Kṛṣṇa. Pure *bhakti* means surrendering to the guru and saying, "Whatever you want, I'll do." Yes, we have to surrender like that. But then Kṛṣṇa and guru say back to us, "What do *you* want to do? Which of these nine principles is most to your liking?" This is not so-called *siddha-praṇālī*, where an immature devotee chooses his eternal *rasa* in all details. But it seems to be a preliminary, valid stage of non-karmic *bhakti*, when we follow our desire to serve Kṛṣṇa in a particular way.

If Kṛṣṇa wants me to shovel dirt and give up my pen, will I do it? I am not really as madly attached to writing as it sounds, but I do love to do it. It is a fact that we have to go beyond all attachments—so that whatever we do, whatever we like to do—the real motive is only to please Kṛṣṇa. I am not yet so surrendered. May Prabhupāda find some use even now in my imperfectly formed *purīs:* "They are not standard, but they will do."

16

Uddhava is out in the greenhouse. Soon I will go out to the bench. What will I say? Will I preach? Worship? Why do I mostly remember something that was in my mind and has since passed out? Can I live in Kṛṣṇa consciousness right now?

Yes, but does now mean I create something artificial or theoretical? Do I recite something and call it "going deeper"? Do I say something that sounds good?

Maybe it's like that. You asked me for food, so it is only natural that I look in the refrigerator or pantry. That's where I keep the food.

I mean, don't you live and breathe Kṛṣṇa consciousness?

Yes, but even for that I have to stop and go to the source of life (*prāṇa*) in order to tell you. If you ask me, "Is your heart beating?" I will answer, "Yes, or I would be dead." But I have to actually hear my heart thumping by going to that part of my body where I can hear it. Then I can tell you, "Yes, it's beating slow and steady." My telling you "I'm alive in spiritual life" is a critical act. It takes observation. I mean, I *know* I am alive, but to be able to describe my state, I have to go to that place where I can look at it. That means that the whole process is many times removed from life itself.

"Are you Kṛṣṇa conscious now? What are you thinking about in Kṛṣṇa consciousness?"

As I look at myself, the false ego wants to butt in and say something clever and motivated. I can't make a simple cry like "No!" or, "Yes!" or, "Help me!"

The free-writing process is an attempt to cut through. We usually don't cut through before we hit an obstacle, so we have to report that honestly.

I prefer it, this chipping away at the coverings of the self, the coverings of the universe. I also like to analyze everything against perfect *śāstra*, but not forget the actual person who is trying to speak Kṛṣṇa consciousness and improve his predicament. That's why writing is *bhajana* and prayer and *sādhana*.

The bench is within reach of Yamunā on her rope. She is getting closer as I write. I will have to abandon this spot or she will lick me up. Her eyes are covered with flies. She is only a few feet away from me now, chewing grass and snorting—snip, snip, snip, snort. Even if she doesn't come right up to me, she distracts me. Plenty of flies. I can't tolerate them as she does.

It is all distraction really, all obstacles. It is our reality as conditioned souls. We *cannot* meditate, most of us, because dependent calves are coming toward us and enemy flies are tormenting us. But we stab at it and sometimes, even in the face of adversity, we are suddenly able to say something Kṛṣṇa conscious even better than we would have been able to sitting quietly like old philosphers in our rooms.

But some comfort is needed, some distance—at least we try to arrange it that way. Therefore a sage lives in a *bhajana-kuṭir*, and even a preacher resides in a temple if he can to save time to hear and chant. Going into the world is only for Kṛṣṇa's purpose. The point is to remember Kṛṣṇa and serve Him wherever we are.

But sometimes I "look within" and it's empty or just full of old, secondhand ideas. That's why I say what I perceive with my senses. Finally I surrender (again and again) and open the *śāstra* and recite. Kṛṣṇa appears in *hari-kathā*, in the words of His devotees. He is actually in His own place doing things His way with His dearmost devotees. This place where we *jīvas* live isn't everything! We can do a lot better than staying here and trying to remember and serve Him from such a distance. He has His abode.

He is here too, through His external energy. The souls in the material world are unconscious. They don't want to be with Kṛṣṇa because they are mad. A few want to reform, but we are stuck in our attachments to the body and the false ego.

Therefore, the best Kṛṣṇa conscious message comes from Kṛṣṇa-loka. That is the definition of *śāstra*. The message also gets through when the *dhāma* (Lord's residence) appears in the heart of the pure devotee. Then we can see a living example of one who is apparently living in the world, but who is steeped in Kṛṣṇa's pastimes.

Śrīla Prabhupāda sometimes said the Lord's pastimes are "televised" into the hearts of devotees. Kṛṣṇa and His *līlā* appear in Rūpa Gosvāmī's heart and he writes down what he sees. Then the *mahā-bhāgavatas* write commentaries on the *śāstras* to create a *smṛti*, a supplementary *śāstra* to educate people who want to know God.

So where does that leave me? Praying at the feet of those great Vaiṣṇavas, tolerating flies on the bench, writing until I get too disturbed. No, it is not a first-class literature, and yet it is within the fire of Kṛṣṇa consciousness. It is in the shelter of my Gurudeva. It's what I must do.

17

I am searching for a perfect place to write. I am waiting for inspiration, the unconscious entry into the perfect subject when all the doors open and I just sail through them with *kīrtana* and praise of Lord Kṛṣṇa and realization and humility, aware of my tiny, joyous place as a punished but rectified servant of Rādhā and Kṛṣṇa, Vraja and the Yamunā.

Where is that perfect occasion? Obviously, being so close to this attic roof is good, but not good enough. The shed would be an improvement in some ways, but still not good enough. "The need of the spirit soul is that he wants to get out of the limited sphere of material bondage and fulfill his desire for complete freedom. He wants to get out of the covered walls of the greater universe. He wants to see the free light and the spirit. That complete freedom is achieved when he meets the complete spirit, the Personality of Godhead" (*Bhāg.* 1.2.8, purport).

18

Why do I write? I write because there is sweat on my upper lip. I write because I came here to do it. I write because I learned how to do it in college. It is a way I have chosen. If I don't write, I won't collect pages.

I write because there is an old woman in a faded *sārī* slowly walking across the field and I want to tell you about it. I write to chase blues, to race ahead of my agitated mind and not dwell on material desire. I write to chase the flies. I write because Prabhupāda told me to.

I write because we came to Vṛndāvana and I am always saying this is the best place to write. There is a bamboo-supported tent up here to protect me from the sun just so I can write.

I write because we have typists and Baladeva and Madhu and everybody, even my high school English teacher, and the dictionary—and what would I do if I didn't write?

I write to join the elite order of eternal Vaiṣṇavas. I write in hopes that Kṛṣṇa will say, "All right, give him some mercy. Let his writing improve and be filled with sweetness." I write to explain myself and to do honest work. I write to serve readers. I write to do something crucial during the crucial hours of the day. When I don't write, I think, "That time could have been spent writing."

I write to use precious health and life duration. After I die, something will be left behind. They will say, "He wrote many books like Bhaktivinoda Ṭhākura. Not *like* Bhaktivinoda Ṭhākura, but for ordinary strugglers like himself."

Here comes Baladeva on a rickshaw. He has a red *gamchā* on his head. The small *walla* is pedaling the heavyset *sādhu* in white cloth. Baladeva may have bought me some India ink—which is why I write. I write also to tell you that last night, after I attended a class, the *pūjārī* handed me some of Rādhā-

Śyāma's flowers. I put them in a reticule. Yesterday was Baladeva Jayantī.

I pray to Balarāma and the *guru-paramparā*—I treasure those yellow daisy petals with the brown whorl that I received. It's worth writing down.

I am foolish. I write in hopes of getting beyond foolishness. It doesn't matter that I am a fool; I write and connect with Kṛṣṇa consciousness. *Anyone* can write, and if he lives a *sādhaka's* life, he can give the most valuable thing.

19

I make a great deal about the fact that I am trying to be honest and that I have to deal with the karma of a *mleccha* upbringing. In writing I try to come clean. I use the writing as a way to rid myself of doubts and to be honest. That means I have to make painful admissions. Those who want reading to take them above that struggle may find it strange that a so-called spiritual author is still struggling, and they may find it even stranger that he insists on writing down the record of his struggle.

It is a private kind of writing made public. I am committed to including the imperfect self, as he exists today, and the reality he perceives—and his act of correcting faulty perceptions by Vedic knowledge. Can such a faulty writer give us perfection? Yes, or he can point to it. It is the same *paramparā* knowledge you get from an author who doesn't include his faulty self (if he has one). But with the writing I do, you get fear of the monkey and the overcoming of that fear—and then the return of that fear, and the toleration of that fear even before it is completely overcome.

20

This is an opportunity. While a white cow eats what it can find amid the thorny bushes, I look within to speak. The broadcast *bhajanas* aren't going to stop me. But I can't remember what I wanted to say. There is something in the breeze I want to capture, if I can just bypass the distractions and the negative mood. I require constant hope and confidence. How detrimental the internal critics are. Yet we are trained to heed them. They say, "You don't have much of worth to say and whatever good is in you, you can't say it very nicely. You better wait a long time and think over a sentence. We'll let you know later whether it needs to be culled or how you should revise it. Don't tell us your dreams, desires, hearty spirit of the moment. Always remember you are a dry stick and your spontaneity is *māyā*."

They've never heard of a book such as I am attempting now. They want to know what category it fits into so it can be listed in the Library of Congress. Is it "Hare Kṛṣṇas," or, "Spiritual Life (Hinduism)," or, "Kṛṣṇa (Hindu Deity)"? Let them do their work after I do mine. They can call it what they like.

21

Now the sun is going down. Cows are pasturing. I am seeking those excellent or good or passable sentences describing a simple operation in Vṛndāvana as I see it. I don't see everyone stunned by love of Kṛṣṇa. I don't hear the flute. But I like to make sentences, like a man who likes to make arrows and would like to make them all day. I am like the person Śrīla Prabhupāda describes who loves his service. Later, he will come to love Kṛṣṇa, but the service itself should not be hated. I dream of crafting excellent sentences in His service. It is ultimately for Him, for use by His pure devotee and the Kṛṣṇa consciousness movement. Why else would I want to do it? It would have no purpose. I can be redeemed only when Kṛṣṇa agrees to accept me and my service.

Someone could say I'm being indulgent. Let them say it. I say it too sometimes. But I am being dedicated. I am feeling the swift chariot of time rushing behind me. I want to do my work before it's too late.

Dear reader, if you were here with me and you looked up, you would see this field. You would see the dirt path that leads across Bhaktivedanta Swami Mārg—and then you would see the temple. My business is to look down toward the page and catch thoughts and feelings. Parrots screech, asking to be included in anything I write. A dog wanders into the courtyard of my mind, his sides heaving and panting. He sits down for a break, his coat tangled and mangy. He is bothered by fleas and he digs at them.

A book-in-progress is threatened in many ways. People take up your time, fill your head with their images. And there are internal threats. I think I may be too poverty-stricken. But I go on anyway. Moment by moment my time is stolen. As I walked home from the temple, two Russian devotees stopped me. "It's important!" I believed it. Then I walked further and the caretaker of the Oriental Institute made his usual friendly greeting, "*Haribol*, Mahārāja." That's usually a pleasant interlude, so I took it that way. But today he went further, "Prabhu . . . " he said, and I stopped. "Diwali *baksheesh*?" I pretended I didn't understand what he was talking about and walked on. But it drained me. I don't know why I felt it so much—a mixture of guilt at not giving and disappointment that his friendliness had turned into asking for *baksheesh*. I've arrived here with forty minutes to spare before the next engagement, but I'm feeling lonely, sorry, tired. I want my time. My time to serve everyone.

Now as I write this, two ladies are outside delivering something, but they see me. This room isn't private. I have an 11 o'clock engagement to speak to young boys in a *gurukula* class. Their teachers have been asking me to do it for weeks. What can I say to them? The teacher said, "They are from five to nine years old and they do not relate to the world of big people, so once a week we have an adult come in so the children can meet them and get some impression that when they grow up, they can be devotees."

I'm going to speak about the childhood of pure devotees. I'll show them pictures of Śrīla Prabhupāda when he was a child, and Dhruva Mahārāja and Prahlāda Mahārāja when they were five years old.

Then tomorrow, another disciples' meeting. This morning in the temple room I positioned myself in front of the closed door of the first altar, waiting for the conches to blow. The devotee standing next to me began speaking to me. At first I didn't remember him, but then I did. He wants to meet with me. Okay, I said, see my secretary and we'll make a time. But after three days, I'm going to stop this.

I want to be so quiet that I can hear a bumblebee in the marigolds and take notice of the voices of the bold-fluffy birds in the front yard. In that state, I should be able to write.

22

Look for Kṛṣṇa. It takes more time than I have tonight. But I know what I am looking for. The well-rounded life—to write about it. Too often, despite our trying to be honest, we write a selected portrait of life. We portray life as we would like it to be or as we think it should be. Are we afraid to face life as it actually comes, as it actually is? Are we afraid we will be exposed as less than Kṛṣṇa conscious? Better to let it come. See what we really are and then we can improve.

For example, tonight I spoke to about thirty disciples on how they should relate to the spiritual master. I told them the burden is on them. I admitted that there is a burden on the spiritual master also: "The spiritual master cannot accept service from a disciple without awarding him spiritual instruction. That is the reciprocation of love and duty" (*Bhāg.* 3.23.52, purport). I didn't raise the question of whether *I* am a spiritual master or not. You might say, "Of course you are!" But both the guru and the disciple may doubt that. I *wanted* to say, "As you are in training and working for improvement, so am I." It's good news, actually, but it stuck in my throat. I couldn't say it. Can a father tell his son or daughter that he's trying to improve in his parenting? Will they hold it against him if he's not perfect?

This is another example of truthfulness. You try to hold all the disciples in some kind of control. One disciple came up to me after and said, "Please forgive me." One asked how he could serve better, but when I told him, he said, "Maybe in the future."

This is the last disciples' meeting in Vṛndāvana. In a few days, many of them will go back to their countries. I will continue to work on their behalf. There's a limit to what we can accomplish by a quick exchange of letters, but something is there too.

The lights went out and as I sat in the darkness, I heard someone come to the gate and ask for me. Madhu gave him a time—11 A.M. tomorrow. So although I call this full-time writing, it hasn't happened yet.

Someone heard me quote Śrīla Prabhupāda on "working to top capacity." Prabhupāda said if we think that we will get the highest grade on the exam, then we will at least pass. If we think that we will just pass the exam, then we may fail. Top capacity? It seems rarely achieved. But I'm looking for it in my writing. Get beyond a sea of faces. Swim out to where it's you facing the truth of your own thoughts and the big sky and the water and your surrender to Kṛṣṇa. Top capacity? I don't know.

I hear the train horn and the sound of its chugging. Take rest and rise. May Kṛṣṇa bless you with full capacity to cry and beg for His mercy. I look forward to a writing day.

23

Writing is a way to prove you are sane, you can make coherent sentences. Psychologists claim writers are trying vainly to create immortality. We try to make experience permanent by recording as much of it as possible. But it's a Pyrrhic victory—it is gained at too great a cost. We write for so many reasons in Kṛṣṇa consciousness. It's a service like any other service. The heart of it is not to create literature, but to incite devotion, both in ourselves and in the readers. When we string garlands, we are not trying to be florists, and when we write, we are not trying to be writers. We are always trying to be the servant of the servant of the servant of those who render service to the *gopīs*.

24

If you keep turning from your human and bodily condition to thoughts of Kṛṣṇa, you will see more the mechanics of it. You will see better *how* to turn to Kṛṣṇa, what act of will is involved. You will see how much you want to do it and what

Kṛṣṇa actually means to you. He has to mean more than a word in a book. Turning to Him has to mean more than duty.

Śrīla Prabhupāda defines Kṛṣṇa as everything, but for our purposes, we will use *The Nectar of Devotion*'s definition: Kṛṣṇa means Kṛṣṇa with His expansions and His pure devotees. I see obstacles: lack of faith *(śraddhā)* and a lack of spontaneous love. These obstacles prevent me from staying once and for all in the ocean of Kṛṣṇa's *nāma*, *rūpa*, *guṇa*, and *līlā*. So I *turn* to Kṛṣṇa—or *steer* to Him. When I veer off, then I again turn to Him by approaching His name, form, qualities, and pastimes by hearing from the *śāstras* and His pure devotees. I have eliminated all other interests in my life; I want only Kṛṣṇa. But I cannot have Him yet.

This situation not only perplexes me, but has become a critical concern. I cannot skip over my reluctance to surrender as if it didn't exist. I *could* stick to recording *śāstra* or writing study notes or philosophical essays convincing people to take up Kṛṣṇa consciousness. But I don't do that. My writing is my *bhajana*, my internal practice of recording first thoughts and then steering to Kṛṣṇa. I have faith that this process will eventually lead me to pure devotional service where all my thoughts are Kṛṣṇa conscious.

I want to explore this act of turning to Kṛṣṇa more in my writing. Sometimes devotees want me to write more expository essays, but I rarely write like that. It is more than a simple choice of one genre over another; I have chosen to write for self-purification and to hope to preach with whatever honest expression I can come out with. I want writing to be more personal and less restrictive than a formal lecture. I'm not satisfied by repeating dogma. I am willing to do it in a lecture for an hour or so, but I don't want to do it in writing.

I am learning more about Vraja Kṛṣṇa. Sometimes things I hear are theoretical to me, but I accept them on authority.

Kṛṣṇa consciousness is like that—it is based on submissive reception. It will only be complete when there is realization. Writing is my means to explore what I am hearing and to pray for realization.

25

Writing things down helps you to remember them. Some people keep "commonplace books" consisting entirely of quotes they want to have on hand. Sometimes they want to add their own appreciation of the quotes.

We write because our memories are faulty. In former ages, *brahmacārīs* were *śrutidhara*—they could remember whatever they read. I have a weak memory, especially for rote memorization. I write in hopes that whatever I write will remind me, and the world, before forgetfulness and death attack us. It may be a vain attempt, but I can't help but try. So much should not be forgotten! Prabhupāda and Kṛṣṇa gave me Kṛṣṇa consciousness in such a palatable way. I was touched. Their words should not be forgotten. Therefore I write.

Fear of death and writing—this is certainly a topic I have emotion for. Intellectually, we can say, "The author feels his death approaching and thinks that by writing, he can stave it off." But when you actually feel impending death you feel urgent. Death is a positive force sending you to the desk with pen in hand. Someone wants to interrupt you, but you think, "No, I must write, before it's too late, now, this evening." Anyone interrupting is an agent of Death. (You can't tell Death, "I'm writing. Don't bother me.") Writing affirms my life. And while I'm alive, I'm going to write. Writing will not prevent my death, but at least in a literary sense, it will outlast my death.

26

The big thing is Kṛṣṇa consciousness. That's my saving grace. I don't have a philosophy of my own; I have Kṛṣṇa consciousness. I'm a struggling human being, but more than that, I'm a struggling devotee, a *sādhaka*. If I didn't have Kṛṣṇa consciousness . . . don't even imagine it. Preserve what you have.

Yes, I want to write here and not just talk about it. But I have to talk about it also.

And if I get loose to write, what will I say? I will respond to *śāstra* and to Kṛṣṇa in my life. I will include portraits, descriptions from my little life, direct experiences as a human being. I long for the day when I can write honestly as a human being and it will coincide with *kṛṣṇa-kathā*. Until then, when I have to think "real hard" before I write of Kṛṣṇa, and be very careful I don't make a mistake or write something against the *siddhānta*, then I am writing as a student, and maybe as a preacher.

But I want more than that. I want to write as a simple, fallible human being who loves Kṛṣṇa and who sees Him in daily life.

"A writer is not so much someone who has something to say as he is someone who has found a process that will bring about new things he would not have thought of if he had not started to say them" (*Writing the Australian Crawl*, William Stafford).

Combine this with Kṛṣṇa consciousness and you've got a winning, revolutionary program. It can be done. It is accepted under the premise of *yukta-vairāgya*. We devotees *do* have something to say. We are struggling to achieve the most wonderful thing. We are dealing with the most interesting phenomena. What we are trying to do is the most important thing in human society. Honest, genuine news from the life of a *sādhaka* is good writing and good reading—as long as he doesn't spoil it with "officialdom," impersonalism, and an illusory covering of his real self. When a devotee breaks through the false covering, he gives more than a nondevotee can ever give—he gives the soul and his loving relationship with Kṛṣṇa. Of course, only other devotees will believe it and be interested, but it is still preaching.

"Some people talk about writing as if it's penmanship: you take dictation from your own psyche that has already done something. Well, I'm interested in the psyche that hasn't done something and then does something. . . . So I always try to get people to relax enough to pay attention to the things that actually occur to them during the process of writing. . . . I think writing is itself educational, exploratory, and worthy of trust while you're doing it" (*Writing the Australian Crawl*, pp. 73–4).

27

I prayed in a wooden pew. Votive candles were flickering. After confession (on Saturday afternoon), you went to the main altar where there was a nice foam edge on the kneeling bench, and made directed prayers to the golden thing that holds the Eucharist. You said your prescribed penance given by the priest in confession: ten Our Fathers, twenty Hail Marys, whatever. A good way for simple minds to be "punished"—by a quota of prayers. I bring it up to question whether I am more advanced now.

Doesn't my mind wander now as it did then? A shout in the street is the same as it always was. And as you used to think of baseball games, TV, and your sister and school friends, now you hear trucks on I-80 and you are a young, old man who the young boys never recognize—especially since you're wearing a *sannyāsī's* dress. But how much different is it?

You want me to answer that?

No, not necessarily.

Let your prayers go up sincerely. *Anyone* who does so is fortunate and blessed. I'm not at the pinnacle of mystical advancement in conjugal humor. I'm a boy-man who can't cry, whether kneeling at a grotto for the Lady of Fatima or looking at a picture of Rādhā and Kṛṣṇa in Vraja. I'm way down in this world. That's why I always write about how we can be Kṛṣṇa conscious from here, how I can write Kṛṣṇa consciousness from here. Will His mercy extend all the way down here? How the hell did I get so overpowered by the mind and the world? Do I have a guarantee that in some future life, I will cry tears when chanting and my voice will choke up? Will I work as hard as I can for the Lord's mission and not slow down when I feel bodily pain?

As if to punctuate this mood, a crow in Pennsylvania caw-caws from the treetops.

28

Since you are writing this for yourself, it seems all right that you are collecting so many proofs of your validity. But is it right? Shouldn't there at least be something more than this? And how often you seem to be posturing, taking a theme because it's what writers do—like writing on solitude, or something like that. I have yet to talk more from my own self. I seem to think that if I do it, I will find myself to be a simple, somewhat ignorant person who will talk like an uneducated relative. Will I be like loudmouthed, greasy Aunt Grace of the Guarino family? "Hey, Ralph! Go get Johnny Boy and bring him to the table!"

But it may not be what you expect. Anyway, you are afraid to venture into that. You keep thinking it means going back to the young man you were with your short, stylish topcoat purchased in Greenwich Village and your tight-wrapped umbrella. But finding the self is not that, although it may mean having the courage to meet each of those past selves and ask, "What was I doing then?" Have I left that posing, or am I posing even now in a different garb? (Prabhupāda says a symptom of Kali-yuga is people will define themselves by their dress, like a *sannyāsī* in saffron or a *gṛhastha* in white, despite their lack of qualification for their *āśramas*.)

I'm a writer, I'm a writer—it keeps coming across on these pages. I am almost desperate to assert that. I've put all my eggs into one basket. What if it doesn't come out? I think I am ready for that contingency and I will just switch over to becoming a chanter of the holy names or even a temple president again (but not a married man in this lifetime, thank God).

All these are temporary designations. You think you are a man, a male ego. You have to go beyond that too. So many things you regard as boorish, but you may not be as clear of them as you think.

You come to drink from the clear stream of your spiritual master's books. Just a sip and then you step back. You talk about it. I say go forward and take another sip, and another.

29

I need to help myself. My inner skeptic is ready to do his quiet, dastardly work. I protect myself by quoting the *Bhagavad-gītā:* "Armed with yoga, stand and fight." I fight with my own word-weapons, and with my thoughts. If the battle subsides, I try to celebrate creativity, happy times in Kṛṣṇa consciousness with Prabhupāda. Devotees aren't always debating; they prefer to discuss Kṛṣṇa's pastimes among like-minded devotees. But we have to be ready to defend from any attack. Writing can be a playground, but it must be ready to switch at once to a military camp. My book is not meant to be a vulnerable place that atheists can ravage through or set afire. I am ready for them. I will throw them out. *Then* I can go on praising the solitary, creative life and the service mood engaged in Kṛṣṇa's service.

For this purpose, I have also had to defend writing itself. It is my *guru-sevā*. These wars that arise are sometimes civil wars. "The doubts that have arisen out of ignorance," Kṛṣṇa calls them. I must take my place in the phalanx of the army *directed by Kṛṣṇa*. He is the best military commander, along with His devotees in *paramparā*. I am their *cela*. On my own, if I choose to take some independent stance, I'll be cut down by powerful adversaries.

Someone may be amused by my chivalrous rhetoric, but I know what's required. I don't want to see this devotee's heart ravaged by my old college friends or the atheist philosophers, psychologists, writers, and poets. Therefore, I include self-defense as one of my themes.

Writing should help me prepare for the journey to Goloka-dhāma. Let it be a record left behind by one who actually took off from here and went back to Godhead. Then it will be a successful journal! It should not be the record of a futile attempt to make a permanent settlement of peace and happiness in this material world.

With this in mind, I can write about how I love to take a morning walk or how I am drawn to fulfill the cravings of my creative side. Keep the cause in mind and work toward it. That morning walk is filled with plans and enactments of devotional service to the transcendent Lord; the book-writing is to increase the library of books by the Vaiṣṇava *paramparā* to go against the imbalance created by nondevotee books. The poems written in a permissive spirit carry the message of loving surrender to Kṛṣṇa and the *desire* to serve Him. Make prayers, efforts, declarations for devotional service. I am your friend in these endeavors.

And *śāstra* is my friend. It lifts me up and makes my writing solid. My life is a touchstone which can help whoever comes in contact with me. If I have *śraddhā* and knowledge of Kṛṣṇa, then I can be a true friend.

30

One of the contentions of this writing is that a book doesn't have to have a conventional form or a specific subject matter. This is also the contention of much modern poetry and art. For example, the old idea was that poems had to be either couplets, sonnets, or rhyming in some other pattern. At least they had to be in iambic pentameter. Since free verse poetry came into being, a poem doesn't have to conform to such models. You don't have to sing while wearing chains. As for subject matter, you don't have to decide, "I will write a series of poems on farms. The first poem will be about the chickens. Then I'll do a portrait of the farmer." Better to write about whatever is touching the heart. The first line may be about a farm, but then it may go off to life in the city or a remembrance of Kṛṣṇa's Vṛndāvana pastimes. I subscribe to these theories that writing needn't be in conventional forms or according to strict subject matters. Whatever is most favorable *(anukūla)* may be used as the form. Choose any or create your own.

The subject matter should always steer to Kṛṣṇa; it should be aimed at Kṛṣṇa consciousness. It should be aimed at going deeper into spiritual life. Find it wherever you are and yearn for it. The subject matter doesn't have to be a thorough analysis of the "nine principles of devotional service." What if, while writing of principle number four, you suddenly remember something urgent about principle number one? What's the harm in digressing or telling it when it comes up—while it's alive in your heart? Just tell me what you believe and what you think and who you are. Help me to be honest as you are, to admit failures, and to put my life in order so that I can serve Kṛṣṇa. This is what I want to get from reading a book.

Lord Caitanya teaches the *catuḥ-ślokī* of *Śrīmad-Bhāgavatam* to Prakāśānanda. Here is verse four: "A person interested in transcendental knowledge must therefore always directly and indirectly inquire about it to know the all-pervading truth" (Cc., *Madhya* 25.125). Śrīla Prabhupāda and Lord Caitanya explain that it is everyone's duty to learn about Kṛṣṇa from a bona fide spiritual master. There is no restriction according to race or nationality. Everyone has access to Kṛṣṇa because He is everywhere. Lord Caitanya said, "As far as religious principles are concerned, there is a consideration of the person, the country, the time and the circumstance. In devotional service, however, there are no such considerations. Devotional service is transcendental to all considerations" (Cc., *Madhya* 25.121). This comment also seems to support the freedom I advocate while writing and reading in Kṛṣṇa consciousness. Just make sure it's Kṛṣṇa in authorized books, and just make sure in your writing that you're steering as best you can to Kṛṣṇa's lotus feet. If you're already at His lotus feet, then please tell us the nectar. Which nectar? Which teaching? *Any*. Śrīla Prabhupāda said Kṛṣṇa consciousness is like a *gulābjāmun*. No matter what side you bite it on, it is sweet.

31

The pattern so often when I write is that I start with whatever my senses can perceive or whatever is on my mind, and feel confident that it is the reality. Soon, my conscience tells me that I want to glorify Kṛṣṇa, that this is the whole purpose of writing. But I cannot turn to a description of Kṛṣṇa in the spiritual world with the same directness as my more perceptual writing. Of course, this is one advantage to writing in Vṛndāvana, that even the sense perceptions are of the holy *dhāma.*

I have to leap from what seems real and tangible to a world I know only from books. I'm sorry about this because frankly, I write as a propagandist, as somebody who wants to convince people of Kṛṣṇa, as somebody who wants to encourage devotees about the reality and beauty of Kṛṣṇa. But I cannot speak of Kṛṣṇa as if I have just seen Him going to play in the fields. I wish I could. I wish I could be filled with emotions of separation from Kṛṣṇa or with joy in telling of His activities the way the Vrajavāsīs do at the end of day. How can I dare to even think of such a thing? And how dare I write like that? It's not even expected of me. Anyway, I'm just explaining the pattern and how I have to work within my limitations as a devotee and a writer. Therefore I hope I can make that leap smoother. I would like to find a way to repeat what's in Prabhupāda's books, and yet have it come directly through my own senses and mind. Then I will be a devotee of Kṛṣṇa who is also an honest, complete human being. I want to tell of the happiness of Kṛṣṇa consciousness and yet be humble. These are things I can perfect as the art of expression.

32

Keep hammering away at this point—how to go from here to *kṛṣṇa-kathā*? We used to talk of a similar transition in writing topical essays for *BTG*. A topical essay treats a situation in the world—disease, war, politics, etc.—and presents it from the Kṛṣṇa conscious viewpoint. Our essays often suffered from too much being cut into two. First we'd state the material problem and then pop! like a jack-in-the-box, out would come the

Gītā śloka or the sudden appearance of the *harināma* party with drums and *karatālas*. There wasn't a sufficient transition. Writing those essays required that a devotee thoroughly consider the material problem and how Kṛṣṇa consciousness could practically solve it.

Similarly, I start to free-write and then realize it's not rich *kṛṣṇa-kathā*, so I make the leap to topics I've read. It reminds me of Greek Tragedy's "*deus ex machina*." God suddenly enters into the flow of human events via some device, and *He* brings the solution. Who believes it? God doesn't appear when we clap our hands and call for Him. "Oh, I forgot. You are supposed to write about God. Okay—God! Kṛṣṇa? Please appear here." It's not like that.

Spray in my face as I ride in the front of a motor boat across a wide river in Guyana. There is danger everywhere. This brown water is filled with crocodiles and the boat is unsteady. Such a wide river.

Why write this? Because it came, friend, don't ask me why. This is not *deus ex machina* when something must appear by itself. Don't worry so much that you're like a tour guide who has to lead the guests through the Fisher Mansion in Detroit or the castle at Rāḍhadeśa, Belgium. Carefully, you say, "Yes, this museum is the work of a community of spiritually-minded people who practice *bhakti-yoga*, but who are actually quite normal. Now I'll take you to the tower where, if the air is clear, we'll be able to get a good view of the hills. This castle was used in World War II by the American soldiers as a hospital. Before that it was . . . " You don't have to be afraid that you will say something that will turn off your nondevotee guests.

Just be yourself. I want to be a devotee, damn it. It's not only the subject—Kṛṣṇa with His devotees—but the mood. I would like to have an overflowing desire to write of Kṛṣṇa, but I want it to come urgently, nonstop. I have a desire to write like that now. I'm committed to writing what comes, because that is me, honestly—but I'm not happy when the results are mostly devoid of glorification of the Lord.

The answer is to intensify my life and consciousness. Then I will have something to write about. But I am preaching and reading to the extent I can do it feelingly. I already have material to write about. Running out into a fresh burst of activities won't supply me with a better impetus to write. Writing is done in the note pad, but it has to come from life. Even if we say it comes from *śāstra*, there has to be life both in the reading and the writing.

Surrender, surrender. I'm touching on some vital areas here but don't know if I can follow them up.

Kṛṣṇa consciousness is already here and I just have to enter it. It's not an artificial imposition on the mind. It's in me. Therefore I write and uncover it. That's why when I'm away from writing, I soon feel distracted from my inner mood. I think if only I could write, maybe I could bring it out.

33

The free-writer has to abandon the idea that all his writing is immortal. He has to keep writing even when he has nothing to say, nothing he wants to get out on paper. Why does he continue to write at such times? Because he has faith in the writing process. He feels he has to keep traversing territory.

For example, if you are crossing a desert and you want to reach an oasis, you have to be willing to walk through the barren land. Otherwise you will never arrive at the oasis. You can't skip over the desert, or circumvent it in any way, if you want to reach something that is only found at its center. This writing method demands commitment. If you want to be an accomplished writer, you must agree to regular, daily practice.

There is something fanatical about it, in one sense, writing even when you don't feel like it or you have nothing to say. Repeated good results, even from days that begin with, "I don't want to; I have nothing to say," prove the effectiveness of writing practice.

The *śāstras* declare that any chanting of the holy name is beneficial. Therefore we persist even if we don't feel the results. Writing doesn't have as many scriptural statements backing it up. We don't find numerous verses or purports advising everyone to write. There are just a few, and of course they are precious to me.

As with other specialized services, we find writing fits under the much-emphasized main practices of ninefold *bhakti*. Writing is *kīrtana* and *viṣṇu-smaraṇam*. It is other things too: *vandanam*, *ātma-nivedanam*. This one practice can be the main form of *sādhana-bhajana* and preaching for a devotee who considers himself a writer.

34

When writing practice succeeds, its virtue is that it is nourishing in and of itself. It doesn't nourish a reader because I purposely tried to prepare something for him, but because it is wholesome on its own. Do you understand the distinction I am making here? If I think, "I shall be a teacher and give them something good," that can be presumptuous. But when I write for my own purification, and when that leads to a personal discovery and I write it down, then the reader gets it with more sincerity and less presumption from the writer.

35

I want to tell you about the picture of Śrīla Prabhupāda I have that accompanies me when I write. I bought it at the gift shop in the Krishna-Balaram Mandir. It is sealed inside a heavy glass frame and I like it very much. I dust it every day and sit it on my desk wherever I go.

In the picture, Śrīla Prabhupāda is sitting outdoors on a pillow. He is wearing a saffron sweater and looking down, his hand in his bead bag. He doesn't have to say anything and neither do I, but sometimes we speak. He appears indirectly in my writing. I may write, "Dear Śrīla Prabhupāda, please let me know . . . " Or, "I want to please him . . . " In each case, I mean *this* Prabhupāda as he appears on my desk.

This picture is far more valuable than anything else I use. He's here, his forehead a gentle golden, his thoughts private. He looks within and invites me to do that too. His feet are bare. I'm all alone, but he is here.

36

A poet should find something Kṛṣṇa conscious to write about. Saying, "I am a poet" is like saying I am a guru or I am a Vaiṣṇava. It's something we shouldn't claim. But I am writing this for myself. I need to make the claim and to assert this side of myself. Why do I write so much? Why do I work to make poetic statements?

Being a poet doesn't mean writing pretty or flowery words. It means transferring feelings from the writer to the reader. A poet wants to share tears and yearning, the nature of being. A poet doesn't always want to polish his expression, and he never wants to polish it to the point where it becomes divorced from the reality from which it sprang. Poets can write poetry within their prose.

We can't sit around waiting for poetic moments to occur. They occur when we write. The more we write, the more likely they are to occur. We can write after Prabhupāda's disappearance, but we cannot write without the inspiration and direction he gives us. Śrīla Prabhupāda can transfer Kṛṣṇa consciousness from his heart to ours.

Let me write for that transference. Let me be a poet and struggle with the poverty of spirit. Let me find my theme and pray to Prabhupāda for mercy.

These are some of the thoughts I had last night. Now I sit facing myself and the photo of Śrīla Prabhupāda on my desk. Can I get deeper? Can I find my own heart and then dive into the fresh streams of Kṛṣṇa conscious expression? "Just writing" is like emptying stores, like fasting and working at the same time. It needs to be complemented by reading Prabhupāda's books.

Writing and Kṛṣṇa conscious life go together. Our lives are flowing—preaching, *sādhana*, and writing. Writing, preaching, and *sādhana*.

37

Śrīla Prabhupāda, you know me, although I don't know you fully. You are my eternal guide. I ache to understand you and how you will guide me eternally. I beg for your help so that I can become qualified to understand it. This is so important that I should be willing to write it again and again in sessions. This is cutting through, this is writing down the bones, the wild mind, the Australian crawl, how to write well, writing with power, writing without teachers, this is it. Don't forget it. One politician in ancient Greece ended all his talks, "Carthage must be destroyed!" I end and begin and go through the middle saying, "Dear Śrīla Prabhupāda, please reveal yourself to me and tell me how I can serve you eternally. Give me faith to overcome obstacles. Give me service to qualify myself. Please keep me. Give me my intimate *rasa* with you. I am begging for mercy."

38

Why have I withdrawn from the material world to write? What is the purpose of the Kṛṣṇa consciousness movement? Am I convinced that we are going about fulfilling that purpose in the best way? Am I doing my share? How is *bhajana* an answer to our problems?

My own field is not to sharpen my language and argument so that it sounds convincing to nondevotees. Drutakarma Prabhu and others are doing that in their books. Don't call me in when you need a quick-thinking spokesperson to appear on a TV talk show. I am working in another important area. ISKCON has divisions of labor. One person can't do it all. I'm fulfilled and happiest when I work on establishing my own integrity and delve into more truthfulness, when I write and enter the sources of expression and creativity, when I read a *śāstra* and tell you what I have been reading.

For those who have already come to Śrīla Prabhupāda's movement, or who are considering it (admittedly a small group of the total world population), I may be a useful source person. That's my humble job. I'm not the savior, the shelter for all, but if I write something honest, I hope it will help people. I mean those who are considering that the material world can't be improved by material methods and that the only escape is

Kṛṣṇa consciousness. To them I offer encouragement. I have been doing this for almost thirty years. You can be a devotee, live away from the world of madness, and still be a real person.

39

I had a few minutes to kill before leaving for a home program. I visited M. in his room filled with boxes and papers, and then I went into the kitchen just to look around. I saw two cookbooks, Kūrma's and Yamunā's, and opened them. I hadn't realized how much personal writing Yamunā put in her book along with the recipes. It's a beautiful book, but I was especially impressed by her lifelong dedication to her cooking service, and her dedication to writing it all down.

It made me want to be dedicated to my service too. But unlike Yamunā, I have no specific topic like cooking. What *is* my topic? The Library of Congress cataloguing people would want to squeeze me into "diaries; autobiography; Hare Kṛṣṇa movement." William Saroyan tells how he looked up one of his books in the library. Under the subject heading they had written, "Nothing." He tells us how he was hurt and insulted by that. His topic was William Saroyan, not nothing.

My topic is rowing a boat. I am rowing down the Charles River, or any river, whether it's cold and foggy or warm and foggy or summer or whatever. I get into my boat and row. Put my books under the "boatman" category, please.

My topic is Kṛṣṇa consciousness, a vast ocean, a series of Mount Sumerus, the inconceivable. How can I claim to always be one hundred percent within that energy? "A Kṛṣṇa conscious author" sounds presumptuous, as if I am always Kṛṣṇa conscious. Or, "I am not always Kṛṣṇa conscious, but when I write my books, I put only Kṛṣṇa conscious things in them. I am not going to put any nonsense in *my* book." Is this the standard of a Vaiṣṇava? Then he should not write until he is a hundred percent liberated. Some would say, "Yes, that is the standard we should follow. Spare the trees from being chopped into paper for imperfect books."

What will the exam be before we are allowed to publish?

I defy those who tell me my writing is a waste of time and paper. I am within my spiritual master's camp. Just give me a little paper and a few readers. Śrīla Prabhupāda wrote to the Indian government when they refused him paper during World War II, "Can't we spare at least a ream to propagate this message? You are spending millions and tons on chemicals for bombs. What's the harm if a little paper is used to broadcast God consciousness, which is the message to deliver us from wars?" I write in that spirit and with that confidence.

I am Kūrma dāsa with the bowl and eggbeater, posing on the back cover of his book. I am another Yamunā dāsī recalling the first time she went to Bombay and how her host cooked hot *capātīs*. They were served with butter, paper thin, and hot from the kitchen. She says, "Not everyone may be able to do this, but it is the standard I try to follow in my kitchen." The *Chicago Tribune* called her book, "The Taj Mahal of cookbooks," and now she has written another one. She writes in every issue of *BTG* on cooking. She's always ready to tell us about *purīs* or rice as something in Kṛṣṇa's kitchen.

I'm like that, although my offerings are not edible. I hope they are food for the spirit—fresh-baked raisin bread, toasted, served hot with butter and natural jam. A spicy ginger tea, and a fresh peach, and ground almonds. That's breakfast. A full lunch plate every day—*dāl*, rice, *sabjī*, *capātīs*, and plenty of sighs interspersed.

So if I come to the page with "nothing" as my topic, what can I say? No, it's not void. There is no void anywhere in God's creation.

Mixed Bouquet

1

Vraja-*bhajana* in the West—a *bhajana* that recognizes the straight downpouring rain as life-bringing; a *bhajana* that savors the cool air; a *bhajana* that acknowledges the gray clouds in the blue sky.

It will also rain in Vṛndāvana and I can write more devotionally there. I won't write farcically—"I am in the land of Kṛṣṇa and the rain appears to be the *gopīs'* tears." If Vraja means love of Kṛṣṇa, then why not feel it here and now with *this* rain? Feel separation. Chant while you have physical energy and facility.

The hard rain is crying, crying, Kṛṣṇa, Kṛṣṇa—it *is* doing that all over the corrugated tin roof and the plastic greenhouse and into the earth, into the calf's soaked skin, into the flowerpots brimming over, into the fresh streams on the roads, the ability in man. Easing off now, only to come on strong in another wave, like waves on a beach, like waves of love and calling to Kṛṣṇa.

Regardless of the increase of *bhāva* that will inevitably come when I go there, or rather, being happy for that future time—let me beg for a tiny drop of mercy here, today. Let me go to Vṛndāvana now, giving up fear and doubt.

I almost want to go out and dance in the rain, and feel it soak and chill me as I dance my primitive dance to God. But I don't. And now it is slowing. It could never keep up for long at such a pitch. Rivulets and drips and drops and new puddles. And the earth breathes in, taking in the water. The fresh aroma . . .

I am a child of the rain. I hope this is somehow connected to Kṛṣṇa's pastimes and that I can convey the same to my readers. This is what I feel now. It is this moment, the rain, my senses, and it is connected.

It *is* possible to feel Vraja's sweetness in a cool summer shower in Eire. You have to be captured by the Queen of Vṛndāvana and the narrations of sweet Kṛṣṇa. Otherwise, it is only rain. I am here to unite two worlds.

Cry out, "Kṛṣṇa! Rādhā! Gurudeva!" When the rain falls harder and harder, my own blood pumps hard. I don't feel like a fifty-two-year-old man anymore, but like a spirit soul ready to fly. It is the *kīrtana* of the inarticulate Nature. And Śrīla Prabhupāda himself said the waves at the beach are like the pounding of the *gopīs*' hearts in separation.

It is a secret world. You don't tell others about it. Under an umbrella you might scurry back to the house and say, "It's sure pouring." That's all. You might add, "It swept into the shed, but then the door shut to protect me." No more.

2

There is a technique in free-writing by which a writer takes two words that wouldn't normally go together and writes on them. Vṛndāvana, pocket. Vṛndāvana is as tangible as the pocket in my *kurtā*. But I can't carry Vṛndāvana in my pocket like I can carry the sugar granules some temples hand out as *mahā-prasādam*.

Kṛṣṇa, belt. Kṛṣṇa wears a golden belt. The secret is in the belt. Kṛṣṇa is not a secret, but the secret is in remembering Him by the word "belt." When we see any belt, we can think of Kṛṣṇa's belt and our secret. Kṛṣṇa, belt.

Brahma-muhūrta is a sacred time for *bhajana*. That's the ordinary way. *Brahma-muhūrta*, hour of switchblades. *Brahma-muhūrta*, a tall blond man in Boston by that name. *Brahma-muhūrta*, motorcycles and mustache.

What do you mean?

I'm not sure. The words *brahma-muhūrta* suddenly became so muscular and rhythmic, so rich in association, that the mind becomes intoxicated. It sounds like the name of an important person in Cuba. It is filled with power and richness like the smell of Cuban cigars. It is the best hour for *bhajana* and writing.

3

A similar exercise is when you try to reach for or discover strong words in your devotional writing. Conservative readers don't usually want to make the leap, but it's only a writing exercise. We don't have to be afraid of it.

In this exercise, you start with a Kṛṣṇa conscious word or image. Such words are sacred, so we don't want to play around with *them*. What we want to play with is our reaction to them. They release little explosions in us when we are conscious and aware and feel their imports.

So write down a Kṛṣṇa conscious word and then write down a strong word, phrase, or sentence. They don't have to be logically connected to the sacred word. We are trying to get below discursive thought.

Japa—overbloomed rose. *Japa* smells like an overbloomed rose. (What is it about the image of a rose just beginning to drop its petals?)

Then you go with the image:

Blossoms hang heavily on their branch, their vibrant colors just beginning to fade. The path is closing in on both sides with the darker green of early summer. The nights are not so chilly and dawn comes early.

Śrīdāmā picked a bunch of roses and put them in a vase on my altar. They bloom out effusively over the shoulders of the Pañca-tattva, a gorgeous pink-red. The six Gosvāmīs take shelter under the bending roses.

4

No tractors on Sunday, just crows. The last bang of pots in the kitchen before he makes his poem. Posies on the window sill. The rush of abbreviated parentheses and the desire to be true and happy and produce sentences that sing and uplift readers. It's not a nonsense waste of time when we pitchfork while M. laughs in the kitchen with his old friend U. But life is so expressible and wants to come out and you would like to write a sentence, but not at the cost of sanity. Annual meadow grass, a balm for the soul. Peaceful navigators come home to Vṛndāvana.

5

Bermuda words crowd out the door, words so strong they give off an odor—like carrots? No garlic, please. Feet washed? Don't smell bad, Prabhu. Words so tumbling that they lose their good manners and even their sense. Crude words of the peasant that I am. Wood chopper's shouts. Words coming out of the ground like vigorous, speedy weeds with such strong roots that my enemies cannot pull them out. They're just like those weeds with the pretty flowers that grow in the wall. If you try to tear them out, the whole wall collapses. You cannot get rid of me.

The clock swings down to the half past and then swings up to the left. I will have to chant soon. Good! I will give up my writer's position and be a chanter of *harināma*. Later I will be back for more words.

The earth returns with the dawn sunlight. Why are we so afraid of the wild creatures, we who live in our houses with cushions? What are we afraid of? The rawness? There is a helpless bug flipping around on the rug. Is it part of the rawness? Close your writing shop, your pen box. It's time for *japa*.

6

The meadow grass is swaying in a stronger breeze than yesterday. I am deep in the weeds, the tenacious, tasty dandelions (also known as "*pis-en-lis*"). The shimmery weeds are beautiful in this strong wind.

We discussed the quality of falling-in-love ecstasy that the *gopīs* had for Kṛṣṇa. Where is *our* enthusiasm? People go to church (or temple) with solemn faces. They don't swoon at the mention of God or at a glimpse of His paraphernalia—a peacock feather, a dark cloud, a golden *campaka* flower (or dandelion or buttercup).

I made a new acquaintance yesterday: sorrel. It is reddish, long, a true, tall weed. Grazing animals avoid it, so it grows abundantly. It is growing near my table and I didn't even notice it until today.

I have to hold my writing page down with my right arm or it flutters up. The clouds are gathering. They look like those marbles you played with as a child, blue and milky-cloudy.

The words punch out. I seem to think brute force has a place in *bhakti* and that I inherited it from my father. Just see my biceps in the loops of my handwriting. I can throw a punch like the best of them. I can leap fences and push and shove. I'm not such an old man.

Do I think that by reaching out blindly and grabbing handfuls of weeds—by ripping them out in one motion—that I can think and write in Kṛṣṇa consciousness? What if I tumble recklessly into a scene I would rather forget? I sprawl and think, "My writing is ruined." And so it is.

Start again. When you start confessing, you have to stop before you reach the worst crimes. Then you feel you weren't truly honest. J. D. Salinger wrote that a person may confess in writing that he was sexually impotent from the ages of 16–20—a painful admission with its resultant loss of face—but the same person won't dare confess that he stepped on the head of his pet hamster in a fit of petulance. What is the use of making such an incomplete confession?

Oh, something is better than nothing. We let it out bit by bit. I turn my face and spit at the things I used to do. Who could guess I have such an unsavory past? Fortunately, devotees aren't like the reporters who dig up the dirt on the politicians who are running for office. "He once backed out of a fist fight when he was in Little League." "He broke his father's pipe." "He has a phobia against roaches." (A whole article was printed in the newspaper during the Gulf War devoted to Sadaam Hussein's fear of roaches.)

He mimicked his Irish priest. He pestered his sister. He broke the TV. He was rejected. He told a dirty lie. He received stolen goods. He shrieked and ran. He fantasized. He thought he was the greatest. He cursed God. God cursed him. He's on the list of most dangerous criminals and also on the list of petty ones. He gambled his life and lost a million times. He wandered from Brahmā-loka to Patāla-loka and back, from Indra-gopa to Indra-loka.

In a past life he was a Dominican priest in Brazil. He desecrated paintings in the museum. He cut off his ear, read trashy novels, wished he were dead. He scratched his arms until they bled, stole, was afraid of the dark, shot squirrels and muskrats and sunk a knife into a man. He wished he had never been born, committed abortion, been aborted as a reaction, killed in the war, ran his car over a dog, stamped on ants and people's rights, played a radio loud at night, not giving a damn for his old mother—where does it end?

There is no sin I haven't committed. I'm exhausted. What else? Blew up Hiroshima, or had a part in it, connected by national karma. Blew up Pearl Harbor. Assassinated Kennedy and Julius Caesar and the second Kennedy and Martin Luther King. Told a lie in order to get ahead. Thought himself better than the next guy. Broke all the rules and threw them out the window.

The meadow grass sways innocently despite my ranting. Surely, my dear grass, you must have done some pretty things yourself. How else would you have ended up in this subhuman state? At least now you don't have to think about it all.

7

The sea is swelling
and I wish I could say
my devotion is too.
The fishermen are netting
silver fish
to eat, to eat

to live, to breathe. You say, "It's a shame. Poor fish," and you squash a mosquito. You breathe in germs. What to speak of ants and machines and De Chirico from the past. De Chirico on the horizon like a ten-foot tall, lonely monument to the dead or a symbol of peace at the heart of two nations, and me chanting like this, whirring under the fan.

8

Sunlight falls into this room. Marigolds are starting to bloom in our yard. The squashes are plumpening (to the monkeys' delight).

The backyard pump stands still as the earth spins fast with everything on it. We all hold steady. The tree muscles into the earth, holding on with its roots, the yellow-tinted leaves are steady in the sunshine, unless a slight breeze tips their edges.

9

The present-day people of Vṛndāvana are mostly not *Vraja-vāsīs* in the eternal sense. But neither am I a typical *sādhu*. Someone praised me recently as learned. He was Indian. I replied, "I'm a sinful person from New York City."

You said that before.

You saw a bird before.

You drank water from a cup before.

You read the same poem by Śrīla Rūpa Gosvāmī before.

How long ago was it that you told us the same story?

When is the last time you shed tears of joy or sorrow? It's been a long time and I can't even remember.

When did you last . . . ?

How long ago? How many births and deaths? What is the purpose of this inquiry? These questions began because I was embarrassed to be repeating myself.

10

In Vṛndāvana, gotta minute? Let me whisper in your ear. Life is more complicated here. For every word you write, ten are passed up. Words surround you like taxi *wallas*, "Hare Rāma, Hare Kṛṣṇa! Vṛndāvana?"

"Govinda, Govinda," that lady is singing. "Govinda, Govinda."

Mādhava dāsa is restless to go out somewhere, but where is the guide to take him? It makes you sad. So many sincere persons trying to understand who is Vṛndāvana and what is Rādhā-Kṛṣṇa.

You said . . . he said . . . a monkey on the brick wall said . . . parrots screeched in your ear and then flew off. The "Hare Kṛṣṇa, Hare Rāma, Nitāi-Gaura, Rādhe-Śyāma" *āśrama* has a new loudspeaker and the International Society for Divine Consciousness has a white, marble dome under construction on Bhaktivedanta Swami Mārg.

He said there's such a huge *Bhāgavata-saptāha* underway that no *āśrama* in town has a spare room. The line of beggars grows.

Leg stump. "Govinda" lady singing the blues. The Hindi lecturer over the PA system is listened to by his immediate audience, but also by two hundred and fifty squirrels and two billion ants.

I just killed an ant unintentionally. By the time I noticed, he was twitching and it was too late. What can I do about it? Absolve it by prayer and preaching? Tell someone they should be nonviolent? If I were kinder, I would see the ant as my brother and take *care* to remove him. I write it down here. I'm sorry about it and I will try not to do it again.

At least I can't understand that Hindi lecturer floating over the airwaves. He's cutting jokes and making dramatic asides. The birds in the sky don't care.

He said, "I think there is a bacterium in Vṛndāvana with my name on it and it's just a matter of time until it catches up to me."

That lady *bhajana* singer bending the notes: "Rādhe-Govinda, Govinda *Rād*-he! Rādhe-Govinda, Govinda *Rād*-he!" Over and over and over.

11

This life is small and contained. It seems to matter less as I read the science of *bhakti*. I mean the details and the step-by-step progress. I have to care about essentials.

Bhāva is rare. The Lord is not inclined to give Himself to impure *bhaktas*. *Bhaktas* can struggle at actually prosecuting the details and working at *bhajana* and *sevā* for many lifetimes, yet fail to attract Kṛṣṇa. We swallow those statements, understanding that they apply to us. Yet we go on. Business as usual. Dullness and slowness as usual. Breakfast and lunch as usual. Where is the keen desire?

The falling snow is still falling. Falling as usual, measuring time and witnessing my story. The snow isn't sticking, just falling and melting, falling and melting. I like to think that if the snow sticks, my devotional practices will stick. I will be buried in a safe world. Kṛṣṇa will come and visit me during the night instead of the ghosts of my past. But the snow isn't sticking, just falling and melting, falling and melting.

12

All up-to-date notes have been delivered to my secretary. All last minute communications have been completed, all flights scheduled and confirmed. The little fleshy organs inside my body are secreting, assimilating, digesting. They should not be crushed or punctured, but nourished by the chemicals or fluids they require. My brain coils and my eyes rest. My lungs breathe on and my heart continues to thump-thump. Satisfaction is gained by a slow, lifelong effort. I will not give up.

This word "Kṛṣṇa" is not yet dear to me, or even as familiar as the words "food," "breath," "blood," "heart," "safety," "water," "work," "friends," "shelter." Why not?

Say it—"Kṛṣṇa." Kṛṣṇa. Rādhā. Holy name, prayer, mystic dimension, self-realization, soul. Kṛṣṇa, be kind to me. Please be kind.